The Public's Impact
on Foreign Policy

The Public's Impact on Foreign Policy

BERNARD C. COHEN

The University of Wisconsin—Madison

 LITTLE, BROWN AND COMPANY   *Boston*

LIBRARY OF CONGRESS CATALOG CARD NO. 72-6872

FIRST PRINTING

Published simultaneously in Canada
by Little, Brown & Company (Canada) Limited

PRINTED IN THE UNITED STATES OF AMERICA

To Barbara and Janie with love

Acknowledgments

I have had the help—the indispensable help—of so many people and so many organizations as I have worked on this book that it is something of a conceit to call it mine.

It all began in 1965–1966, when I was the Visiting Research Scholar at the Carnegie Endowment for International Peace in New York; I am very grateful to the Trustees of the Endowment, to its then-President Joseph E. Johnson, and to the rest of the very cooperative staff for providing me with such a comfortable and congenial launch pad and for making possible the interviews with State Department officials without which there would have been no book. The Endowment, of course, bears no responsibility for the conclusions I have reached.

I wish it were possible to thank, individually, the State Department officials who were so generous in sharing their time and their thoughts with me, but they were promised anonymity in exchange for their confidences. They may not share my conclusions, but I hope at least that they see in these a shared concern for the road we travel together.

In 1967–1968, through the generosity of the Research Committee of the University of Wisconsin Graduate School, I was able to engage the research assistance of Leanora Dreisinger Scheingold. Possessing a competence and an efficiency not ordinarily given to three mortals, let alone one, Lee helped me carry forward the coding and analysis of my interview material.

In 1969–1970, with a Ford Foundation Faculty Research Fellowship, I spent the year as a Fellow at the Center for Advanced Study in the Behavioral Sciences in Stanford, California, where I completed the draft manuscript. My gratitude to both the Ford Foundation and the Center is boundless: in a year in which productive scholarship on the campus was nearly impossible, they whisked me off to green pastures, where there was freedom to concentrate and to write. Meredith Wilson, Preston Cutler, and Jane Kielsmeier—the Officers of the Center—are masters in the art of magic carpetry. I should add, for the record, that the judgments and conclusions reached here are my own and are not necessarily shared by the Ford Foundation.

A number of people have read the entire manuscript and have been uncommonly helpful in their comments; I especially want to record my thanks to Leon D. Epstein, Alexander L. George, Nelson W. Polsby, Robert Trice, and two anonymous readers for Little, Brown and Company. I am grateful also to Melvin Small for his reactions to the early portions of the manuscript and for the many conversations that preceded it. In 1967 I contributed a paper to a conference under his direction at Wayne State University; subsequently published as "The Relationship between Public Opinion and Foreign Policy Maker," in Melvin Small, ed., *Public Opinion and Historians: Interdisciplinary Perspectives* (Detroit: Wayne State University Press, 1970), it represented my first thoughts on the questions that are covered here in Chapter 1. The material is used with the kind permission of the Wayne State University Press.

Hildegarde Teilhet, Lou Ann Karter, and Marjorie Kritz have each had a hand (more accurately, two hands) in the typing of successive versions of the manuscript. Basil G. Dandison and Freda Alexander at Little, Brown and Company shepherded my manuscript into a book, and Cheryl Wurtz transformed my marginal scrawls into an index.

With paternal pride, and with apologies for the delay, I dedicate this book to my two daughters; while I have been trying to finish it, they have wisely concentrated on growing up.

Contents

The Public's Impact
on Foreign Policy

ONE

**The Study of Public Opinion
and Foreign Policy**

The literature purporting to deal with public opinion and foreign
policy is mountainous. It is so extensive that a suitable measure of
it might be by weight rather than by number or volume. Given the
desirability of preserving our scarce resources both of timber and of
time, I feel an obligation to try to justify my intention to add one
more book to the pile. My justification is brief and simple; and if it
seems arrogant it is not meant to be so. This *is* a book about public
opinion and foreign policy. Or perhaps I should say, this is a book
about public opinion *and* foreign policy — not public opinion *on*
foreign policy, which is what most of the works in the genre are
about. I want to explore the linkages between opinion and policy
in the United States, a political nexus which this vast and sometimes incandescent literature has notably failed to illuminate. But
this is obviously more than a statement of intention and a justification; it is also a simplified characterization of a complex literature.
To say that we do not know very much about public opinion *and*
foreign policy is to claim a significant gap between what we would
like to know and what we *do* know about public opinion as an element in the formulation of foreign policy. I owe it to my colleagues
who toil in this vineyard as well as to my readers to defend that
claim. I will try to do so in this chapter, in two stages: first, in a
descriptive, distributive way and, subsequently, in a qualitative
way. The existing literature — as it deals with the United States, at
least — seems to me not only inadequate in its scope but also, insofar as it deals with the articulation of opinion and policy, unsatis-

1

factory in its contents. Eventually I will arrive (p. 26) at what should be by then a more readily comprehended statement of what *this* book is all about and what the reader can expect to find in it.

THE SCOPE OF THE LITERATURE

To spell out all that we would like to know about the role of public opinion in foreign policy making is an elaborate task. I propose to keep it as simple as possible, referring the reader to some of the "models" of the public opinion–foreign policy relationship that are available in the public opinion literature, if he wishes to explore any of these categories in greater depth.[1] I found especially useful the framework proposed by Lee Benson for historians who are seeking to understand the opinion-policy relationship in a particular historical period, and I draw on it heavily in the following paragraphs.[2] Its special merit lies in the coherent, systematic way in which it relates public opinion to decision making in concrete circumstances, aiming at an enlargement of our factual, empirical knowledge of real events. Presumably, any general theorizing we do about the impact of public opinion on foreign policy has to be rooted in this kind of information.

What we want to know about the role of public opinion in foreign policy making may be summarized in the following general categories.

The characteristics and distributions of opinions. We want to know what opinions are held concerning foreign policy subjects, and by whom, and the manner in which they are held. This summarizes a vast array of specific questions dealing with the political, social, cultural characteristics and location of persons and groups identified as holding particular opinions, what those specific opinions are on actual or proposed policy questions and how they are interrelated, and the general properties or qualities of those opinions, such as intensity, stability, saliency, knowledgeability, and so forth. In other words, for all or for a fully representative range of foreign policy questions, we would want a map or grid that identified all opinion-holders and opinions and specified their attributes and interrelations.

The formation and transmission of opinions. We want to know how opinions are formed and transmitted and by whom. We are concerned here with all the processes by which "agents" or "actors," governmental and private, attempt to shape the development of individual and group opinions, their purposes in so doing, the skills, resources, techniques and strategies they bring to the task, the consequences of these efforts, and their modes of transmitting opinions to political targets. The reason why I include the transmission of opinions to decision makers together with the formation of opinions is simply that in many cases the attempted formation and transmission of opinion are a single process or act — e.g., a public speech or a "teach-in." Analytically, of course, they are quite distinct processes.

The impact of opinions on foreign policy makers. We want to know how governmental officials perceive opinions, since political messages transmitted are not necessarily identical with political messages received; we want to know how officials evaluate opinions and what effects those opinions have on specific decisions. In order to make a valid assessment of the impact that public opinion thus perceived and evaluated has on any specific decision, we also want to know what impact *other* factors have on the decision — i.e., we want to know about the overall process of decision making on foreign policy. Only this way can we understand how much of the final decision is properly attributable to the influence of external opinions. (By "external opinion," here and elsewhere in this book, I mean domestic opinion that is outside of the governmental decision making process. I could as well use the phrase "outside opinion" or even "nongovernmental opinion," so long as it is understood in all cases that I am referring to domestic, American opinion and not to opinion abroad.)

The relation of causes and consequences of opinions. There is an important additional requirement for information, of a different order from the above. We want to know the above kinds of information sequentially — that is, with respect to the development of the same foreign policy matter — so that we can relate causes and consequences when it comes to impact on decision making. Knowing the characteristics and distributions of public opinion on the question of returning Okinawa to Japanese authority, for example, does not necessarily have any bearing on the impact of public opinion on the decision to intercept all drug traffic from Mexico to the United States. Only by the development of coherent and full explanations of the role of external opinions on foreign policy making in a variety of specific circumstances and issues can we proceed with confidence to the building of predictive theories concerning the public's influence.

This, then, is a model of what we would *like* to know. How much of it do we actually know? Where is the mountainous literature of public opinion and foreign policy found once it has been arrayed in the categories of this model? Recognizing the difficulty of doing it justice in so short a compass, let me begin with a summary answer: we know bits and pieces all over the place, though very substantially less about *impact,* or the linkages between opinion and policy, than about anything else. "Bits and pieces" is another way of saying that our knowledge is partial, unsystematic, disconnected, and discontinuous. Most studies are located in discrete sectors of the model, or they cut across several of these categories; exceedingly few of them attempt systematically and sequentially to treat the full range of relevant questions. I do not mean by these comments to pass a summary judgment on the quality of this literature. Many of these studies are excellent; they are frequently indispensable contributions, opening up new subjects, making first approximations. But they are isolated lights in a very large city at night: they give us only the most general clues to the contours of our subject, and they leave us almost wholly in the dark about its vital processes.

The most extensive and sophisticated studies — sophisticated conceptually, methodologically, and analytically — lie in the first category, the characteristics and distributions of opinions. The refinement of survey research techniques over the past third of a century gives us ever more insight into the nature and the location of foreign policy views among the American people and into the thinking that shapes particular views. The work of all the survey agencies is relevant here, but most particularly that of the Survey Research Center at the University of Michigan and the National Opinion Research Center at the University of Chicago.[3] The survey research instrument has been employed chiefly in the study of national samples, however, and thus we know most about the foreign policy opinions of the people who, overall, are least likely to participate in foreign policy discussions and activities; conversely, we know less — in a comparably systematic way — about the characteristics and distributions of opinions at the more active leadership levels — what is often called elite opinion.[4] We are able, however, to talk with some assurance now about the limited contribution that an individual's opinion on foreign policy makes to his voting decisions, which is one link — though a tenuous one — between public opinion and the government's behavior in foreign policy.[5] And the first steps have been taken to explore the connections — also limited, apparently — between the opinions of constituencies on foreign policy matters and the votes of their Congressmen on those matters.[6]

Rather extensive but uneven work has been done in the area of the formation and transmission of opinions, which is itself a very broad area. Focusing first on government officials and political leaders as "agents," to use Benson's phrase, in the formation of foreign policy opinion, we do have much information on the foreign policy bureaucracy. There are many detailed studies of offices and institutions,[7] a large literature of personal recollection,[8] and some case-study reconstructions that center on the work of foreign policy agencies in the development not only of foreign policy but of a supportive base for it in external opinion.[9] In the millions of words written by and about the media of mass communications, there is finally the beginning of an approach to the mass media as instruments in the formation of public awareness of foreign policy issues and in the expression and transmission of opinions concerning them. In my own work on this subject I have tried especially to link the work of the press with the perception and evaluation of it by government officials, but systematic inquiry of this kind across a range of specific substantive policy areas has yet to be undertaken.[10] Interest-group activity in the foreign policy field has on occasion been moderately well described.[11] But the consequences of this activity, the linkages both with "publics" and with policy makers, are the subject more of continuous speculation than of research.[12] The study of individual foreign policy activists or influentials has lagged considerably behind these generally institutional studies, with no clear projections at hand as to its future development.[13] In sum, we have a fairly good overview of the people and institutions who try (or have tried in the recent past) to shape and express foreign policy opinions, and of their resources and strategies, though a lot of the detail is missing. A major problem in this area is that the relevant literature spans at least a generation, and we have no uniform basis for judging its present worth. Both institutions and individuals have passed away, beyond the reach of first-hand investigation. The issues themselves have faded from man's memory, and documents are often no substitute. And the methods involved in some of the early works are of questionable merit. One of the major weaknesses of V. O. Key's discussion of the role of the mass media in the formation of public opinion, for example, is that he swept along the findings of about twenty-five years of scholarship, some of it of dubious validity by current standards, so that the final product was an unusual mixture in which one could have little confidence.[14]

When we look at the area we variously call the nexus, or the linkages, or the impact of opinions on decision, we find a quite different situation from that I have described above. The literature here is exceedingly sparse — a fact which has been often noted though little remedied.[15] There is a handful of studies, some conceptual and some empirical, which attach major importance at least to the *problem* of officials' perception of public opinion on specific political issues.[16] But there is almost nothing reliable on the consequences of officials' perceptions — i.e., on the actual impact of opinions. This is not to say that no claims are made concerning the real impact of opinion; as we shall see later in this chapter, assertions of the influence of opinion on policy are not uncommon. But reliable evidence to support these claims is not part of the literature — and for good reasons, or at least for reasons one can sympathize with and understand. It is immeasurably difficult to get at this question. Data that relate to it are simply not part of any historical record in convincing or persuasive amounts.[17] And even in contemporary research, the problem of ascertaining the impact of opinion, in relation to the impact of other relevant factors impinging on policy decisions, is so enormous as to discourage researchers whose access to officials and to resources is limited (which covers most of us, regrettably). Yet without fair comparison of the influence of opinion with the impact of other participants in the policy process, any single-factor explanation — whether it be about the impact of public opinion or the impact of the President's kitchen cabinet — is inescapably suspect.

I specified above, as an additional desideratum, sequential studies of policy making across a range of issues. There is a mounting literature that fits loosely in this category, most of which may be described as "case studies." From the point of view of the development of a body of testable generalizations or propositions, "case studies" are often a frustrating diversion of talent. They involve extensive human resources in the acquisition of knowledge which, however enlightening and suggestive, is frequently noncumulative. Various issues in American foreign policy have been studied over a period of years, each one more or less "unique" in the categories of analysis employed and in the kinds of data used and propositions (if any) put forward. The unsystematic exploitation of the history of the policy making process has as a result been even more haphazard in its treatment of public opinion, further compounding all the unevenness and discontinuities of the rest of the literature. In particular, the case-study literature, which has presented the best opportunities to trace the effects of all factors including public opinion on the decision making process, has shed only a fitful light on this process.[18]

Finally, we have a small body of literature that seeks to explain in a more general theoretical way the place of public opinion in the formulation of foreign policy.[19] These are books of interpretive and speculative virtuosity, and they have substantially enlarged our vision and our aspirations, but their authors would be the first to recognize the limitations placed on *their* vision by the inadequate data available to them. We are left, along with V. O. Key, with the unsatisfactory conclusion that public opinion is important in the policy making process, though we cannot say with confidence how, why, or when.

But we are left with more than just that. We still have the concern and the curiosity about foreign policy and about the democratic process that led us to try to understand this problem in the first place. And so we are drawn back irresistibly to the core of our concern, which is the point where our knowledge is the weakest: how does public opinion get related concretely and specifically to acts of foreign policy in this country? What is the public's impact on foreign policy, insofar as we can comprehend and describe it? This book is an attempt to provide some answers to these questions. If we can make headway here, then I think we may simultaneously revalue the rest of the literature in some small way by providing connective paths among some of the landmarks. The more we know about the impact of opinion on policy making, the more value we can find in and the more direction we can give to studies of all the other aspects of the public opinion–foreign policy relationship.

THE CONTENT OF THE LITERATURE

Any evaluation of the body of knowledge in this particular field has to pay attention to its quality as well as its scope. The problem that confronts the student of public opinion and foreign policy is not only the relative void right at the point where the problem gets interesting. It is also the tendency of scholars to try to fill that vacuum when they lack the data to do so adequately. Most of what has been written about the impact of public opinion on foreign policy decisions, limited as it is to begin with, is unsatisfactory. I will summarize it under four different — though not always mutually exclusive — headings. The reader will readily recognize the most common kinds of generalizations that are put forward concerning the role of public opinion in foreign policy formulation.

Nonevidential assertions or implication of influence. In his recent effort to provide systematic direction to the study of public opinion in prior historical periods, Lee Benson wrote: "Different officials . . . may have radically different perceptions of the distribution of public opinion on an issue, or set of issues. Researchers . . . must therefore specifically identify the officials about whose perceptions they make claims; if they cannot do so with some reasonable degree of specificity, they are not entitled to make claims about the impact of public opinion on public policy." [20] Such a blunt admonition of the irrelevance of unsupported claims of influence is as applicable to political scientists, public officials, and journalists as it is to historians, to whom it was directed. The admonition should, in fact, go even further. It is not enough simply to "identify the officials about whose perceptions they make claims." The *consequences* of those perceptions must be visible to the observer, before claims about those consequences can be made.

The classic formulation — and the classic irrelevancy — about the public's impact on American foreign policy is the flat-out assertion that "the long-range foreign policy of the United States is determined by the American people." [21] No evidence to support such a statement is offered; and it takes little reflection to understand that without very considerable refining and defining of its terms such a statement simply cannot be factually proved or disproved. It is offered, rather, more as a statement of faith than as a statement of observable, testable fact.

An alternate formulation of this position puts it that "all policies depend, for their ultimate effectiveness, upon the support of public opinion." [22] "There are 148,000,000 Americans. These are the people who ultimately make or break our foreign policy." [23] These statements, too, are not only offered without proof; they are incapable of refutation by empirical test. If a policy is "ultimately ineffective," it can only mean that it has not had the support of public opinion. On the other hand, if it *is* "ultimately effective" (or even if it has not clearly failed), obviously public opinion is giving it direct, positive, effective support. A host of other, easily imagined, alternative possibilities are thus ruled out by definition. And an enormous burden of responsibility is subtly transferred from the shoulders of policy officials to an undefined public opinion.

Benson believes that even though there is little hard evidence to support an assumption that public opinion influences public policy, such an assumption "probably serves as the main scholarly justification for opinion research in general and historical opinion research in particular." [24] The perverse fact, however, is that scholarly research on opinion bears the major responsibility for the continued viability of the unsubstantiated assumption; at the very least, it lends its good authority to the assertion of public influence, while it persists in overlooking opportunities to test or even to question the proposition. It is no doubt invidious to single out particular scholars by way of illustrating this point; perhaps it will mitigate the sting if I insist that these are merely examples of a common thrust in American scholarship and that I myself have been guilty of it in the past.

In Chapter 10 of my book *The Political Process and Foreign Policy*, I attempt to discuss the perceptions of public opinion concerning the Japanese peace settlement in both the Executive branch and the Congress. In fact, however, I am actually discussing my *own* perceptions of the flow of opinion in these places. I

am, in other words, confusing activity and intention in the opinion
area with effect and consequence, without proper evidence for the
latter.[25]

Robert Browder, in *The Origins of Soviet-American Diplomacy*,
performed a prodigious task of scholarship in portraying the views
of individuals and organizations on the subject of American recognition of the Soviet Union. But his conclusions and his judgments
concerning the *impact* of that opinion are inconsistent, contradictory, supported by indirect inference rather than by direct evidence. For example, he states: "Among all the other facts which
Roosevelt had taken into account before he sent his historic invita-
tion to Kalinin, none perhaps was more instrumental in deciding
him to act when he did than his realization that American public
opinion in the main supported a resumption of relations with Russia." [26] But Browder does not at that point supply more than fragmentary evidence concerning American public opinion; nor does
he relate this evidence to the causal or motivational sequence he
has presumably identified. Furthermore, this statement about the
influence of public opinion on Roosevelt's decision or on its timing
contradicts the clear import of many of Browder's prior statements
to the effect that Roosevelt was determined to recognize the Soviet
Union all along. In fact, if the reader relied on Browder's generalizations about the general nature of American public opinion — i.e.,
its isolationism and anti-communism — one would have to conclude that, if public opinion had *any* bearing whatsoever on foreign policy, recognition could never have taken place.

In similar fashion and on a similar issue, A. T. Steele, in *The
American People and China*, has attributed a substantial part of
the "reason for congressional caution" on the question of the recognition of the Communist Chinese regime to public pressures:
"These pressures come in part from the Committee of One Million
and its allies and in part from organizations of the extreme right
with a special penchant for letter-writing. As one author observes:
'A large part of the history of American foreign policy since World
War I might be interpreted as a series of successful intimidations
by pressure groups.' The applicability of this statement to the
China situation is self-evident." [27] Although it may have been self-
evident to Steele, he has not made it so to his readers; what he has
done is argue by historical generalization rather than by specific

evidence of "successful intimidation." What is worse, the historical experience which he quotes (without identification) is, in its original form, also offered to the reader substantially as a self-evident assertion rather than as a generalization supported by evidence.[28]

At the risk of beating a sick (if not dying) horse, I will quote without further comment three passages by a noted historian of American foreign policy. At the Washington Arms Conference of 1921–1922, Dexter Perkins writes, Secretary Hughes "secured that parity with the British which American opinion (for no very clear reason, it must be conceded) demanded." [29] "As early as 1925, eschewing the very cautious view of the matter expressed by Secretary Hughes, and responding, no doubt, to the pressure of powerful elements in American opinion, Secretary Kellogg permitted the United States to take part in the deliberations of the Preparatory Commission on Disarmament that assembled at Geneva." [30] "Let us summarize at this point the policies of the United States with regard to peace and security as they relate to Europe. We shall have to begin by saying once again that these policies were narrowly circumscribed by public opinion." [31]

The "osmosis" hypothesis. Somewhat different from assertions of opinion-influence unsupported by evidence are statements or models of the influence process that obscure the mechanisms by which opinion is absorbed and translated into policy. In the absence of precise mechanisms or procedures, one is left with the impression that opinion is absorbed, by osmosis, into the political bloodstream. Or, if the process of opinion-absorption is not osmotic, it is treated as automatic, thus minimizing, in the first instance at least, the need for further study of it.

In his study of *National Leadership and Foreign Policy*, James N. Rosenau elaborated a model of opinion formation and public policy which took it for granted that the state of opinion among leadership groups would be reflected in foreign policy. At the start of his book, he wrote: "Because they are spokesmen for diverse segments of the public, in other words, national leaders have an informal authority which . . . officialdom cannot ignore, and which thus enables them to prevent or permit the selection of alternatives that are formulated, modified, and proposed by government leaders." [32] At the conclusion of his study, Rosenau found the essentially osmotic premise that public consensus "will be translated into official policy" inadequate: "the model does not presently account for a contrary — and seemingly contradictory — situation in which officialdom vetoes a consensus widely shared by diverse groups of national leaders." [33] So he is led to speculate, by way of conclusion, on possible mechanisms that link — or fail to link — external opinion with public officials.

One sees the subtleties of one's own ideas more clearly than those of other people's; nevertheless I should include as an example of the osmosis hypothesis the conception of the "climate of opinion" which, I once argued, "by creating in the policy-maker an impression of a public attitude or attitudes, or by becoming part of the environment and cultural milieu that help to shape his own thinking, may consciously affect his official behavior." I went on to say, of the isolationism of the 1920's and 1930's, "Many officials . . . were not so much buffeted by the winds as they were busy blowing them, or unconsciously reflecting their pressures." [34] Believing that this was a fundamentally correct interpretation of that particular situation, I should have explained with some precision how, when, and why opinion became internalized, and not have left the essential processes hanging in the inaccessible realm of unconscious absorption.

V. O. Key was well aware, after his extensive survey of both the literature and the data concerning public opinion and public policy, of how little we properly knew. His book on the subject is studded with qualifications which, while meant precisely to convey these areas of doubt, had the opposite effect of affirming interactive relationships without specifying how they work: e.g., "Yet presumably actions at the governmental level are conditioned by the distributions of opinions within the mass public, especially on those matters that generate intense opinions among large proportions of the people." [35]

A variant of the osmosis hypothesis is the common explanation — a nonexplanation, really — that policy makers take public opinion into consideration or into account before making a decision. Since the notion is uniformly phrased, one example may suffice. Stanley Hoffmann argues, in *Gulliver's Troubles,* that "there is such a thing as a *specific public opinion on foreign policy;* this is a force that directly affects the president; he must take it into account before formulating or executing policy." [36] My objection to

hat statement is not that it is always incorrect but that it is a
ruism which apparently frees its users of further obligation to explain what it means to have opinion "taken into account" and what
he effects of that process are. The implication clearly is that "tak-
ng opinion into account" means adapting policy in some fashion
o the demands of external opinion; in practice, however, it may as
often be the case that "taking opinion into account" means formally acknowledging it and then rejecting it out of hand, or using
t to inform public relations efforts.[37] These are quite different phenomena, and obscuring the mechanisms by which opinion impinges upon policy is very likely to obscure the nature of the impact itself.

The highly improbable relationship. Another type of unsatisfactory statement about public opinion and foreign policy is
hat which claims or posits a highly improbable relationship be-
ween them. By this I mean a relationship that offends or violates
our common-sense notions of political events or our commonly understood theories about them. In a way this classification is not
wholly separable from the others, in that improbabilities tend to
creep in wherever the canons of evidence are not upheld, for whatever reason. But the wilder the claim, the greater our need for supporting evidence, and the quicker we are to doubt the accuracy of
what we are hearing.

Browder's analysis of the weaknesses of the Soviet-recognition
movement during the 1920's will serve as an example. He lays
much stress on the indifference of the American people: "But the
American people were too engrossed in their own prosperity and
too confident of their national security to be greatly concerned
about nondomestic problems." [38] By lumping together two such
disparate factors as prosperity and national security, Browder
makes it extraordinarily difficult for anyone to factor out the con-
ribution of each to the overall result. I want to concentrate for the
moment on the first of these factors: the presumed distractions of
prosperity. Such an explanation flies in the face of logic, evidence,
and history. If it were true of the American people at that time
hat they were too preoccupied with their prosperity to be concerned with foreign policy issues, one would presume that it would
be true equally of the proponents and the opponents of recogni-
ion. How then does one account for the fact that "the opponents

of recognition" were "more numerous and better organized than their adversaries"? [39] And if the American people were too engrossed in prosperity in the 1920's to be concerned about external relations with the Soviet Union, why was this not equally true at the time of recognition in the 1930's, when the American people were engrossed in their poverty? Everything we know about the correlates of interest and information on foreign affairs confirms that these two items vary directly with income, rather than inversely as Browder suggests. Instead, Browder ascribes to the American people, then in the pit of the Great Depression, a major role in the basic political strategy of the recognition effort: "Apparently, no American official questioned the advisability of settling the major issues [associated with the establishment of United States–Soviet diplomatic relations] before or at least contemporaneously with the granting of recognition. The unsatisfactory experiences of other nations which had left negotiations until after relations were established, together with the realization that the American people demanded all proper precautions be taken before extending the hand of friendship to Russia, were the basic considerations affecting the decision." [40]

In his insider's account of the development of the Truman Doctrine and the Marshall Plan in 1947, Joseph M. Jones writes, "There is no question whatever that Secretary Marshall's proposal at Harvard [for a European Recovery Program] was to an important degree the consequence of public pressure built up and suggestions advanced, during the weeks following the announcement of the Truman Doctrine, in an interplay of ideas between the nation's leaders and the public." [41] But neither direct experience nor retrospective analysis of the revolution in American foreign policy in 1947 gives any prima facie support for the implication that the government was responding to external stimulus at that time. The very suggestion, in fact, denies the fundamentally creative act of statesmanship that marked the whole episode, and that Jones himself was celebrating in his book.[42] Furthermore (leaving aside the ambiguity of his phrase "to an important degree"), Jones makes it amply clear in his volume that by "public" he means "press," and by "interplay" he means external responsiveness to governmental initiatives. By using Aesopian language, in other words, he has attributed a major role to external opinion when he does not mean it in the conventional sense at all.

Herbert Feis, a sensitive interpreter of policy and history, gives us a striking example not so much of a highly improbable relationship as of a highly improbable expectation of such a relationship. He describes the State Department's inability to act decisively against Italy during the Italian-Ethiopian War in 1935: "There was in the Department a thin hope . . . that public opinion might finally awaken to what was at issue, and demand further and more decisive action. This hope, however, fed largely upon itself. Officials could not find, either in the mail received at the State Department or in the press, evidence that public opinion was insistent upon more vigorous control of trade with Italy. . . . The ruling science . . . was interrupted mainly by those who were hostile [to League sanctions]." [43] Feis does not tell us what such evidence of public insistence would consist in or how it would be recognized, measured, or evaluated. But the very notion here that the government does not act in foreign policy except upon the "insistent" demand of public opinion is simply not credible; we have far too much evidence to the contrary. By putting the State Department's problem this way, Feis suggests either that the State Department was looking for the wrong thing — i.e., that it had set an impossibly high standard of external political support — or that it was seeking someone with whom it might share, or to whom it might comfortably and publicly transfer, the responsibility for inaction.

The empirically irrefutable proposition. I have already noted some formulations of public participation that were not readily subject to confirmation or disconfirmation. Here I would like to explore some additional and quite common statements about the impact of public opinion on foreign policy which are fundamentally meaningless either because they too can be neither proved nor disproved or because they can mean anything at all or all things at once.

Robert Browder, once more, has observed that President Franklin Roosevelt "was remarkably sensitive to public opinion and throughout his tenure as Chief Executive seldom moved politically or diplomatically until he was sure that the majority of his countrymen would follow either from previous conviction or, on occasion, because they were fascinated by the boldness of his actions." [44] This is to say that Roosevelt always followed or moved with public opinion except when he did not. Such a statement does not enable us to differentiate the times when Roosevelt moved in the certainty of public support from the times when he moved in the expectation that he would subsequently have public support or to differentiate either of these from the times when he really did not know what would happen. Thus as a summary statement inter preting Roosevelt's perception of and responsiveness to public opinion, it tells us nothing because it includes everything at once

A proposition which is clearly beyond the reach of empirical in vestigation is the following, by A. T. Steele: "Members of Congress are of course well aware of this powerful body of opinion and of the hardened attitude of a large and influential section of the pop ular press. They consciously or subconsciously take it into consid eration in weighing any legislation that involves a change in our relations with Communist countries." [45] Compounding the total ambiguity of the phrase "take it into consideration" is the observa tion that this is done "consciously or subconsciously." The subcon scious, of course, is not accessible to empirical observation except perhaps to psychiatrists; the author thus is saying that all behavior in this realm which is not conscious and thus potentially observ able is nonetheless there and operating in identical form except that we cannot see it. I do not deny the possibility that this might sometime be the case; but we are entitled to be skeptical nonethe less and to regard the burden of proof as falling on the psychia trist, be he amateur or professional.

Another familiar form of the assertion of public influence on for eign policy which is irrefutable (as well as nonevidential) in nature is what Walter Lippmann called the "latent veto." In dealing with foreign policy, Lippmann argued, "democratic politicians have pre ferred to shun foresight about troublesome changes to come, know ing that the massive [public] veto was latent." [46] Lippmann has been taken to task so often and so well for both his faulty logic and his faulty history that we need not dissect him in detail again.[47] I want only to stress the patent impossibility of observing and hence knowing — in the true sense of the word — that which is latent, and thus of demonstrating its power to others. It may be that, at times, individual politicians did prefer inaction out of fear of an adverse public (or, more likely, political) response; but to as sert the general potency of latency is to deny all purpose in even asking whether and when other causes for inaction may have been at work.

Lippmann has borne the brunt of the attack on the inherent mysticism of the latency notion, but he is not the only one to argue thus. That many others who (like Lippmann) should know better nevertheless slip into that mode of thinking about public opinion is some sort of testimony to its hold on us. V. O. Key correctly pointed out its attractiveness: "If one encounters analytical obstacles as he seeks to tie governmental action to public opinion, he can blandly assert that actions are based on estimates of latent opinion." [48] But knowing its lure did not protect him from eventual seduction: "Insofar as considerations of opinion enter into decision, governmental decisionmakers must calculate how much they should discount the clamor of immediate opinion and what weight they should give to latent preferences that are remote, both in communications and in time, from the point of action." [49] And I have known a touch of sin myself: "And even if public opinion remains quiescent throughout the development of a given policy issue, the wise policy-maker still has to take advantage of opportunities to mend his public fences, to lessen the chance that opinion may become aroused later on and wreak its vengeance on other issues, including electoral ones. The influence of public opinion on the making of the Japanese peace settlement was of this indirect variety." [50]

We come, lastly, to what may be the most common conception of all regarding the influence of public opinion on foreign policy, the notion that "widely held popular attitudes . . . unquestionably serve to set up the 'dikes,' or mark out the limits, within which our leaders feel free to act." [51] Like channel markers or gravitational fields, public opinion is presumed to hold foreign policy makers to a clearly delineated area of acceptable decisions. This proposition, or assumption, is found on all sides: Witness, for example, V. O. Key: "Mass opinion may set general limits, themselves subject to change over time, within which government may act." [52] "Nonparticipators, it should be fair to assume, have little role in shaping the dikes of opinion within which the day-to-day policy of government flows." [53] "The opinion context . . . fixes the limitations within which action may be taken." [54] Former Secretary of State Dean Rusk varied the metaphor: "Throughout my long years in government, I have found that the American people expect their government to travel a broad highway of policy which responds to their own simple and decent purposes and that when government wanders over toward the soft shoulders on either side of the road the people have a dozen ways to nudge the public vehicle back onto the hard surface." [55] Theodore Sorensen, in trying to make the point that President Kennedy had much more freedom of initiative in foreign affairs than in domestic affairs, nonetheless described the impact of opinion on foreign policy in these familiar terms: "His foreign policy actions were still constrained within bounds set by [Congressional and public opinion]." [56] At a different level, a recent study of the State Department's information activities argues that the Department's study of public opinion "furnished the professional diplomat with a much more realistic appraisal of the limits imposed by general public opinion on foreign policy." [57] James N. Rosenau speaks of "the ordinary citizen who contributes vague feelings to a public mood that sets outer limits on the policy commitments which can be undertaken." [58] And Harwood L. Childs writes: "In the final analysis, a state of public opinion, known or assumed, seems to set the outer limits of governmental action within which public officials exercise much discretion." [59]

There is something comfortable and reassuring in the notion that even if the general public cannot easily control the daily decisions of foreign policy makers, it (we) can still control the set from which they come. Though this notion is attractive, it nonetheless defies rigorous analysis. The image it evokes is sharp: policy makers may not stray too far off the path — but where is the path, and where are the woods? Is policy-making space so clearly defined or understood that one can specify its left and right margins? How can those margins or limits be established or even identified? If there is a clear line on each side of the policy space, it would have to be drawn through a number of connectable points, or specific instances, in which public opinion restrained foreign policy officials in clear and unambiguous ways on issues that are related both in substance and in time. The historical record does not provide us with enough of such points to draw clear lines. The best it offers is an ambiguous point perhaps once in a generation. The "limits," then, can only be implicit or "latent"; that is, they are subject not to precise observation, identification, or measurement but rather to different readings by different men. They are, in other words, not bounds or dikes at all, but clouds. They suggest sub stance, and they may sometimes constrain action; but one can move right through them on other occasions without even knowing it. They are a figure of speech, designed to suggest specific meaning; but few men try to specify that meaning, because in practice it can be done only at such a general level as to be — really — meaningless.[60] When Key says of these "limits" that they are themselves subject to change over time, he implies that they can be identified before and after change, but he does not tell us how to go about the task of identification. Furthermore, to endow the limits with flexibility of this order is in fact to deprive them of all meaning; when the government acts outside those limits, it means only that the limits themselves have changed.[61]

This is devastating criticism — much more devastating than that which merely points out what scholars have failed to do. The unhappy part of it is that it is directed at the very heart of what we have to say about the public's impact on foreign policy, at the very language of the discipline, and not at a few scholars. These are not random or esoteric usages, as I indicated earlier, but rather the most common ways of conceiving and talking about the relationship between public opinion and foreign policy. They make painfully clear the conclusion I drew earlier after reviewing the scope of the literature: we know next to nothing about the subject. We have as yet no satisfactory way of explaining something as apparently visible as the impact of opinion on Vietnam policy, never mind being able to forecast or predict it! We once talked about the Korean War experience as having set "limits" on our policy makers' freedom to engage in limited wars — the "Never Again Club" — but those limits were ignored as the country slipped easily into the Vietnam War. As that war stretched on and on, dissent raged, and there was more talk of "no more Vietnams."[62] But still in 1972 we had no sound basis for predicting whether Vietnam is indeed a parameter case for this generation. Does it constitute such a clear and unambiguous example of a "limit" which has been exceeded that no policy maker will attempt a remotely comparable intervention again for as long as a generation?[63] Or a few years from now will our leaders interpret our national interest as requiring military intervention somewhere else? We have almost limitless data about opinion at the micro level, but it should be clear by this time that those data do not by themselves provide reliable answers to questions about public constraints on foreign policy five years from now.

THE SOURCES OF OUR MISCONCEPTIONS

Why is this so? Why should the practitioners of political science and history and journalism have done so badly when they have tried to talk — in passing, usually — about the link between public opinion and foreign policy? It is worth our while to explore some possible reasons for these inadequacies of our disciplines; by getting closer to the root of the difficulties, we may all get a better understanding of the whole problem. The sources of our troubles seem to me to lie in the interplay between the weaknesses of our theoretical understandings and explanations and the strengths of the prevailing political and ideological perspectives on the subject. The latter flourish because there are so few compelling empirical theories or even good descriptive propositions about the process of making foreign policy. And because they flourish they provide continuing rationalizations and alternatives — i.e., "answers" — to scholars, thereby inhibiting the scholars' search for explanations. Since these sources do interact, it does not make much difference where we cut into them; let's start with the ideological and political, and then move on to the intellectual-disciplinary.

In the first place, there are the pervasive principles of normative democratic theory about public opinion that are aided and abetted in many ways — some strange and some customary — and effectively challenged in few. Our political myths all tell us that the people rule; and we see it happen regularly at election time. We do not often see it happening on other occasions, but ideological if not cognitive consistency leads to a mechanical assumption that the public rules or at least participates extensively in policy making, and to a readiness to assert the assumption as unquestioned fact. Lacking good empirical theories about the role of opinion in foreign policy making, which is to say lacking other satisfactory or compelling modes of explanation for policy outcomes, we have drifted into the habit of accepting normative theories as explanations of what has happened in specific policy instances. We have been encouraged to do so, furthermore, by the behavior of both policy makers and scholars.

Observation, recollections, and public statements of foreign policy officials concerning the policy making process seem to have a special claim on our attention, partly because of their proximity to the seats of power, to "the action," and partly because other sources of authoritative information are not readily found. We are regularly and ritualistically reassured by our Secretaries of State in such statements that public opinion shapes foreign policy, that the policy maker is guided by public sentiment, that governments cannot function without it, and so forth. One would expect the Secretary of State to say such things, if only because he believes they are expected of him; but we do not have to believe it when he says it. It is precisely the importance we are obliged to attach to statements from the Secretary and his associates that should compel us to look at them with a cold and fishy eye, to ask whether they are reasonable or verifiable, and to consider whether there are not other, more proximate and practical reasons why officials talk this way. When a policy maker is attributing a decision to the dictates of public opinion, he may be explaining away a variety of complicated, delicate political constraints on his and his colleagues' behavior by passing them off onto the one "legitimate" political actor that cannot answer back, defend itself, or take offense at the charge. He may have been led to a particular decision because it was the only action which made sense to him or on which he could get any agreement from the interested parties within the State Department or the Executive branch; or he may have concluded *not* to do something — held back by the clear, if unpublicized, intimation of Congressional reprisal or by personal unwillingness to shoulder responsibility for all the risks involved. To explain his decision by blaming himself or his colleagues or the Congress could have disastrous political consequences; but to lay it all on the shoulders of the public might even be construed as flattering.[64] This is not necessarily a conscious and deliberate subterfuge; it could as easily be an automatic set of euphemisms and rationalizations, an institutionalized response to the felt necessity of saying *something* about ultimate responsibility for decisions, wise or unwise.[65]

Large parts of the scholarly enterprise that we reviewed at the beginning of this chapter also contribute unwittingly to the strength of a normative, nonempirical theory that the public makes foreign policy. Most of this research, I pointed out earlier, is concerned with public opinion *on* foreign policy, ignoring or side-stepping the relationship between them. Such a massive research investment in the study of public opinion about foreign policy finds its justification, explicitly or implicitly, in the presumed importance to democratic process and/or to policy outcome of such opinions.[66] Thus the scholarly community involved in this research is inescapably attributing a fundamental role to public opinion in the formulation of foreign policy in the absence of empirical evidence to that effect and even though its long-range purpose may be the elaboration of a possibly quite different empirical theory concerning it.[67]

A long-prevailing political perspective on the role of public opinion in foreign policy making, like the ideological one, seems to me to have interfered with the search for understanding also. By "political perspective" I mean the common association of initiative and responsibility in foreign affairs with the Executive branch of the government and of ignorance, apathy, and inertia with the public and its representatives in the Congress.[68] This perspective is still part of our political culture today, having supplied direction or content to the ideological or normative perspective for half a century. That is, it has told us *how* the public exercises the fundamental role we attribute to it. It seems to have begun with the group of liberal internationalists whose policy aspirations were defeated in 1918 and who struggled thereafter, by organizational, educational, and political means, to keep the flame of "responsible international participation" alive.[69] This perspective now dominates historical interpretations of the 1920's and the 1930's, when supposedly an apathetic, uninformed isolationist public kept us from assuming our international responsibilities, as well as the 1940's and 1950's, when allegedly an equally indifferent and uninformed public was, only by dint of great effort and crash-and-crisis programs, persuaded to give its support to the active interventionist policies of our national leaders.[70] With varying degrees of explicitness over the years, it has dominated the widespread network of community organizations for world affairs education during this past half-century. Two generations of publicists and community leaders have justified the importance of citizen education in world affairs on the grounds that, since the public makes foreign policy, it is public ig-

norance and apathy that handicap responsible American participation in world politics.[71]

In a practical sense, this perspective was reflected for at least
thirty years in a nearly open alliance between the foreign policy
establishment in the Executive branch, regardless of political
party, and the internationalist foreign policy elite outside of government, also regardless of party, against the forces of darkness on
the outside — in the general public, in the Congress, in the Mid-
western press. This alliance has been subjected to unprecedented
strains by the Vietnam War, and its future is problematic. At the
early stages of the rupture, in 1966, a high official in the State Department described the situation to me as follows: "There is a considerable sort of feeling of unhappiness here that elements in the
population that used to be thought of as our 'natural constituency'
are not doing yeoman service for the Department now. We do
have a constituency of sorts — the Foreign Policy Association, the
Council on Foreign Relations, and all the other groups like that.
These people have helped us all along for years, with the United
Nations, the Marshall Plan, NATO, Korea, and all the others. But
they are not helping us with the American public on the Vietnam
issue. When they come to town to be briefed on Vietnam, they do
not leave with marching orders, as they used to." Not just the alliance, but the political perspective itself, is jeopardized by the Vietnam War; the outside critics are claiming, in effect, that the association has been reversed — that initiative and responsibility now
lie with the public, and ignorance and inertia with the Executive
branch. This experience has already stimulated new studies of public opinion and foreign policy and may ultimately lead scholars to
a fundamental reevaluation of their prior assumptions, perspectives, and work.[72]

These ideological and political sources of our troubles feed into
our more narrowly defined intellectual-disciplinary ones. They give
us a good crutch to lean on when the intellectual problems of empirical research and theory construction become difficult, which
they do early on. To begin with, any empirical analysis or historical reconstruction that seeks to measure or even describe the role
of public opinion as one among a number of causal agents in the
shaping of a particular policy quickly confronts the problem of
finding some researchable indicators of "influence." Furthermore,

in tracing the influence of opinions on policy, one needs to be prepared for "branching" paths and multi-step processes. The complexities and difficulties are so enormous, both practically and conceptually, that one student of the subject has proposed abandoning the concept of influence altogether in favor of empirically more manageable concepts.[73] No wonder that others take refuge in nonempirical formulations!

Another intellectual problem is the absence of any general agreement on what constitutes the "public." Established practice is diverse, with only one generalization seemingly appropriate: "public opinion" is treated on the whole as a residual category. It is a catchall for any actors or opinions that do not fit the authors' schemes of formal participants in the policy making process. Sometimes it means editorial opinion in the press; sometimes it means mass opinion as revealed in public opinion polls; sometimes it means interest-group opinions or positions; sometimes it means the mailbag; sometimes it means any combination of these ingredients. Consequently, public opinion is generally a nonoperational concept; that is to say, no agreed measures or indicators or even descriptions of behavior, no ready processes of analysis, can be applied to it, since we do not agree on what we are — or should be — studying in any given instance.

At the heart of the intellectual problem, however, is an even more profound disciplinary failure, a failure of political conceptualization that has afflicted political scientists and historians equally, though I suppose that political scientists bear the greater responsibility for the situation. This is our failure to conceive of foreign policy making as a set of processes involving calculable political strategies (and it may help to explain why it has been so easy for statesmen, scholars, and journalists to get away with patently absurd statements).[74] For reasons that can be explained if not justified, foreign policy as a subject matter has been treated as a special thing in American political science, substantially divorced from the theories and concepts of the political process that specialists in American politics have developed. Even in textbooks about American government, foreign policy is invariably treated in two or three chapters at the end, as a major *problem area* of American government rather than as a central set of questions and issues which define and shape (as well as illustrate) the very way that the

American government and American politics operate. Thus, although there are now some well-developed theories of the political process in areas such as budget making and military policy, for example, foreign policy still appears as a subject that is more appropriately studied from the point of view of international politics than of national politics.[75] This blindness to the political strategies of foreign policy making no doubt owes much to the fact that a considerable portion of foreign policy making is invisible to the casual observer, being carried on within the confines of the Executive branch and often under the wraps of national security, and to the fact that the Congress has less of a role to play in comparison with areas of domestic policy. Public opinion and nongovernmental actors generally have tended, consequently, to be conceived as external to the decision making process, and as operating more or less directly on the foreign policy officials, rather than more subtly being engaged in a complex political process that envelops large sections of the national political system. One result of this primitive theory of foreign policy making is that it is easy to portray as a contest between "good guys" and "bad guys," the latter being not political opponents or competitors — people trying to implement different goals or value structures — but all the unenlightened people on the outside who impede or thwart the "rational" policies of Executive foreign policy officials.

Historians of diplomacy and foreign policy who want to explain the political and social forces that led to particular policies have had to work without realistic political conceptualizations of the politics of foreign policy making. But unintentionally they have had their revenge on the students of politics (and the authors of high-school civics texts) who have (unintentionally) failed *them:* lacking any independent analytical constructs to guide their search for the historical political reality, the historians have leaned heavily on the available "documentary" record of public opinion, seeking persuasive explanations for past decisions chiefly in the newspapers and the memoirs or recollections of officials. I have already suggested some reasons why the latter are unreliable. Newspaper accounts are equally unreliable, not only because they may be quite wrong when they accept the rationalizations of officials, but because they are always fragmentary and partial, responding to conceptions of "news" rather than to the search for truth.[76] And because it *is* "news" rather than truth, it rarely gets supplemented or revised or corrected at a later date. Once caught in print, like an etching on a rock, it is history; and the historian transfers it with few questions to *his* pages, where it is subtly transformed into truth. And the political scientist, in search of data from the past to help him understand the present, is lightly hoist by his own petard.

THE RESEARCH FOCUS

Like an old-time movie that drew the curtains as the couple went into the bedroom, the literature of political science and history has veiled the crucial coupling of public opinion and foreign policy. My aim here is to lift that veil, to explore, as I said at the very start, the linkages between opinion and policy. I propose to examine the mechanisms of articulation between public opinion and foreign policy makers, by studying the ways that policy makers perceive and evaluate external opinions and the effects these may have on their policy-making behavior.

My "working view of public opinion" is close to that of V. O. Key but is not identical.[77] It seems to me that *public opinion as a political force has bearing on foreign policy to the extent that foreign policy makers perceive in the environment outside of their political orbit some encouragements or limitations that facilitate or modify preferred behavior.* I want to enlarge on four different aspects of this working view, since they are of fundamental importance to my whole approach to the problem and to what follows in this book.

1. My focus here is on the policy maker himself, on the way that *he*, as a responsible official in a policy-making institution, sees and reacts to the opinion environment. I am concerned not with "objective reality," or the external reality that I as a scholar might discern from an independent appraisal of all the available opinion materials. Rather, it is the "perceived reality" of the government official that will concern us. We have persuasive evidence, in the case of Congressmen, that these two "realities" may diverge greatly in the foreign policy field.[78] Since I am concerned with many foreign policy issue areas and with potentially national constituencies, and thus with an enormous attendant proliferation of the

relevant objective realities, it has simply not been possible for me systematically to compare perceived with objective realities in most instances. In any event, for our purposes here the divergence between objective and perceived reality is not nearly so important as the patterned ways in which policy makers institutionally experience, define, and accommodate the external environment.

2. As a first approximation I define public opinion very broadly as residing in the environment outside the immediate political orbit of foreign policy makers. The point is that public opinion is not a clearly defined and autonomous political actor, and is not seen as one by policy makers, no matter how it may be conceived by external analysts. The question that concerns us, then, is how does the policy maker define his field of action outside his official circle? I am concerned, thus, not to discover how officials perceive and react to what *I* may think of as public opinion, but to discover what aspects of the external environment come into *their* consciousness as politically relevant factors. By asking the question that way, we will learn some surprising things about the way the external environment impinges on policy makers.

3. I noted above that the prevailing political perspective has long been that public opinion is retrogressive, irrational, indifferent — in short, that it is a negative force in policy making, restraining or thwarting policy makers in their pursuit of wise, rational actions on behalf of the national interest. My perspective here is not so predetermined, on either side: officials may see in their external environment encouragement and support for their policy positions as well as opposition to them — and they may even seek to mobilize supportive opinion or to convert opposition into neutrality or into permissiveness or support. There is reason to believe, from the figures on public reactions that policy makers sometimes release following public addresses or major policy statements, that in such circumstances officials hear more often from those who agree with them than from those who disagree — and they may also be more aware of opinions that agree.[79] To the extent that this happens, it is clear that the impact of opinion may be to encourage policy makers to do foolish things as well as to prevent them from doing wise things. The important point is the necessity to be sensitive to these and all other possibilities.

4. The actual determination or measurement of impact is the

most difficult question of all. If someone merely listens to opinion and then ignores it, that cannot properly qualify as an impact. Opinion may be said to have political consequence if it alters the preferred behavior of officials in some policy-relevant fashion. It can be a restraint or a modification of a preferred or intended course of action, or it can be an encouragement to remove restraint and act in ways that are preferred. If officials fully intend to behave in a certain way, opinion designed to persuade them to behave that way may be cordially received but have no effect whatever on behavior. If officials prefer to behave in a certain way but do not see their political environment as permitting it, particular opinions supporting that behavior may have the effect of modifying the perceived environment and thus facilitating the behavior. On the other hand, opinion may be said to have a limiting or restraining effect only when it has persuaded officials to refrain from behavior they would otherwise have set in train.[80] One can hone these various possibilities even finer, but the point should be clear. In his book on President Kennedy, Theodore Sorensen discussed the President's efforts to mobilize public opinion behind the Nuclear Test Ban Treaty; the impression he creates is that public opinion shifted as a consequence of the President's efforts, and as a consequence of that shift in public sentiment there was a shift in the sentiment of Senators which resulted in the Treaty passing the Senate.[81] That is an assertion of public impact for which no convincing evidence is offered. In the context I have presented here, it would be important to learn whether public opinion in fact induced a shift in the behavior of Senators or whether all the discussion in public merely provided a backdrop that made it "easier" for Senators to do what they were going to do anyway. The latter case is deserving of study as a type of political action, perhaps, but it clouds the issue to call it an example of the impact of public opinion on foreign policy.

I shall be concerned, in the ensuing chapters, with the following kinds of questions, though I cannot answer all of them with equal confidence: How do foreign policy officials perceive the nongovernmental public? In what ways do they experience, or come into contact with, this public? How do they evaluate expressions of public views? What are the ways in which they "take them into account," or respond to them? Is there any discernible relationship between sources of opinion and modes of evaluation and response or between the content of opinion and the modes of evaluation and response? Are there any differences in the perception and evaluation of opinion as among officials having different substantive responsibilities in foreign policy? As among officials in different policy making divisions, or in different levels of political and administrative responsibility, or with different career commitments? What differences do different constituencies make? Or different modes of public participation? In addition, I want to work toward a theory of the public's impact on foreign policy that accounts for the accommodations of opinion both in periods of calm and consensus and in periods of challenge and change. More precisely, then, what is involved in changing the terms of an apparent consensus on foreign policy? How does it happen?

Chapter 2 of this book examines the way the State Department operates in the public opinion field: its lack of internal machinery and the attitudes, outlooks, and modes of evaluation that prevail in the absence of, or as substitutes for, such institutional machinery. Chapter 3 explores in detail the diverse ways in which officials experience "public opinion": the many shapes it takes at the points of conjunction. In Chapter 4, I try to relate the patterns in the political interpretation of opinions to the patterns in the responses they elicit; my purpose is to discover what kinds of opinion seem to have what kinds of effects on officials. Chapter 4 is concerned only with the effects that public opinion has on the substance of foreign policy questions. Chapter 5, on the other hand, considers the consequences of opinion for information policy — the Department's public relations responses. Finally, in Chapter 6 I explore the larger problem of the responsiveness of our foreign policy institutions to public preferences and how that responsiveness might be enhanced.

The material for this study comes broadly from two sources: from personal interviews with foreign policy officials and from the literature discussed earlier. The interviews give us the policy makers' perceptions, the insiders' perspective; they provide a framework, a context, for the reexamination of varied data of all sorts from past studies. Despite all the defects in this literature, it remains a source of occasional data which, in conjunction with other information, give us new insight into past experience. The interviews are of two sorts. I have relied chiefly on a group of fifty which I undertook in the Department of State and the Agency for International Development during the academic year 1965–1966; I have made secondary use of a group of sixty-eight, of now quasi-historical value, undertaken in 1953–1954 by students in the Graduate Program of the Woodrow Wilson School of Public and International Affairs at Princeton University, under the supervision of Gabriel A. Almond and myself. These latter interviews were with foreign policy officials of both the Truman and Eisenhower Administrations, and, in those occasional instances when they are comparable with interviews from the Kennedy-Johnson years, they provide both depth and counterpoint.

Why do I confine a study of public opinion and foreign policy so narrowly to the Department of State, when foreign policy is scattered more widely around the government and when there is a growing feeling that the State Department is a declining factor in the formulation of American foreign policy? [82] At an early stage in the development of this work, I had intended to interview a larger sample of foreign policy officials throughout the Executive branch and of Congressmen active in foreign affairs too. But I soon concluded that, no matter how widely I might want ultimately to cast a net, it made more sense as a research strategy to concentrate my efforts, to focus on a place at or close to the center of the foreign policy process, and to do as thorough a job as possible there before moving farther out. I chose the Department of State rather than the White House, for several reasons. The major administrative responsibility for the development of most areas of foreign policy lies in the Department of State. It is not "cut-off" from most policy areas, even though the White House is involved in major policy choices and may even take over certain policy areas as its special preserve. Over the last forty years, Presidents have played a more direct role in foreign policy than they had customarily played before then; but the exercise of that role has varied substantially, ranging from distant supervision of State and other departments to personal control of certain policies through operations and/or through interagency coordinating machinery such as the National Security Council. At the time of my interviewing for this study, the White House staff for "national security affairs" was heavily invested in one area — Vietnam. In the years following, the Nixon Administration transferred considerably more political responsibility for foreign policy into the White House. But I am not moved by arguments that this is one further step in an inexorable, even inevitable, secular decline in the power of the State Department.[83] The evidence for such a projection simply does not exist — and it is just as easy to write credible scenarios for the next decade that would involve the strengthening of the State Department's influence as to write those that foretell its eclipse.

In periods when — or in policy areas where — the White House directly exercises the President's constitutional power in foreign policy, there is of course an additional source, or locus, or dimension of foreign policy decision making that it would be profitable to study. But one does not study the White House as easily as one engages in research on other political institutions in the United States, and one has to accommodate to that fact. Access to the White House in 1965–1966 was not very good, to understate the matter.[84] On the few occasions when I thought I had made it even to the working level, Vietnam always turned out to have a prior claim on my respondents' time. But an inability to study foreign policy making in the White House very easily or very closely does not mean that there is no point to our studying it as best we can elsewhere. The varying exercise of Presidential control over foreign policy does not seem to have very much effect on the way that the State Department goes about its business in that share of the market it may still control in any particular period. And I believe we are entitled to make reasonable extrapolations about "normal" approaches to other parts of the market from what we can learn about approaches to policy and opinion in these areas.

But can we extrapolate as easily from the lower levels of political responsibility and political significance that are represented in the State Department's share of the market to the higher levels that are represented in what the White House has taken over? In one sense, to be sure, we cannot: the very fact that policy questions are "appropriated" by the higher level suggests that they may be thought to be different in some ways from those that are left behind to be dealt with by lower-level officials. They may be deemed politically more sensitive, or more vulnerable, or simply more rewarding — all of which implies that "public opinion" may enter into their disposition in ways that are different from the routines of the State Department. An important question remains, however: are these differences of degree or of kind? I am persuaded — for reasons that I believe are manifest in the pages that follow — that the intellectual and political processes which seem to be involved in the perception and evaluation of, and accommodation to, external opinion are substantially the same throughout the foreign policy establishment, no matter the location or the level. The institutional and environmental constraints that affect the bureaucracy also affect its political leadership. Even the President is part of this establishment and subject to many of its constraints. Though he is the least accessible member of it, at least to a researcher, I think it is possible to make some relevant extrapolations to him, and I shall do so from time to time. Though I think it likely, then, that these differences between the State Department level and the White House level are mostly differences of degree, I must stress that this is nonetheless a surmise, whereas the question itself is in principle at least open to empirical investigation. It would be nice to *know* whether or not there were significant differences as between these levels — and I am hopeful that there will be future opportunities to find out. In other words, I do not conceive of what I have done thus far as embracing the whole process or as marking the end of the inquiry; it is merely the practical expression of a research priority made more compelling by the passage of time.

The interviewing that I did in 1965–1966 represents an effort to sample the State Department both horizontally and vertically, so to speak. This was not intended to be a scientifically representative sample of the Department. Rather, I tried to balance a reasonably broad range both of responsibilities and of substantive competences with some depth in particular offices so as to minimize the risks of idiosyncratic responses. And, as is inescapable in "elite interviewing" of this kind, my choice of respondents was on occasion remade for me by the vicissitudes of official life in Washington: unexpected trips abroad; interviews cut off by the press of events or by calls from above, with substitute respondents rushed into the breach; sudden shifts in assignments; even the chance availability of an official not on my list. The sample horizontally, or by level of responsibility, is as follows: two at the higher levels of the Department, above the rank of Assistant Secretary; six at the Assistant

Secretary level; ten at the Deputy Assistant Secretary level; eleven at the Office Director level; three at the Deputy Office Director level; nine at the Desk Officer (Officer-in-Charge) level; [85] and ten Special Assistants who performed at all levels, from the Office of the Secretary on down.[86] Vertically, or by bureau, the breakdown was as follows: three "generalists" at the secretariat level, five in Public Affairs, five in African Affairs, ten in European Affairs, seven in Far Eastern Affairs, four in Near Eastern and South Asian Affairs, four in International Organization Affairs, five in the Agency for International Development, and seven scattered through six other major subdivisions of the Department.[87]

The interviews averaged about an hour in length; they were all held in the respondent's office or a nearby lounge; and they were recorded in extensive shorthand notes taken on the spot, with the respondent's permission in every case. (The 1953–1954 interviews were conducted by two-man teams, one man asking questions and the other taking notes.) The respondents were all promised anonymity, and I have resorted to varying techniques to accomplish that: I have sometimes identified a respondent by rank, sometimes by bureau, but I have withheld the combinations of information that would identify individuals.

The interviews were not highly structured. I went into each with a common set of general questions, designed to elicit a range of information about the respondent's perceptions and evaluations of external opinion, but I almost always found it necessary to adapt those questions to the special circumstances and interests of respondents, in order to get comprehensive replies. Furthermore, I found it both a matter of common courtesy and a productive interviewing strategy to let an official run for a while with a question after he had it securely in his grasp. These practices yielded a wealth of information, but it most often requires qualitative rather than quantitative treatment.

Can I be sure that my respondents were giving me accurate responses? When I first started the interviewing, I was troubled by the apparent difficulty of officials to comprehend readily what I thought were very simple questions; and I had some concern for the value of my material. It soon became evident to me, however, that the problem was rooted in the not unimportant fact that officials simply do not think about public opinion very much or very explicitly. My confidence in the accuracy of my material grew steadily as I saw the repetitive patterns of response once officials began to think about the subject and to articulate their experiences. Beyond that, the exercise of judgment and the capacity for drawing inferences from rich data have to substitute for independent, objective confirmation.

NOTES

1. See, e.g., V. O. Key, Jr., *Public Opinion and American Democracy*, New York: Knopf, 1961; Robert E. Lane and David O. Sears, *Public Opinion*, Englewood Cliffs, N.J.: Prentice-Hall, 1964; and Bernard C. Hennessy, *Public Opinion*, Belmont, Calif.: Wadsworth, 1965.

2. Lee Benson, "An Approach to the Scientific Study of Past Public Opinion," *Public Opinion Quarterly*, Vol. 31, No. 4, Winter 1967–1968, pp. 522–567.

3. One of the earliest attempts to make some order out of the mass of survey data in the foreign policy area was Gabriel A. Almond, *The American People and Foreign Policy*, New York: Harcourt, Brace, 1950 (2d ed.; New York: Praeger, 1960). For recent examples of the insights available in this area, see James N. Rosenau, ed., *Domestic Sources of Foreign Policy*, New York: Free Press, 1967, esp. the chapters by Herbert McClosky, Milton J. Rosenberg, Johan Galtung, and Warren E. Miller; Sidney Verba *et al.*, "Public Opinion and the War in Vietnam," *American Political Science Review*, Vol. 61, No. 2, June 1967, pp. 317–333; and Alfred O. Hero, Jr., *The Southerner and World Affairs*, Baton Rouge: Louisiana State University Press, 1965.

4. See Key, *Public Opinion and American Democracy*, pp. 536 ff.; and William C. Rogers, Barbara Stuhler, and Donald Koenig, "A Comparison of Informed and General Public Opinion on U.S. Foreign Policy," *Public Opinion Quarterly*, Vol. 31, Summer 1967, pp. 242–252.

5. Angus Campbell, Philip E. Converse, Warren E. Miller, and Donald E. Stokes, *The American Voter*, New York: John Wiley & Sons, 1960; Richard A. Brody, Benjamin I. Page, Sidney Verba, and Jerome Laulicht, "Vietnam, the Urban Crisis, and the 1968 Presidential Election: A Preliminary Analysis," paper prepared for delivery at the annual meeting of the American Sociological Association, September 1969.

6. See Warren E. Miller and Donald E. Stokes, "Constituency Influence in Congress," *American Political Science Review*, Vol. 57, No. 1, March 1963, pp. 45–56.

7. See, e.g., William O. Chittick, "The Domestic Information Activities of the Department of State," unpubl. Ph.D. dissertation, Johns Hopkins University, 1964; Samuel P. Huntington, *The Common Defense:*

Strategic Programs in National Politics, New York: Columbia University Press, 1961; and James A. Robinson, *Congress and Foreign Policy-Making,* Homewood, Ill.: Dorsey Press, 1962 (rev. ed., 1967).

8. A recent example is Dean Acheson, *Present at the Creation,* New York: W. W. Norton, 1969.

9. See, e.g., Joseph M. Jones, *The Fifteen Weeks,* New York: Viking, 1955; and Raymond A. Dawson, *The Decision to Aid Russia, 1941,* Chapel Hill: University of North Carolina Press, 1959.

10. Bernard C. Cohen, *The Press and Foreign Policy,* Princeton: Princeton University Press, 1963. See also Dan D. Nimmo, *Newsgathering in Washington,* New York: Atherton Press, 1964; and William O. Chittick, *State Department, Press, and Pressure Groups,* New York: Wiley-Interscience, 1970.

11. See, e.g., Robert A. Divine, *Second Chance: The Triumph of Internationalism in America during World War II,* New York: Atheneum, 1967; Walter Johnson, *The Battle against Isolation,* Chicago: University of Chicago Press, 1944; Wayne S. Cole, *America First: The Battle against Intervention, 1940–41,* Madison: University of Wisconsin Press, 1953; and Selig Adler, *The Isolationist Impulse: Its Twentieth-Century Reaction,* London and New York: Abelard-Schuman, 1957.

12. Bernard C. Cohen, *The Influence of Non-governmental Groups on Foreign Policy-Making,* Boston: World Peace Foundation, 1959; Lester Milbrath, *The Washington Lobbyists,* Chicago: Rand McNally, 1963.

13. E.g., James N. Rosenau, *National Leadership and Foreign Policy,* Princeton: Princeton University Press, 1963; Ernest R. May, *American Imperialism: A Speculative Essay,* New York: Atheneum, 1968; and William C. Rogers and Barney Uhlig, "Small Town and Rural Midwest Foreign Policy Opinion Makers," *International Studies Quarterly,* Vol. 13, No. 3, September 1969, pp. 306–325.

14. Key, *Public Opinion and American Democracy,* Chaps. 14 and 15.

15. Note, e.g., Key, *Public Opinion and American Democracy:* "At elections public opinion is clearly controlling; that is, it determines who shall govern. The vexing analytical problem comes in the comprehension of the extent to which, and the processes whereby, public opinion is linked to the actions of government in the periods between elections" (p. 413). And at a later point he says: "The interaction between government and public opinion in the day-to-day work of government presents, it must be conceded, a phenomenon about which our systematic data are limited" (p. 431). James N. Rosenau has made the same observation, but since he cites me as a reference, it would be incestuous to carry it further. See also Ernest R. May, "An American Tradition in Foreign Policy: The Role of Public Opinion," in William H. Nelson, ed., *Theory and Practice in American Politics,* Chicago: University of Chicago Press, 1964, pp. 101–122; Richard C. Snyder and James A. Robinson, *National and International Decision-Making,* New York: Institute for International Order, 1962, pp. 61ff.; and William O. Chittick, "Public Opinion and

Foreign Policy: Three Problems of Analysis," paper prepared for presentation at the annual meeting of the Organization of American Historians, New Orleans, April 15, 1971.

16. On the conceptual side, see Richard C. Snyder, H. W. Bruck, and Burton Sapin, "Decision-Making as an Approach to the Study of International Politics," in Snyder, Bruck, and Sapin, eds., *Foreign Policy Decision Making*, New York: Free Press, 1962; and Norman R. Luttbeg, ed., *Public Opinion and Public Policy: Models of Political Linkage*, Homewood, Ill.: Dorsey Press, 1968. Luttbeg explores, through a collection of readings, a variety of theoretical models of the linkage between the public and its leaders that are either explicit or implicit in contemporary political science. His conclusions (e.g., p. 453) reflect his discouragement over the state of theory and over its practical implications for democratic government.

For studies using historical evidence, see Doris A. Graber, *Public Opinion, the President, and Foreign Policy: Four Case Studies from the Formative Years*, New York: Holt, Rinehart & Winston, 1968; May, *American Imperialism;* and Dawson, *The Decision to Aid Russia, 1941.* For analyses using contemporary data, see, on the Congressional side, Raymond A. Bauer, Ithiel de Sola Pool, and Lewis A. Dexter, *American Business and Public Policy: The Politics of Foreign Trade*, New York: Atherton Press, 1963; and on the executive side, Bernard C. Cohen, *The Political Process and Foreign Policy: The Making of the Japanese Peace Settlement*, Princeton: Princeton University Press, 1957.

17. See Graber, *Public Opinion, the President, and Foreign Policy;* and Manfred Landecker, *The President and Public Opinion*, Washington, D.C.: Public Affairs Press, 1968, p. 57. Dean Acheson, *Present at the Creation*, argues that *all* causal factors are lost in the documentary records (p. xv).

It should be noted that there is an extensive historical literature on the European side that tries to deal with this question, with equal lack of success. See, e.g., Lynn M. Case, *French Opinion on War and Diplomacy during the Second Empire*, Philadelphia: University of Pennsylvania Press, 1954, and other works that are cited therein. Case himself presents interesting material on "public opinion" gathered throughout France by *procureurs generaux* and by *préfets*, some of which contains internal evidence that it was examined, at least, by high French officials. But Case does not go much farther than that in his claim for the influence of opinion on policy — nor does he go very deeply into the question of whom the *procureurs generaux* and the *préfets* talked to as they prepared these regular reports on "French public opinion."

18. See, e.g., Robert Browder, *The Origins of Soviet-American Diplomacy*, Princeton: Princeton University Press, 1953; Jones, *The Fifteen Weeks;* and Dawson, *The Decision to aid Russia, 1941.* A. T. Steele, *The American People and China*, New York: McGraw-Hill, 1966, studies an issue-area rather than a particular case, with no more substantial results. And Harwood L. Childs, *Public Opinion: Nature, Formation, and*

Role, Princeton: Van Nostrand, 1965, reports in Chap. 13 some case studies by Princeton students which are equally inconclusive. In my own case study *The Political Process and Foreign Policy,* I tried to be systematic in my approach to this question, but it is inescapable that in the process I produced one more case study using categories and data not readily comparable with those that went before. (My hope, of course, was that they might be comparable with those that came after!)

19. See esp. Almond, *The American People and Foreign Policy* (2d ed.), and James N. Rosenau, *Public Opinion and Foreign Policy,* New York: Random House, 1961.

20. Benson, "An Approach to the Scientific Study of Past Public Opinion," p. 548.

21. This particular formulation was used by Secretary of State Dean Rusk, in an address to the American Political Science Association on September 7, 1965, and was published in the *Department of State Bulletin,* Vol. 52, No. 1370, September 27, 1965, pp. 506–507.

22. Lester Markel, "Opinion — A Neglected Instrument," in Lester Markel, ed., *Public Opinion and Foreign Policy,* New York: Harper & Bros., 1949, p. 23.

23. Martin Kriesberg, "Dark Areas of Ignorance," in *ibid.,* p. 49.

24. Benson, "An Approach to the Scientific Study of Past Public Opinion," pp. 543–544.

25. Cohen, *The Political Process and Foreign Policy,* pp. 209–230.

26. Browder, *The Origins of Soviet-American Diplomacy,* p. 119.

27. Steele, *The American People and China,* p. 219.

28. See Robert A. Dahl, *Congress and Foreign Policy,* New York: Harcourt, Brace, 1950, pp. 52–57. Dahl does explore one example in summary detail, the fate of the 1935 resolution of adherence to the World Court; but in this example he cites only Cordell Hull for his interpretation of the fate of that resolution. It is at least arguable that Hull's — or the Administration's — optimism that the resolution would pass handily before Hearst and Coughlin went to work on it was factually unwarranted. Thomas Bailey, e.g., who *implies* that Coughlin and Hearst did the foul deed, is much more conservative in his interpretation of the estimated margin of victory than Hull. Cf. Bailey, *A Diplomatic History of the American People,* 7th ed.; New York: Appleton-Century-Crofts, 1964, pp. 629–632. And Selig Adler stresses the "half-hearted fashion" in which the Democratic leadership, and President Roosevelt, argued on behalf of the resolution. *The Isolationist Impulse: Its Twentieth-Century Reaction,* London and New York: Abelard-Schuman, 1957, p. 255.

29. Dexter Perkins, "The Department of State and American Public Opinion," in Gordon Craig and Felix Gilbert, eds., *The Diplomats, 1919–1939,* Princeton: Princeton University Press, 1953, p. 298. On the subject of the Washington Arms Conference, Donald S. Birn has written: "The historian, even of an event as recent as the Washington Conference, cannot hope to measure the influence of public opinion on policy with any precision. . . . The historian must also be wary in accepting

the claim of the politician who says he is pursuing a course of action in deference to public opinion. At the Washington Conference such claims were made so frequently on such obscure and technical issues that they appear ludicrous." But despite this warning Birn goes on, immediately and perversely, to claim that "At Washington, public opinion not only helped determine the direction of each nation's policy; it also played a more direct role in shaping day-to-day tactics." Donald S. Birn, "Open Diplomacy at the Washington Conference of 1921–2: The British and French Experience," *Comparative Studies in Society and History*, Vol. 12, No. 3, July 1970, p. 298. For further information — but little enlightenment — on the American experience, see C. Leonard Hoag, *Preface to Preparedness: The Washington Disarmament Conference and Public Opinion*, Washington: American Council on Public Affairs, 1941.

30. Dexter Perkins, "The Department of State and American Public Opinion," p. 300.

31. *Ibid.*, p. 301.

32. James N. Rosenau, *National Leadership and Foreign Policy*, p. 17.

33. *Ibid.*, p. 335.

34. Cohen, *The Political Process and Foreign Policy*, p. 29.

35. Key, *Public Opinion and American Democracy*, p. 70. See also Charles O. Lerche, Jr., *The Uncertain South*, Chicago: Quadrangle Books, 1964: "If the South persists in moving outside the national circle of agreement on important issues of international affairs, the overall vigor of American action will obviously decline" (p. 17).

36. Stanley Hoffmann, *Gulliver's Troubles, or the Setting of American Foreign Policy*, New York: published for the Council on Foreign Relations by McGraw-Hill, 1968, p. 233. For another example of the use of this notion, see W. Phillips Davison, "More Than Diplomacy," in Markel, ed., *Public Opinion and Foreign Policy*, p. 131.

37. See Chap. 5 of the present volume.

38. Browder, *The Origins of Soviet-American Diplomacy*, p. 22.

39. *Ibid.*, pp. 21–22.

40. *Ibid.*, pp. 112–113.

41. Jones, *The Fifteen Weeks*, p. 226.

42. See also Acheson, *Present at the Creation*, pp. 217–235. The title of Acheson's memoir itself speaks to this point.

43. Herbert Feis, *Seen from EA: Three International Episodes*, New York: Knopf, 1947, pp. 256–257.

44. Browder, *The Origins of Soviet-American Diplomacy*, p. 119.

45. Steele, *The American People and China*, p. 119.

46. Walter Lippmann, *Essays in the Public Philosophy*, Boston: Atlantic–Little, Brown, 1955, p. 18.

47. See, e.g., Kenneth Waltz, *Foreign Policy and Democratic Politics*, Boston: Little, Brown & Co., 1967; and Henry M. Wriston, *Diplomacy in a Democracy*, New York: Harper & Bros., 1956.

48. Key, *Public Opinion and American Democracy*, p. 264.

49. *Ibid.*, p. 429.

50. Cohen, *The Political Process and Foreign Policy*, p. 209.

51. Foreign Policy Association, *Intercom*, Vol. 8, No. 2, March–April 1966, issue on Public Opinion and Foreign Policy, p. 26. Leon Epstein calls this "the customary way of explaining the role assigned to the public." See his "Democracy and Foreign Policy," in W. N. Chambers and R. H. Salisbury, eds., *Democracy in the Mid-Twentieth Century*, St. Louis: Washington University Press, 1960, p. 133.

52. Key, *Public Opinion and American Democracy*, p. 97.

53. *Ibid.*, pp. 199–200.

54. *Ibid.*, p. 424.

55. Dean Rusk, "The Anatomy of Foreign Policy Decisions," *Department of State Bulletin*, Vol. 52, No. 1370, September 27, 1965, pp. 506–507. (One wonders whether Rusk would have put this differently three years later.)

56. Theodore Sorensen, *Kennedy*, New York: Harper & Row, 1965, p. 509.

57. Chittick, "The Domestic Information Activities of the Department of State," p. 209.

58. Rosenau, *National Leadership and Foreign Policy*, p. 3.

59. Childs, *Public Opinion*, p. 315.

60. Note the following attempt by Leroy N. Rieselbach: "There are constraints within which the President must operate. He cannot go beyond what the public, or at least the attentive segment of the public, will acquiesce in, for while most citizens will willingly yield day-to-day policy determination to the executive branch, they will reject policy moves which go beyond the broad, and vague, area of popular consensus. Recent events suggest, for instance, that a President who talked seriously about either preventive nuclear war or unilateral disarmament would be confronted by an immediate public outcry and the very real possibility of a crushing defeat at the polls' in the ensuing election. In short, the chief executive is constrained by what the public will, or can be persuaded to, accept." "The Public, Congress, and Foreign Policy: A Review," *Journal of Conflict Resolution*, Vol. 9, No. 2, June 1965, p. 243. I believe it is safe to say that it is not the possibility of an eventual crushing defeat at the polls that constrains a President from serious public discussion of preventive nuclear war or unilateral disarmament; it is the possibility of an eventual crushing defeat on the battlefield or at the diplomatic bargaining table (as well as the related fear of being thought by one's close associates to have lost one's marbles). Furthermore, to conclude that the President is "constrained by what the public will, or can be persuaded to, accept" is finally and precisely to beg the question of where the limits are.

Robert A. Dahl's argument, in his *Preface to Democratic Theory* (Chicago: University of Chicago Press, 1956, p. 72), that elites operate within limits "set by their expectations as to the reactions of the group of politically active citizens who go to the polls," is subject to this same criticism.

61. See Ole R. Holsti, "Cognitive Dynamics and Images of the Enemy," in David J. Finlay, Ole R. Holsti, and Richard R. Fagen, *Enemies in Politics,* Chicago: Rand McNally, 1967, p. 91: "While public opinion may set broad limits on policy beyond which the decision-maker cannot move, it is also true that public attitudes are in large part shaped by decision-makers."

62. See the discussion summarized in Richard M. Pfeffer, ed., *No More Vietnams? The War and the Future of American Foreign Policy,* New York: Harper & Row for the Adlai Stevenson Institute of International Affairs, 1968.

63. Most of the participants in the discussion reported by Pfeffer, *ibid.,* seemed to believe that the Vietnam experience would bequeath an inviolable "limit."

64. Cf. Dean Acheson: "But I could not overcome two stubborn facts: that our delaying research [on the H-bomb] would not delay Soviet research . . . and that the American people simply would not tolerate a policy of delaying nuclear research in so vital a matter while we sought for further ways of reaching accommodation with the Russians after the experiences of the years since the war" (*Present at the Creation,* p. 349). In view of Acheson's remark on p. 21, however — "Over the years I have been impressed by how often political leaders have misjudged the people's willingness to follow a strong lead" — and his scattering of contemptuous remarks about public opinion elsewhere in his book, one may be forgiven for thinking this comment about nuclear research disingenuous.

65. The radical historian's view of this is not radically different. See Gabriel Kolko, *The Roots of American Foreign Policy: An Analysis of Power and Purpose,* Boston: Beacon Press, 1969, pp. 12–13: "The theory of public attitudes as the fount of the decision-making process reinforces a democratic theory of legitimacy, which, for reasons of sentimental tradition at home and ideological warfare abroad, is a useful social myth. But the close and serious student of modern American foreign relations will rarely, if ever, find an instance of an important decision made with any reference to the alleged general public desires or opinions. What is more significant is the fact of ignorance and lack of interest among the vast majority of the population during a period of crisis as to the nature of essential issues and facts, a condition that neutralizes their role in the decision-making process even more and cultivates an elitist contempt for the inchoate role of 'the people' as nothing more than the instrument or objective, rather than the source, of policy."

66. For an explicit justification of this sort, see Rosenau, ed., *Domestic Sources of Foreign Policy,* esp. the introduction by Rosenau. For an implicit justification, see Divine, *Second Chance.*

67. See Melvin Small, "Historians Look at Public Opinion," in Melvin Small, ed., *Public Opinion and Historians,* Detroit: Wayne State University Press, 1970, p. 14: "After thus delineating the frame of reference, the student must verify the assumption that public opinion plays a role in the policy making process. No studies *prove* this traditional piece of

folklore. On the other hand, few historians or political scientists challenge it, either on empirical or intuitive grounds. Until more work is done in this area, the scholar must practice a not very admirable form of intellectual obfuscation and point to legitimizers who have accepted the all important assumption."

68. E.g., Lippmann, *Essays in the Public Philosophy*, esp. pp. 3–87. Cf. also Jones, *The Fifteen Weeks:* "The tragedy of government is usually that farseeing leaders in positions of power find themselves thwarted in their desires and efforts to achieve new solutions by the pull of established institutions and rigid patterns of public thinking. This was not so during the Fifteen Weeks" (p. 239); and Kriesberg, "Dark Areas of Ignorance": "An uninformed electorate acts as a drag upon the government. Prejudices which fetter the ignorant and apathetic voters hang heavily upon the hands of their representatives also" (p. 63).

69. See Divine, *Second Chance.*

70. In a reversal of this interpretation, Rosenberg suggests that an uninformed anti-communist public has constrained otherwise intelligent officials to follow a Cold War policy. Milton J. Rosenberg, "Attitude Change and Foreign Policy in the Cold War Era," in Rosenau, ed., *Domestic Sources of Foreign Policy*, pp. 150–151; and Milton J. Rosenberg, "Images in Relation to the Policy Process: American Public Opinion on Cold-War Issues," in Herbert C. Kelman, ed., *International Behavior*, New York: Holt, Rinehart & Winston, 1965, pp. 278–334.

71. See Bernard C. Cohen, *Citizen Education in World Affairs*, Princeton University: Center of International Studies, 1953.

72. E.g., Sidney Verba *et al.*, "Public Opinion and the War in Vietnam."

73. Rosenau, *Public Opinion and Foreign Policy*, pp. 9–16.

74. Roger Hilsman, *To Move a Nation*, Garden City: Doubleday, 1967, is an interesting exception to the usual neglect of political strategy.

75. On the politics of military policy, see, for example, Huntington, *The Common Defense.*

76. See Walter Lippmann, *Public Opinion*, New York: Pelican Books, 1946; and Cohen, *The Press and Foreign Policy.*

77. Key, *Public Opinion and American Democracy*, p. 14.

78. Cf. Bauer, Pool, and Dexter, *American Business and Public Policy;* W. Miller and D. Stokes, "Constituency Influence in Congress."

79. Cf. Bauer, Pool, and Dexter, *American Business and Public Policy*, esp. Part V; and Leila Sussman, "Mass Political Letter Writing in America," *Public Opinion Quarterly*, Vol. 23, No. 2, Summer 1959, p. 209. In the absence of major efforts to mobilize support, however, officials are more likely to hear from those who disagree with them. See Chap. 3 of the present volume.

80. See Robert A. Dahl, "The Concept of Power," *Behavioral Science*, Vol. 2, July 1957, pp. 201–214.

81. Sorensen, *Kennedy*, p. 739.

82. See Terence Smith, "Foreign Policy: Decision Power Ebbing at

the State Department," *The New York Times,* January 18, 1971, pp. 1, 14.

83. *Ibid.*

84. The suggestion is powerful that good access was related to one's disposition to be "helpful" to the Johnson Administration: witness Henry F. Graff, "How Johnson Makes Foreign Policy," *The New York Times Magazine,* July 4, 1965.

85. This was before the levels between Office Director and Officer-in-Charge were compressed into the position of Country Director.

86. These figures total fifty-one; one man among the fifty occupied two distinct positions, and I interviewed him in both capacities. A simpler breakdown of these fifty officials, which also locates Special Assistants at the level in which they are serving, results in the following: four at the secretariat level, eighteen at the bureau level, nineteen at the office level, and nine at the desk level.

87. The discrepant figures for the secretariat are owing to a Special Assistant who was serving the secretariat but who was administratively located in one of the subdivisions of the Department.

**The State Department and
Public Opinion: An Overview**

The opportunities for the public to have an impact on foreign policy reside in the mechanisms within the foreign policy establishment for understanding public opinion and for dealing with it in a
policy-relevant way. The mechanisms may be formal or informal,
institutional or personal. This is more than a question of the "internal allocation of jurisdiction [which] may affect the types of
opinion that enter effectively into the settlement of particular
questions." [1] It says, rather, that public opinion can impinge on foreign policy only to the extent that, and in such ways as, policy
makers are aware of and/or receptive to it. I shall begin, then
(and for reasons which I specified in the preceding chapter), by in-
quiring into the operations of the State Department in the public
opinion field. The State Department handles the vast bulk of our
foreign political relations, and in the ordinary course it develops
most of our foreign policies. What are the various procedures,
practices, and orientations of Departmental officials in the handling of external opinions as they bear on the conduct and development of these foreign relations and policies? If there are formal
institutional mechanisms for the discovery and the consideration of
opinion, then we have to inquire into the way they operate and
into their consequences. If there are no such institutional devices,
or if they function very imperfectly, then we shall have to ask
whether there are informal functional substitutes, what forms these
take, and what they signify for the perception and evaluation of
opinion.

THE DEPARTMENT'S
PUBLIC OPINION INSTITUTIONS

Since the middle of World War II, the State Department has had a major section devoted to Public Affairs. Now called the Bureau of Public Affairs (designated the *P* area within the Department) and headed by an Assistant Secretary of State, it has — like all State Department offices — gone through many organizational changes over the last twenty-five years. Although all the details of those changes need not concern us, their consequences do: for they have progressively converted the bureau from an organization at least ostensibly devoted to public affairs into one devoted almost wholly and rather openly to public relations. But the transformation may be more apparent than real, for the internal tension between these two aspects of the bureau's work — that of opinion analyst and of opinion maker — has always been high, and the public relations role has always been dominant.[2]

Those who were involved in the early efforts of the Office of Public Affairs, as it was then called, referred to it even then as the effort "to sell the State Department to the American people,"[3] "to bring closer to our fellow citizens the work of the State Department."[4] While the Department has often assured citizens that their voices count, that someone *is* listening, the prevailing view in the Department clearly is that the Public Affairs task is to interpret the Department's policy to the American people, rather than to interpret American public opinion to the Department. One knowledgeable participant described the efforts of the *P* area as the development of "mechanisms to absorb and cushion the arrows of public opinion," much like the cadmium rods that absorb neutrons in a nuclear reactor. Another said, "Our job is first of all to get information out and to be aware of what is being said and reported." Officers within the Department are little aware of the work of the bureau, since it affects them so little; one person, who had once held a high position within the bureau, mused: "It is interesting; because I served in the Bureau of Public Affairs, I thought I would be especially sensitive to it for a long time thereafter. I don't even hear of the bureau any more; I wonder when it was that I stopped being aware of them?"

The evolution — or perhaps I should say "fate" — of the various divisions within the Bureau of Public Affairs reveals starkly the de-

cline of the bureau's role as public opinion analyst. The main offices (excluding that of Historical Publications, which publishes the
Department's documentary series) for many years were Public
Opinion Studies, Public Liaison (later Public Services), and News.
Public Opinion Studies had the task of "placing accurate summaries of American public opinion before officers of the United States
government who are responsible for the formulation and conduct
of foreign policy." [5] Public Services maintained contact with outside organizations interested in foreign affairs, helping them to develop and staff programs on the subject. And the News Division
was the Department's formal contact point with the press, providing a daily press briefing, handling press conferences, and getting
answers to reporters' questions.[6] While both the News Division and
the Public Services Division provided some possibility of two-way
channels of communication with outside agencies of opinion, their
orientation was substantially outward; the Division of Public
Opinion Studies, on the other hand, was clearly the Department's
institutional mechanism for systematically exploring the state of
public opinion (defined chiefly as press and interest-group opinion)
and conveying it inward. From 1952 to 1971 there has been an almost uninterrupted decline in the fortunes of the Public Opinion
Studies Division and a parallel rise in the importance of the News
Division. The News Division, in fact, has risen to such an extent
that in 1969 it was given separate status, no longer under the authority of the Assistant Secretary for Public Affairs. The job of
Assistant Secretary for Public Affairs is now much more a personal public relations position and less an administrative
post.[7]

From 1946 to 1952 the staff of the Public Opinion Studies Division (then called Public Studies Division) ranged in size from nineteen to twenty-five. Under the Eisenhower Administration, the division was cut in half, ranging in size from ten to twelve between
1953 and 1960. In 1961 the Kennedy Administration again cut the
staff of the division in half, this time to six.[8] And by 1965 it was no
longer a division, merely a position (Public Opinion Adviser) en-
tailing a staff of three, and preparing opinion summaries mainly on
request. It is obvious from these figures that the fate of Public
Opinion Studies has not been a partisan issue, since both parties
have contributed to its demise.

The reasons for its disappearance are simple: one can find

hardly a soul among the contemporary potential users of the division's summaries of press and organizational opinion who found them helpful and who had a good word to say on their behalf. High officials in the Department during the late 1940's and early 1950's, when the division was in its prime, were generally aware of its output and in general terms were sympathetic toward it. Several Assistant Secretaries of State who were interviewed at that time described the opinion digests as "helpful in giving us a feel as to what the country was thinking on issues." Yet as early as 1949 an academic observer reported that this material did not meet the needs of Departmental officials, not only because of its type and its quality but also because of the customs and habits of Department personnel.[9] And interviews with officials serving since that time simply confirm the point. In 1959 the Director of the Office of Public Studies, H. Schuyler Foster, wrote: "The requests which the Public Studies Division receives from Department officers and from overseas posts make it clear that there is great interest in public opinion — especially at the higher and middle levels of the Department and Foreign Service." [10] But in my interviews in the higher and middle reaches of the Department, I found not great interest but indifference and even hostility. Referring to the disappearance of the opinion summaries, an Office Director said, "I haven't missed any of it. There is too much paper here anyway. We all read the press carefully . . . so we know pretty well what the country is thinking. These newspapers, plus the stuff that comes from the Congress, tell us all we need to know, and we do not need anyone to feed us this pap." [11] A Deputy Director of a different office made a similar remark: "I've never read their material. . . . Most people in the State Department do not use these opinion summaries; they read the same sources anyway, and they want to make their own judgments." Still another Office Director who had once worked in the *P* area observed: "As restrained as my support was for the operation in running the opinion summaries, I was probably the most sympathetic of all those who had anything to do with it." The kindest thing I heard about the opinion summaries came from a Deputy Assistant Secretary: "This is very helpful as a tool for people who do not have time to go into detail and do their own research in these matters." But the class of people whom he thus described was apparently minuscule. Opinion was divided on the worth of these opinion summaries for officers abroad. A few officials recalled that they had had more tolerant attitudes toward the opinion digests when they were serving in foreign posts and found it less easy to keep up on their own. "But here in Washington," as an officer then in the *P* area remarked, "everyone has his own two or three newspapers he reads regularly, and he gets his own feel of the situation that way." But other officers were even more contemptuous of the irrelevance of the summaries for the man in a foreign post than for the official here at home.

The treatment of incoming mail as a form of opinion, which I shall discuss in greater detail subsequently, also reveals the weakness of the Department's machinery for opinion analysis. It is a matter of some interest, to begin with, that letters have been handled not by the Public Opinion Studies Division but by a branch (Public Correspondence Branch) of the Public Services Division, whose function is liaison rather than opinion analysis. In his sympathetic description of these activities, Elder noted that the analyses of mail opinion were "forwarded to the Public Studies Division for its consideration." [12] Apart from figures on the distribution of mail by subject, however — itself a matter of some sensitivity in the Department — further analysis of mail opinion seems not to have been widely distributed (or at least not perceived to have been widely distributed). A Deputy Assistant Secretary observed, "We do not get a specific reading from the Public Affairs people on the letters that bear on our particular business. . . . No one keeps tabs for us on the public correspondence, in terms of particular subject matters and so on." An Office Director complained, "In the Public Affairs area, they all believe that the mail should be analyzed, so that they know where it comes from, what the relative interest is in various issues, and so forth; but somehow they never get around to analyzing it — at least I don't think they do."

The institutions mentioned above represent substantially all of the Department's basic machinery for public opinion analysis. One additional position, the Public Affairs Adviser (PAA) attached to the various bureaus in the Department, has no opinion-analysis function, whatever expectations to the contrary may be engendered by the title. The PAA is a point of contact between the bureau he serves and the press. His job is to handle the press, to get answers to their questions, to stand, as a Politico-Military Adviser in one of the regional bureaus put it, "between us and the outside groups, and in this sense [he does] serve to insulate us." The reporters are frequently critical of the PAA's performance and do not allow him to insulate all the officials in a bureau; but they cannot endow him with additional functions, such as opinion analysis, which he is neither authorized nor equipped to perform.

It is a fair conclusion, I think, that this machinery for opinion gathering and analysis does not work very well. The institutions have apparently never performed very useful services for Department staff, and now they scarcely perform them at all. A good measure of the perceived inadequacy of existing institutions is the creation of ad hoc ones to perform the same functions. In the public opinion and foreign policy field, this took the form of the International Cooperation Year, a program involving hundreds of people — they were described by one official as "the top people in American life" — in the work of thirty substantive committees over a period of ten months in 1965, analyzing problems of international relations and making recommendations for governmental policy. The work of the ICY was novel and prodigious, and the recommendations were detailed, specialized, and extensive. But the effort as a whole recapitulated prior experience in the public opinion field. The evaluation of the program by Department officers was on the whole so negative — damning with faint and especially reserved praise — that no one has ventured to suggest that the exercise be repeated. An official who had worked with one of the ICY committees subsequently had a brush with the *Foreign Service Journal* and concluded that he "simply could not promote the point of view that the recommendations were worth the time of Foreign Service officers."

Until quite recently, the Assistant Secretary of State for Public Affairs had at least a vestigial institutional role in trying to claim the Secretary's attention for public affairs work; though that role was substantially for the purpose of improving the Department's public relations, it nonetheless implied some responsibility on the Assistant Secretary's part for "knowing" the state of those public relations or for having some good intuitions about them. But recent changes in the Assistant Secretary's authority and responsibility, symbolized by the brief appointment to that position of a space hero who presumably could communicate directly to the young, have virtually closed off even that tiny route of formal access.[13]

I do not mean to suggest, by all this, that there are now no means whatsoever by which the State Department learns things about the condition of external opinion on subjects dear to its heart. On the contrary, many other aspects of the Department's work yield opinion information, and I shall examine them all in subsequent chapters. The important point, however, is that I will no longer be talking about an organized, relatively systematic effort on the part of the State Department to learn something about public opinion that might simultaneously inform all of the officers and persons in the Department who could be affected by it, since such a thing does not exist.[14] As a result of this situation, and despite any preferences of their own on the matter, Department officials all the way up to the Secretary of State have to rely on their own varied resources both for the acquisition of opinion data and for its analysis and interpretation. These resources, and the states of mind that inform their use, are thus of fundamental interest to us.

It is necessary to resist, as premature, the temptation to speculate here about the stream of consequences that flows from all this. The prevailing view has certainly been that the Department's summaries of press and organizational opinion were of no value to Department officials anyway and that nothing has been lost in their demise. The reasons for that view were complex; they related in part to the specific nature and quality of the opinion digests — rather mechanical and repetitive summaries of the policy positions of masses of newspapers and interest groups — and in part to the more general problems of trying to make politically meaningful sense out of this kind of information and of integrating it into all the other kinds of information that bear on policy preference and choice. But whether that kind of centralized and institutionalized opinion information is on balance to be preferred to the present decentralized, individualized alternative; or whether there may be still other, untried institutional approaches like the International Cooperation Year that seem more promising; or whether what I referred to above as "the more general problem" of making use of such information really precludes any significant possibilities in this area — the answer to such questions is not something that we can readily address ourselves to at this early point in the analysis.

First we have to explore the present decentralized alternative and, even antecedent to that, the way that Department officials themselves approach the whole subject of public opinion and conceive of the "problem" it presents.

PERCEPTIONS OF PUBLIC INTEREST IN THE STATE DEPARTMENT

Officials come up against opinion not as something separate or separable from the larger field or context of political action but as an interwoven part of that political field or context. As a first step in unraveling these threads, or in understanding this gestalt, it is useful to ask how officials perceive and define public interest in their work. To put this subject in a more familiar light, these perceptions by foreign policy officials of the extent, volume, and character of the public audience for their work are central to definitions of the "constituency" of the Department of State.

The argument over whether the State Department, like the Labor or Agriculture Departments, has a domestic constituency is enduring but hardly momentous. It never quite disappears; yet it is not often carried to the point of precision in specifying what such a constituency does or should consist in and what its consequences may be for the institution itself and for its policy output. The argument is reflected in some of the conflicting notions within the State Department on what a constituency is and what the Department's real situation is with respect to such a public. One view is that a constituency exists only in relation to services performed. Those who subscribe to this premise disagree on the true situation in the Department. One conclusion is that since State is not a service department, it has no constituency: "The State Department is one of the few agencies in the government that does not have a clientele in this country." In AID, however, an official pointed proudly to a service-related constituency: "We started it [i.e., tying aid funds to purchases in the United States] for balance of payments reasons, but we have kept it going because it has created a real constituency for us — a sizeable collection of groups of people in this country who have an economic interest in keeping the program going as it stands." Still others conclude that since its services are performed for everyone, i.e., since foreign policy is a collective public good which everyone consumes, "The State Department has no constituency except the entire country." Another official quoted Secretary of State Rusk as saying that "our constituency is the American people."

Others define the constituency not in service terms but in terms of interest, attention, concern — some of it passive, some of it involving active participation in efforts to influence policy. One official described the knowledgeable and active participants in the ICY conference as "really all of [Secretary Rusk's] constituents." Another concluded: "I guess we're not totally without a constituency. We have the universities — they have a special interest in foreign affairs." Another, whom I quoted in Chapter 1, said: "We do have a constituency of sorts — the Foreign Policy Association, the Council on Foreign Relations, and all the other groups like that." Andrew Berding, a former Assistant Secretary for Public Affairs, has extended this view to its fullest logical development. Disputing the "conviction" of Foreign Service Officers (which he called their "major inferiority complex") that State is the only Department without a domestic constituency, he argues that it "does have a constituency, and it is ever acquiring a larger one. Partly this is made up of the hundreds of thousands of persons who now demonstrate an active concern in our foreign relations. . . . Partly it comprises the families and friends of the vast number of our military overseas. . . . Partly it is formed of the many scores of thousands of Americans who have some contact with foreigners who come here under exchange programs. . . . Partly it is comprised of the many thousands of Americans who . . . take part in People-to-People activities. . . . Partly it is contributed to by the major portion of the torrents of American tourists who pour overseas each year." [15]

These divergent (and illustrative) viewpoints are not simply definitional or even interpretive quibbles. More fundamentally, they reflect the fact that people in the State Department and elsewhere in the foreign policy establishment have very different experiences with and perceptions of public interest in their work. The relationship between the State Department and the public looks different to different people because it *is* different; it varies from issue to issue, over time, and from one location in the Department to another. It also depends on the breadth of vision of individuals, on how large a segment of the political and policy horizon (and thus on how much comparative data) they take in at any given time. Narrow peripheral vision may be a personal limitation as well as a function of very narrow institutional responsibilities. But it would be a mistake, as we shall note, to assume that narrow vision sees only small constituencies or that wide vision sees large ones.

Just how large or small the constituency actually appears, then, depends on where one sits in relation to issues and what one sees. The few men in the State Department who were familiar with the flow of letters to the Executive branch on all foreign policy questions (most of those letters ended up in the State Department even when they had been addressed elsewhere) would have no reason to disagree with the very restricted estimates of the size of the interested and involved public made by recent academic observers.[16] The total number of those letters in the year 1965, less than 200,-000, was equivalent to less than one-tenth of one percent of the United States population, without making any discount for the many "repeaters" among the letter-writers and for the many form letters received. That total, incidentally, also included an indeterminate number of letters to Congressmen, which the latter felt were important or complex enough to send on to the State Department for its assistance in preparing replies. Furthermore, more than half of the total number of letters were on a single subject — Vietnam — leaving the rest (i.e., equivalent to less than one-twentieth of one percent of the population) divided in interest among all other issues of American foreign policy current at that time.

At the level of the bureaus and the desks, however, there is great variability and fluctuation in the awareness or perception of constituency. In approximately fifteen of the country-areas of the State Department in which I interviewed, officials were in no great doubt that there was "little public interest in what we do." Not surprisingly, perhaps, for areas like Malta, Cyprus, Mauritania, Portuguese territories in Africa, or even Lebanon or Australia; rather more surprisingly for Germany and for policy areas like the Multilateral Force (MLF) proposal that so embroiled U.S. relations with NATO countries in the Kennedy years. An Office Director: "Public interest in our area has been very minor. The problems in —— are a low-key irritant rather than a major issue . . . we have no domestic constituency at all. There are no interest groups or outside reference groups. Academics don't really get into this policy area very much either." Another Office Director: People "have opinions on Vietnam but not on anything else. . . . But why should they be aware of the problems of ——? They have enough trouble keeping the crabgrass out of the lawn." [17]

In other and fewer areas of the Department, officials perceive a public interest or a constituency which they recognize as narrowly specialized and clearly "minority." The Eastern European countries are a good example of these; the interested public is seen not as all those Americans of Slavic descent, but as particular "emigré groups" with special political interests and positions. "Most of the issues that we handle here are issues which only a minority of Americans feel deeply about, and the ones who do feel deeply are likely to be critical of our policy."

In still other areas (again, at the time of my interviews) officials worked in the light — or, for some, in the shadow — of clearly identified and strongly felt constituencies. And if my interviews are a good sample, there are almost as many of these "hot spots" as there are areas where no public interest makes itself felt. They are all familiar, as one would expect of places or issues that had attracted substantial public interest over a sustained period of time: first and foremost even then, Vietnam; Communist China; Rhodesia; Israel; the Soviet Union; the United Nations; population control; immigration. The Vietnamese question is particularly interesting, in that its characterization as an area of enormous public interest came as strongly from officials who were in *other* policy or geographic areas as it did from those with Vietnamese responsibilities. This is no doubt a measure of the gross differences between this issue and all other issues in the public market place, clearly visible as such to all comparison-shoppers in the State Department. For example, a desk officer in Europe: ". . . Compared to Vietnam, we get just a shadow of this." And a desk officer in the Far East: "All of this amounts to very little as far as I am concerned; when a person is working on Vietnam, on the other hand, he gets a lot of pressure." Even though the White House had appropriated the Vietnam issue in its public and political dimensions, drawing some of the fire away from the State Department's Vietnam Working Group, the men closest to the issue in the Department described the manifestations of public interest as "tremendous," "insatiable."

The Israeli and African situations are also instructive in their differences from the Eastern European question. In the latter case, an interested public was perceived as a small minority, a marginal constituency, of rather circumscribed electoral significance. In the former instance, however, the minorities that make up the interested public are seen as large and/or politically important. On African questions, for instance, this observation: "Where you get up to 10 percent of the population *possibly* concerned with this, it is an interest of the American people of a rather substantial magnitude. No other bureau in the Department has such a sizable public interest in a special policy. Lots of people are interested in the UN or in the Alliance for Progress, but when you start thinking about a potential interest of 22 million [black] Americans, I would propose the proposition that this is a different kind of problem from the normal variety in our policy formulation." In the Public Affairs area the view was expressed that questions involving Israel, such as policy toward the United Arab Republic, were the only ones in the Department for which there was a public audience that would react directly and significantly upon the State Department rather than indirectly through other institutions, especially the Congress.

It seems clear from these descriptions of public interest in the issues confronting the State Department that there are some public audiences who follow particular issue-areas with close interest and express their views with sufficient clarity, frequency, and force to be perceived and identified by officials as interested and involved in more than a passing way. If that seems like an inordinately trite observation as well as a pedantic formulation, perhaps it can also be taken as an acceptable definition of what I have been calling "constituency." It is enormously suggestive that officials working in several of these issue-areas seem to think of their constituency relationship as unique in the Department. To Africa and Israel, above, we can add the United Nations — "There is more public interest in what we do than in the work of any other bureau. . . . To the extent to which we have a constituency . . . it is the community of the internationally minded." And Consular Affairs can be added as well — "[We] get the largest volume of mail in the State Department. . . . We have a constituency that others do not have." There is no doubt a trace of institutional pride or ambition in these claims; but one cannot avoid the conclusion that the claimants do believe — rightly or wrongly — that an identifiable constituency, a continuing public following, is a rare bird in the foreign policy aviary. Apparently it is not as rare as they think, however, since it seems to be nesting in quite a few places at any one time.

Although it may be understandable that officials who are immersed in the problems of a particular area do not have very good peripheral vision, one might expect that the higher a man stands in the Department hierarchy, the more opportunity or occasion he would have to aggregate these particular experiences of active and sustained public interest into a larger view of an overall foreign policy constituency in the United States. Yet there is no clear or convincing evidence that such is the case. There are not very many people in the Department above the bureau or Assistant Secretary level to begin with; and those I interviewed did not talk as if they had such a larger view. From the Assistant Secretary level on down within the bureaus, on the other hand, there is no discernible difference by rank between those persons who saw little evidence of public interest and those who saw a great deal. In other words, even within the bureaus there was no noticeable tendency for higher-ranking persons to aggregate "constituency" experiences within their purview. Andrew Berding, whom I quoted earlier, may appear to be an exception to this, but I do not really interpret him in that way. His "larger view" of the foreign policy constituency has no policy or issue-area base; it rests on classes of people who are presumed to be interested in foreign affairs, not on any explicit evidence that they have and exercise such interest. One suspects his conception or definition of having large doctrinal and philosophical components, as well as an ego-satisfying function. One can understand how a former Assistant Secretary for Public Affairs who saw the public relations function of his job in the widest possible terms might be equally expansive in defining the broad targets for his efforts as the foreign policy constituency.

We have here an apparent paradox: At nearly a dozen points within the State Department, including some of the politically most troublesome issue-areas in recent years, I found a clear perception of a sustained "audience," of an identifiable segment of the population watching them with great interest and periodically participating in their policy discussions; yet there seems to be no generally accepted view in the Department — in fact, not even a strong minority view — that these pockets of public interest collectively define a national foreign policy following or constituency for the Department. Three somewhat interrelated possibilities suggest themselves as explanations for the apparent inconsistency.

First, the perceptions of public interest and involvement may be idiosyncratic, the result of highly individualized and essentially unshared experiences and standards of comparison or evaluation. In this sense, what looks like great public interest to one person, because of his very intimate involvement with outsiders, may be written off as negligible by another, because he does not deal with it directly. This is conceivable within any particular issue-area and much more likely across areas, where observers in a different, and especially a higher-level, office are out of range of the details of public contact. If the latter are too far away to see what is going on in the trenches, so to speak, it may also be the case that the men in the trenches are so close to the action that they have lost all perspective on its magnitude and significance.

Second, we cannot dispute the fact that issues and issue-areas come and go in foreign policy and that some of them attract more attention than others as they transit our lives.[18] The areas we have been discussing here are those where the transit has been slower than most, and the amount and variety of public attention greater. In these circumstances, an observer has some freedom of choice in his interpretations: he can focus either on the transitory nature of the phenomena or on the spectacular life they lead during their historically brief existence. It is quite reasonable, thus, that experienced officers, men who have been through many skirmishes during their careers, may define most of these particular issues as transient phenomena, scattered through the Department in no pattern, the product of the vagaries of press coverage and publicity and the object of temporary, artificially created "attention groups" rather than of enduring and structured foreign policy audiences. Certainly they would find support for this interpretation in the reams of public opinion data on foreign policy questions.[19] From this perspective, then, they might take note of the public attention given to certain issues but fundamentally depreciate its significance.

Third, the explanation may lie not in the interpretation of the opinion phenomena officials confront but in what they believe a constituency to be. It is perhaps the fate (or is it the definition?) of a very common word in the lexicon of both the political scientist and the public official that it has a variety of meanings. "Constituency" is sometimes used in a neutral sense, as in the definition of a particular electorate or, as I used it above, a particular audience. At other times it is used in a partisan sense to describe one's followers or supporters. In the foreign policy field — and this is true of outsiders as well as of State Department officials — the prevailing definition is the partisan one: a constituency is a group of supporters, people who throw their weight behind the State Department, facilitating its difficult work of making and carrying out high-cost, high-risk policy that is (by definition) "in the national interest." For example, Andrew Berding's definition of the Department's domestic constituency is "a solid section of the American public working in its interests." [20] Similarly, Charles Frankel, who was Assistant Secretary of State for Cultural Affairs from 1965 to 1967, has described his office as "a troubled one, out at the fringes of the State Department, with no strong constituency behind it." [21] This is a naive view of agency-constituency relations, one that owes nothing, certainly, to the experiences of other government departments and agencies that propose and administer policy in domains where there are stable and recognized "consumers" of that policy. It may have grown out of the special relationship which I noted in Chapter 1 between the State Department and the small group of liberal internationalist citizen-education organizations, whereby for a generation the organizational leaders came in, as one official put it, for their "marching orders." [22] Indeed, this official described "the liberal forces" as "the people and the groups that can properly be called the foreign policy clientele in this country."

In any event, the character of the identifiable public interest in foreign policy questions as it is now generally perceived in the Department does not meet this definition of constituency as supportive groups. "We don't have anything like the Navy League, that will fight to support the Navy's position. The people who invite us out to talk are not necessarily supporters of our foreign policy." The interested, active, and involved public, far from being the front-man for the Department's views of the national interest, is seen rather as embodying a variety of negative characteristics: it is held to be suspicious, hostile, and critical, above all else; but it is also resentful, prejudiced, unrepresentative, dogmatic — "a monster." The public debate on issues is seen mostly as uninformed but also as irrelevant, narrow, inaccurate, unrealistic, and unreasoned. Favorable characterizations are much fewer, and they fall short of identifying a partisan group of supporters: tolerant, persuasive, intelligent and informed, enthusiastic, friendly on an individual though not on an institutional basis. In brief, the public that plays an active part in the foreign policy debate displays few of the characteristics of a natural ally. Officials may feel some satisfaction and pride in doing something "important" in the public's eye, at being the object of at least some public interest — that, after all, is one of the rewards of public service; but this isn't the girl they want to marry, the constituency they want to settle down with for life.

THE OTHER SIDE OF THE COIN: OFFICIALS' INTEREST IN THE PUBLIC

In the preceding section we looked at the insiders' perceptions of outside interest in the State Department and its work. Here I want to turn the coin over, to examine the insiders' own interest in the public and the general affect or emotional tone which pervades that interest. In a real sense, the rest of this book is concerned with aspects of the government official's interest in and responsiveness to the outside public on foreign policy matters; any attempt to compress all that into a few paragraphs here would be either pointless or misleading. The "outside public" means different things to different people; and there are many forms of "interest" in these different publics, not all of them commensurate and — truth to tell — not all of them credible! Hence I want at this point to stay on the surface, to try to delineate what I see as the major features of the Department's attitudinal posture toward the outside, as a preliminary to my subsequent detailed inquiry.

One might reasonably expect that the interest which State Department officials take or at least express in the public, and the attitudes they hold toward it, would be related in a direct fashion to their perceptions of public interest in what they themselves are doing. But such a hypothesis cannot be properly tested from the data at hand. Officials perceived outside interest as attaching to policy issues and issue-areas and not to particular individuals; in their own experience, consequently, they had sometimes seen themselves and others as the object of much interest, and sometimes of little, and it is simply not possible for me to identify and specify current views and attitudes toward the public as being related to one or another of these experiences or perceptions. The problem seems to me to be of sufficient import, however, to warrant further research designed to factor out these elements.

Not surprisingly, there is great variation in the interest that State Department officials take in the outside public, both as they express that interest and as they demonstrate it in concrete behavior. Some officials are extensively involved with the public, whereas others have little or no expressed or demonstrated interest.[23] The situation here is rather similar to what I found operative in the relations between the State Department and the press: a relatively few officials are "outside men," so to speak, taking on heavy burdens of contact not only with the press but with all other organized or institutional forms of public opinion, while a larger number of officials are "inside men" who have only limited or occasional contact with outsiders, and much of that through intermediaries such as the Public Affairs Advisers. And as in the case of the press, it seems to me that the differences in these two roles have more to do with personal skills and personality factors than with institutional or positional factors.[24] Of course the Public Affairs people have differential interests in the public, just as the Public Affairs Advisers and the men in the Office of Press Relations have in the press; but these formal responsibilities do not begin to define or circumscribe the Department's connections with the outside. Those connections are much more significantly the work of officials who enjoy public contact and are effective with outside groups, *no matter what work they happen to be doing in the Department at any particular time.* They may move from one bureau to another or from one responsibility to another within the same bureau, taking with them as their own personal attribute a disposition and an ability to cultivate outside contacts. In the next office, however, and perhaps even sharing the same secretary, there are officials who want and have very little contact with outsiders on policy questions, who seek shelter from the press in the protection of the Public Affairs Adviser and from other outsiders in the protection of Foreign Service Officer professionalism. An Office Director expressed it with unusual clarity: "The role of public opinion is in some sort of ratio to the level or height of one's job, and to one's background and personality.[25] Our Assistant Secretary, for example, is far more sensitive to public opinion than are some of the other Assistant Secretaries who have area responsibilities. But there are some obvious generalizations one can make. The professional, the Foreign Service Officer, and I am one, is likely to be more remote from public contact for a series of reasons. First, he expects to serve his government loyally, no matter what the Administration. Secondly, as a matter of principle, the Foreign Service Officer is disinclined to get involved in political activities — I don't mean partisan politics here, but rather working out a solution to one's policy problems through political channels. Third, there is the Hatch Act, which is a legal bolstering of the Foreign Service Officer's point of view. He is not isolated as a result of this calculated remoteness, but still he does not expose himself to certain points of view. This means that I do not expect to be the object of numerous outside pressures or to exert outside political pressures myself."

More important even than the degree of interest (or lack of it) which officials express in contacts outside of government is the emotional content of that interest. Here, it seems to me, lie in one bundle the accumulated personal experiences of officials in public contacts, the institutional experiences and norms that officials absorb and share as part of their job, and the mind-sets that shape the way officials define nongovernmental participation in foreign policy matters and respond to it. That emotional content or affect is overwhelmingly negative; even among those officials who have high interest in public contact, negative affect is general. Of all the persons whom I interviewed, only two had both a high level of interest and an unalloyed positive affect regarding public involvement in foreign affairs — one was a noncareer official who had been in the Department only a short time and was soon to return to private life, and the other, also not a Foreign Service Officer, was clearly disaffected and was using external opinion as a device to criticize the Department. Positive affect is rarely evident and is invariably particularistic: "Good newspaper correspondents are the

best source of information a man can have." "We will get businessmen visitors, either on their way to ——— or just back from there.
I am always glad to see them, to get their comments and their observations on things that are going on there." "We look on the Advisory Council as a good way to open up new doors." Negative
affect is pervasive and is both particularistic and universal. It is directed at the press: "The press is full of distortions." "All these guys
[i.e., Lippmann, Reston, Alsop, Hightower] are writing muddier
stuff these days than ever before." "You can't satisfy the press anyway, so why try?" It is directed at ethnic groups: "I have a hell of
a problem trying to get them to work on something together." "We
certainly weigh all the views of ——— groups, but if a man comes
in here with a specific proposition he is going to get nowhere." It is
directed at scholars: "Why is it that academicians in this country
see all the sores on our body and never see them on the other
guy?" And a reverse twist, "I deplore the lack of aggressive behavior toward us on the part of academia. I'll be damned if I'm going
to call ——— for advice, but he never calls me." It is directed at
business: "You have to explain a lot to businessmen; they don't
know a great deal about ———." It is directed at all of them together, and at none of them in particular: "By and large, the American business community, the academic community, the American
press, the American Congress, other agencies in the government,
all have a net effect of complicating and hindering the work of the
State Department and the Foreign Service." "The greatest problem
— a serious problem — is that so often the debate on policy that
takes place in the public is unrealistic; the premises are often inaccurate. . . . It is so silly for us to have to waste our time on these
kinds of topics." "I will not listen to Walter Lippmann unless he
accepts responsibility for the consequences of actions which he rec-
ommends. That is a widespread attitude here, and a widespread
attitude toward public opinion generally." "Our efforts have always
tried to put into proper focus what we stand for, and to put
in proper perspective the errors, misinterpretations, misstate-
ments, that the other side, the [outside] opposition here, makes
about ———."

All institutions have norms, quite informal, that define operative
group standards and serve to orient members, new and old, to acceptable modes of behavior. These norms may differ greatly from

the formal doctrine that justifies the institution's existence and supposedly guides the behavior of its members. That there may be, in most public institutions, a gap between formal doctrine and informal norms, or that such a gap is wide or narrow, is not in itself a novel or significant finding; it is only a mirror of life, an outcropping of the everyday hypocrisy to which we are all prey, young and old alike, and without which we might not even be able to function in a social sense. Of vastly more importance is the nature of the operative norms themselves, for they tell us how our institutions function in fact rather than in theory.

If the State Department has any formal doctrine concerning its relationship with the public, it is the doctrine of all democratic institutions — that it and they can function only in symbiosis, that the public is to the State Department as the placenta is to the foetus. There is some ambiguity in this doctrine as to the level of generality or specificity at which the public is presumed to give nourishment, guidance, advice, support to its leaders. The working norm or operational code — call it what you will — as it is expressed and implied by Department officials cuts right through this ambiguity, denying to the public any but the most passive, general support functions.[26] Speaking from the Defense Department, Adam Yarmolinsky made a rare public statement of this usually internal point of view. Explaining to public opinion analysts why there was little room for public opinion research in government, he said, "There are surprisingly few operationally significant questions for the policy maker as to which any public opinion, in my view, exists at all. By an operationally significant question, I mean a question the answer to which will affect specific actions of government officials." [27]

Most officials, whose policy work involves questions of just this kind, echo this sentiment in private. Thus, instead of the norm being something on the (meaningless) order of "We try to be as responsive to public opinion as possible," we find people all through the Department sharing the idea, if not the exact words, of the Office Director who said, "To hell with public opinion. . . . We should lead, and not follow." The prevailing view is precisely that the job of the official — whether he is a Foreign Service Officer or not — is to use his own best professional judgment in determining and pursuing the national interest. Another Office Director: "The

Executive has to *lead;* it often has to take unpopular stands. This is where you pay off, where you do what you are supposed to do." And still another: "We have a responsibility for moving against the stream because that is what we are being paid for." A Deputy Office Director: "I thought that our problem there should be solved, as Foreign Service Officers are wont to do, by arranging the components that were at hand, rather than listening to the conservative view of the U. S. public. . . . We have to put the pieces together, to fashion initiatives, and public opinion makes that task difficult." The irrelevance or pointlessness of public opinion for State Department officials on an everyday basis was most vividly put by a Deputy Assistant Secretary who was greatly concerned that I understand the basis for his view that *consent* was all that they wanted from the public: "I don't want to leave the impression that I am a conservative about all this; rather, I am trying to be accurate. I cannot say that out of all this [i.e., the public] comes a fresh flow of ideas or inspiration. If it did, we would be out of our minds. We spend twelve-hour days, day after day, worrying about these problems and considering all possibilities relevant to them; and we should close up shop if, after all that, we get fresh ideas on these things from a high school teacher in Oklahoma."

These contemporary expressions of the prevailing norm are unchanged in any particular from the views expressed in the early 1950's; the continuity is so striking that we can only conclude that this is a central element in the institutional ideology, conveyed effectively to newcomers in the Department. A former Assistant Secretary for Public Affairs: "You should study the problem carefully in terms of the national interest and decide on the ideal course. Only then should you consider congressional and public opinion with an eye towards educating such opinion in the necessities of the situation." An official then in the Public Opinion Studies Division, during its better days: "The policy officers must make decisions on the basis of what is the best thing for the United States. If the public doesn't understand the issue, the only solution is to educate the public." And a desk officer then on an Eastern European desk: "Our business is to figure out what the best policy is for the United States; it is *not* to let every group which has its own political interest in that policy have it." [28]

What officials *do* want from the public amounts to a substantial measure of freedom in the exercise of their professional judgment concerning the national interest. Mostly what they ask for is "support," a vague and variable notion which I shall subsequently look at more closely. From near the top of the Department hierarchy comes this observation: "Most people here are interested in public opinion not in the sense of being shaped by it, but rather in gaining support for something they want to undertake, or measuring support that may already exist for what they want to do." From Public Affairs: "The participants in these affairs [regional conferences] want to influence policy; the State Department wants support for the policy it has now. . . . We are really looking for public *acquiescence.*" From European Affairs: "Unless you have a degree of public support, you will have a hard time carrying out what you want to carry out. If you are on some line of public policy and you lack a degree of at least elite support and understanding, you are in constant trouble." [29]

If positive support is too much to ask for, or to expect, then some prefer an absence of criticism: silence, the lack of opposition, even apathy or indifference. From African Affairs: "There really is no great public interest in ——— at the moment, and we soft-pedal it because we do not want to stir up any public interest there." From Far Eastern Affairs: "You can sure live much better without opposition." From Public Affairs, two very different views and a closing of the circle: "We want silence rather than vocal support, since we can't get that in any unanimous way anyway." And a sharply contradictory position: "When there is silence, the Foreign Service feels safer, but I don't; because when you move on issues, you need public support and you don't have it."

SCIENCE VS. INTUITION IN THE
DEPARTMENT'S APPROACH TO PUBLIC OPINION

In the light of these patterns of attitudes toward external opinion, let us take a look now at the characteristic modes of evaluating such opinion within the Department. How do officials measure support for what they want to do? As a first approach to this question, I will distinguish only two modes: "science" and "intuition." This simple dichotomy, or some variant of it, actually does less violence to the simple reality than one might expect at first glance:

the choices — and they are by no means mutually exclusive — are, on the one hand, fairly sophisticated, systematic techniques of opinion appraisal and, on the other, intuitive, impressionistic hunches about the state of opinion. The social scientist is likely to believe that the more systematic techniques will produce more accurate appraisals of opinion than will intuition.[30] I do not want at this stage, however, to equate the "science-intuition" dichotomy with an "accuracy-inaccuracy" dichotomy; it is simply not that clear that, *given the uses to which it is put,* intuition in these matters generally produces more inaccurate or misleading information than does scientific appraisal. It is also not clear that officials have realistic alternatives to intuition most of the time, in any event.[31] Since these points will recur often in the pages that follow, I will develop them subsequently, in relevant and appropriate contexts. What the practitioner and the observer/critic both want is accurate or at least adequate appraisal; the question is, how does the practitioner, the policy maker, go about getting it or trying to get it? And ultimately, of course, we will want to know how well he succeeds.

Intuition is the prevailing mode of opinion evaluation in the State Department. This is not at all surprising, and might even be considered inescapable, given the facts that the institution itself has more or less abdicated all responsibility in the public opinion field and that officials are not looking for detailed guidance anyway. Department officials, not unnaturally, lack the research and data-analysis skills involved in specialized public opinion studies, and the Department as a whole does not make up for that lack. As I said earlier, officials are thereby thrown back upon their own resources; one Foreign Service Officer put it this way: "Each of us who works in the field [i.e., a foreign post] develops his own system of political analysis." These resources, or these individual systems of analysis, are strikingly dependent on intuition.[32] This is expressed both as a positive evaluation of intuition and negatively as a sense of unease with system or science in opinion analysis.

Positive evaluations of intuition. Fully a third of the Department officials interviewed in the mid-1960's spontaneously and specifically singled out their own or their colleagues' intuitive sense of public opinion as an important skill. A Public Affairs Adviser remarked: "We are all trained to react to political situations on an intuitive basis. Your reaction to public opinion has to be intuitive. We are all well-antennaed. You have a sense of how the body politic is moving." This notion of "a sense" of how opinion is developing recurs. A Deputy Assistant Secretary discussed it in general terms: "You live with it for a while, and you begin to get a sense of what things in foreign policy are impossible, what things are difficult, what things would need a lot of explaining and clarifying . . . what has broad general support." Another Deputy Assistant Secretary described it a little more specifically: "We knew that there had been changes in public opinion [on a particular problem], though they had not yet made themselves felt. We sensed it, in terms of small straws in the wind. The violence was suddenly gone from public arguments and public discussions of the whole subject, in the same way that it was gone from discussions of our trade policy before the Trade Expansion Act of 1962. Call this expert intuition — a feeling in the bones that the obstacles can be dealt with. You can feel these things, especially if you have an instinct for action rather than a bureaucrat's preference for inaction." And in the Public Affairs area itself, an official said, "Our images of public opinion are intuitive rather than scientific. . . . Really, it is just a bunch of personal impressions from what people everywhere say to me when I travel around." A high official in the Department noted that "each man has his own feel for the situation" and added, "Public attitudes are often the subject of discussion in [our senior staff] meetings, and people sitting around the table chip in with their various impressions."

There is a strong suggestion, in these data, that the ability to "sense" public opinion is somehow related (or at least thought to be related) to experience and seniority (and thus authority also). For one thing, intuition is often expressed as a special attribute of senior Foreign Service Officers and the political appointees, who may or may not be career people, serving at the policy level (Assistant Secretary and up). A Deputy Assistant Secretary: "Many officers develop this kind of radar sense." A Public Affairs Adviser: "That sense [of how the body politic is moving] exists at the political level and at the experienced, senior Foreign Service Officer level." An Assistant Secretary: "Most Assistant Secretaries don't rule out their intuition; they like their intuition, and they are rather proud of it." Another Assistant Secretary complained that the Department was concerned only with the conservative forces on the outside, never the liberal forces; "deference is paid to the right." He saw in this situation the intuitive capacity of the Foreign Service Officer: "An articulate senior F.S.O. is part of the public he is talking about — he is the same type."

For another thing, intuition as an important and affirmative attribute is more likely to be expressed by senior level people, though not disproportionately by Foreign Service Officers. Of the total sample of officials whom I interviewed, 57 percent were Office Directors or higher in the Department hierarchy; but 76 percent of those who singled out intuition as an important skill were Office Directors or higher. Not a single desk officer, the man in charge of primary contacts with specific countries, was found in this latter group. But Foreign Service Officers were found in the group recognizing and extolling intuition in virtually the same proportions as they were found in the total sample (60 percent).

Negative attitudes toward "science." Positive evaluation of intuition is paralleled by a negative assessment of scientific or systematic techniques of opinion appraisal. This negative assessment is evident both in the attitudes that individuals express and in the things that the Department does and does not do by way of the systematic study of public opinion.

The opinion survey, or public opinion poll, is of course the most obvious encroachment of science in this domain. Up until 1957 the State Department periodically and quietly commissioned opinion polls on foreign policy questions. Congressmen saw in this practice the makings of a strategy of opinion manipulation, and their strong criticism was clearly a factor in the cancellation of polling contracts in 1957.[33] Since then the Department has been gun-shy about polls, and officials do not talk freely or fondly about them.

But this experience accounts only in part for the fact that officials do not attach great importance or trust to polls — even though they do look at them and learn something about public opinion from them, as we shall see in the next chapter. A high-level career officer, serving as a Deputy Assistant Secretary, expressed a commonly held view when he said, "I have reservations about computer methods of assessing opinions." This represents no great change from the opinion expressed in 1953 by a former service Secretary in President Truman's cabinet: "Our people didn't watch the Gallup polls. . . . This is the way it should be. You can't run a government on IBM machines." [34] An official at the Assistant Secretary level who praised the public opinion instincts and intuitions of his colleagues said of them, "They also look over the polls —but they don't do very much of that!"

So we have to go beyond the Department's "hands off" attitude toward opinion polls to understand this downgrading of them. Much of the reason, I think, is broadly cultural: an intellectually traditionalist hostility toward numbers that are, or seem, dissociated from real people. This is compounded by the difficulty — which even specialists share, for diverse reasons — in interpreting the polls, in knowing what the data mean. The Department official, thus, is likely to regard polls as marginal; when they "fit" other kinds of evidence, they have meaning, and when they do not, they may be set aside. A Foreign Service Officer who was serving as an assistant to a senior official expressed it this way: "We pay attention to public opinion polls. And if the polls are reinforced by what influential journalists are saying, it can be a significant index in the eyes of policy people." [35]

It is not only public opinion polls that are downgraded or dismissed; more inclusively, Department officials tend to the view that the type of public opinion they are dealing with is not accessible to systematic measurement of any kind, that it is beyond the reach of any practical technique save intuition. The official who candidly acknowledged "I don't know any other way to do it" except impressionistically and intuitively was giving expression to the art of political judgment as practiced by government officials. One of the most astute, insightful, and articulate officials, then a Deputy Assistant Secretary, talked candidly about the importance of particular groups in particular policy areas but repeated, "This really is not capable of very precise formulation. . . . You simply cannot get precise. It is intuitive." Another official, higher in rank and equally impressive in his abilities, acknowledged wryly: "We impute to outside people and groups all kinds of strengths which we really are not able to measure and have no clear idea of. This building is filled with men who are amateurs in politics, people who think they know what others will buy and what they will not buy." There are, no doubt, patterns in the exercise of these political intuitions, as there are in most repetitive behavior. The fact

that these patterns are implicit does not make them any less systematic, but it does have the effect of obscuring — not least in the
eyes of officials themselves — their accessibility to precise measurement.

The Department's reluctance to engage in the systematic analysis of *any* of its exposures to opinion information, especially those
which are amenable to a more precise or accurate appraisal, is further evidence of the low or negative value it attaches to such
modes of analysis. The "systematic" treatment of opinion information in the State Department now seems to be limited to the count-
ing of the mail, its separation broadly by issue, and its division
into "favorable" and "unfavorable" piles — though it is by no
means certain that even these simple compilations receive any
great distribution within the Department. The low level of the
analysis accorded this one source of information on external opinion is suggested by the following breakdown (which was given to
me orally by the person who made it and which never surfaced
again anywhere in my discussions within the Department over the
next four months). In the week of February 21–25, 1966, after Secretary of State Rusk had appeared before the Senate Foreign Relations Committee in a televised and highly publicized session, the
Secretary received 4,114 pieces of correspondence; 3,510 of these
were addressed to Rusk by name, and 604 were letters to Congressmen on the subjects of his testimony. Of these letters, 1,207
concerned the Vietnam War; 1,028 were deemed favorable, and
179 unfavorable. In discussions of the mail situation and the way it
is handled by the Department, several officials noted, "We do not
get a specific reading from the Public Affairs people on the letters
that bear on our particular business." Only one of them, however,
was moved to the view that they *should* get such a "reading," and
even in his case it was clearly a thought that struck him only as he
talked with me. "Perhaps we should," he repeated a few times, half
to himself.

In sum, then, the foreign policy official operates in an opinion
environment in a sensory way, using political antennae that have
rarely been developed for this purpose. Since State Department officials are shifted every two or three years to new assignments involving new problems and sometimes even new substantive areas,
they confront additional obstacles to the development of orderly

theories and orderly knowledge about relevant publics. But these are additional obstacles and not basic causes. The intuitive mode of evaluation is so pervasive in government that one has to entertain the hypothesis that it is simply a manifestation of political behavior, as prevalent among administrators as among elected officials.[36]

THE DIFFICULTIES IN APPRAISING OPINION

We cannot at this point estimate with any confidence the accuracy of the opinion information the foreign policy official gets through his impressionistic exploration, because we have so far looked only at *how* he approaches the problem and not yet at the sources themselves or at the way he uses them. To be sure, there are tremendous difficulties in appraising opinion when the exploration itself is unsystematic, haphazard, accidental, and subject to not-wholly-conscious self-selective screening processes; the possibilities of error seem on the face of it to be very great. But there are also tremendous difficulties in appraising opinion when the exploration is continuously systematic and "scientific," as the experience in trying to interpret poll data on the Vietnam War suggests.[37] Each mode of appraisal is subject to errors of different sorts; we do not have very good empirical evidence on this, however, because most of the time the issues — unlike Vietnam — are not important to many people, and the errors in appraising opinion are either never discovered by officials themselves or never revealed by them. The American recognition of the Soviet Union in 1933 seems to have been a case where the Administration read more public opposition into its political environment than was actually warranted, although the chief historian of that event has so obscured it that one cannot be sure.[38] Secretary of State Cordell Hull and the State Department apparently believed that American public opinion was so isolationist that the Administration needed to proceed on the recognition question with great caution, so as not to frighten anyone. Yet Browder reports — amid his own repeated judgment that American public opinion was isolationist — some evidence that recognition was favored by 63 percent, and opposed by only 27 percent, of 1,139 newspapers throughout the country which responded to a questionnaire sent out by the Committee on

Russian-American Relations of the American Foundation.[39] Whatever qualifications one might wish to attach to these returns, they
are an indisputable sign that "isolationism" was not a very discrim-
inating way to characterize opinion on that issue. In the outcome,
Browder notes, "the volume of protest was evidently considerably
less than the Administration had anticipated." [40]

The situation in 1937, after President Roosevelt's "quarantine
speech," was much more complex than in 1933, suggesting not only
the difficulties of accurate appraisal but also the pressing need for
external analysts to understand the way that officials interpret politically relevant opinion. The historical legend is that Roosevelt
was forced by a frightened and hostile public opinion to retreat
from a program to isolate Germany and Japan.[41] In fact, however,
there was substantial support for the President in the public prints,
in organizational policy positions, and in his mailbag — enough
support to allow him some freedom in deciding how to interpret
the public reaction.[42] Dorothy Borg says that Roosevelt's mail
"consisted overwhelmingly of expressions of approval," [43] and Norman Graebner reports that "In his personal correspondence Roosevelt himself accepted the national reaction as favorable." [44] But
Roosevelt had no clear plan or program of action in mind, and he
seems also to have run immediately into opposition from more cautious people within his own Administration, like Cordell Hull, as
well as from isolationists in the Congress. Characteristically he
chose to temporize, thus leaving the field to his isolationist opponents who ran their flags up, proclaiming a battlefield victory.[45]

Another incident, in 1941, underlines these difficulties of accurate appraisal. President Roosevelt was edging cautiously in May
1941 toward a policy of convoying shipping across the North Atlantic to Great Britain, to provide protection against German sub-
marines. According to Robert A. Divine, the President "carefully
watched the public opinion polls, noting that a slight majority was
in favor of convoys." [46] On May 27 he gave a radio address in
which he stressed the vital need to keep the sea lanes to Britain
open. Divine describes the reaction: "Almost as soon as he finished
talking, telegrams praising his speech began pouring into the
White House. 'They're ninety-five per cent favorable!' exclaimed an
astonished Roosevelt to Robert Sherwood. 'And I figured I'd be
lucky to get an even break on this speech.' " [47] Apparently uncer-

tain about how to interpret this opinion situation, Roosevelt disavowed any convoy proposal at his morning press conference the next day, just as he had disclaimed any plans for a quarantine when pressed by reporters after that speech.

To summarize: There are no formal mechanisms of opinion analysis within the State Department any longer; it is every man for himself, so to speak, and so we are perforce concerned with everyman. There is no broad, well-developed sense of constituency for foreign policy or for the State Department; external attention is focused irregularly on issues and areas, creating within the Department varied perspectives on the question of who is listening. Among Departmental officials, interest in the outside public is mixed; negative feelings toward it are rampant, and the appropriateness of its having an active role in day-to-day issues is explicitly rejected. Clearly, public opinion is not high on anyone's list — but it *is* there; officials do pay attention to it. Institutionally abandoned, deemed inappropriate for scientific inquiry, it is informally and impressionistically perceived. The risks of intuition are that individuals will hear what they want to hear, see what they want to see, using opinion information to confirm support for other voices in other rooms. We want to know, then, what *do* they hear and see? What are the sources of opinion inputs into this policy-making structure?

NOTES

1. V. O. Key, Jr., *Public Opinion and American Democracy*, New York: Knopf, 1961, p. 93.

2. See William O. Chittick, "The Domestic Information Activities of the Department of State," unpubl. Ph.D. dissertation, Johns Hopkins University, 1964.

3. John Dickey, then second-in-charge in the Office of Public Affairs, to his Assistant Secretary, Archibald MacLeish, as quoted by Dean Acheson, *Present at the Creation*, New York: W. W. Norton, 1969, p. 102.

4. Acheson's own phrase, in *ibid.*, p. 101.

5. Robert E. Elder, "The Public Studies Division of the Department of State: Public Opinion Analysts in the Formulation and Conduct of American Foreign Policy," *Western Political Quarterly*, Vol. 10, No. 4,

December 1957, p. 791. See also Elder, *The Policy Machine*, Syracuse: Syracuse University Press, 1959.

6. Bernard C. Cohen, *The Press and Foreign Policy*, Princeton: Princeton University Press, 1963, Chaps. 5 and 6.

7. Note the public announcement of the appointment of former astronaut Michael Collins as Assistant Secretary of State for Public Affairs, and the accompanying comment, *The New York Times*, November 29, 1969. The United Press International story on the nomination called the job "downgraded" as a result of the departure of the News Division. At the time of Collins's swearing-in ceremony, Secretary of State Rogers observed that "we need an aggressive public affairs bureau to help convey our message to the American people." *Department of State News Letter*, No. 106, February 1970, p. 5.

8. Chittick, "The Domestic Information Activities of the Department of State," pp. 51, 71, 77.

9. W. Phillips Davison, "More than Diplomacy," in Lester Markel, ed., *Public Opinion and Foreign Policy*, New York: Harper & Bros., 1949, pp. 128–131.

10. H. Schuyler Foster, "American Public Opinion and U.S. Foreign Policy," *Department of State Bulletin*, November 30, 1959, p. 797.

11. One of the men in the *P* area who helped to carry out the first 50 percent cut in the Public Opinion Studies Division in 1953 made a similar remark at the time: "We just don't get time to read all the reports and analyses they put out." W. Phillips Davison quotes a high official in the State Department as saying, "We don't need to call in the experts on information; we know pretty well what the public is thinking." Davison, "More than Diplomacy," p. 131.

12. Elder, "The Public Studies Division of the Department of State," p. 784.

13. At the time of his appointment Col. Collins, the former astronaut, suggested that the door was not really shut tight: He "said also [i.e., in addition to remarks about Vietnam War dissenters having oversimplified the conflict] that communication should be a two-way street, that he would pay attention to the thinking of the public on foreign policy while he was trying to inform the public." *The New York Times*, November 29, 1969.

14. This is also the conclusion reached by the National Policy Panel of the United Nations Association of the United States of America, in its report: *Beyond Vietnam: Public Opinion and Foreign Policy*, New York: UNA-USA, 1970; see esp. pp. 17, 19.

15. Andrew Berding, *Foreign Affairs and You!* Garden City: Doubleday, 1962, pp. 140–141.

16. Gabriel A. Almond, who has been attacked as an "elitist" in these matters, is in fact the most generous in suggesting a constituency (he never used the word) that might translate into ten or more million people (he never made the numerical translation, either). See Almond's *The American People and Foreign Policy*, 2d ed.; New York: Praeger, 1960.

James N. Rosenau, using a different measure, concluded that "the full range of foreign policy issues encompasses no more than several hundred thousand national opinionmakers and no fewer than fifty thousand." *National Leadership and Foreign Policy*, Princeton: Princeton University Press, 1963, p. 8. Rosenau subsequently predicted "slow and continuous growth" for the "attentive public"; see his *The Attentive Public and Foreign Policy: A Theory of Growth and Some Evidence*, Research Monograph No. 31, Princeton University: Center of International Studies, 1968. Sheldon Appleton limits the extra-governmental group "which often plays a significant role in setting foreign policy goals and devising the means to implement them" to "the thousands or tens of thousands." *United States Foreign Policy*, Boston: Little, Brown & Co., 1968, p. 303.

17. Congressional perceptions of opinion at about this time were remarkably akin to this, according to *The New York Times* report, April 18, 1966: "As the Congressmen filtered back into Washington for tomorrow's resumption of House and Senate sessions, their impressions were the customary blur of local issues strongly felt and of national and international problems only vaguely apprehended." Vietnam, however, was high on every Congressman's list of troublesome questions.

Former Secretary of State Dean Acheson's evaluation of the quality and level of public interest in foreign affairs in general is of a similar order: "In the State Department we used to discuss how much time that mythical 'average American citizen' put in each day listening, reading, and arguing about the world outside his own country. Assuming a man or woman with a fair education, a family, and a job in or out of the house, it seemed to us that ten minutes a day would be a high average. If this were anywhere near right, points to be understandable had to be clear. If we made our points clearer than truth, we did not differ from most other educators and could hardly do otherwise." *Present at the Creation*, p. 375.

18. See Cohen, *The Press and Foreign Policy*.

19. See Almond, *The American People and Foreign Policy*.

20. Berding, *Foreign Affairs and You!* p. 140.

21. Charles Frankel, *High on Foggy Bottom*, New York: Harper & Row, 1968, p. 11.

22. See above, p. 23.

23. From the perspective of the Department of Defense, Adam Yarmolinsky has argued that one reason why opinion research is of so little value to officials in the Executive branch of the government is that they are interested in the views of only one small group of people — Congressional committee or subcommittee members. "Confessions of a Non-User," *Public Opinion Quarterly*, Vol. 27, No. 4, Winter 1963, p. 545.

24. Cf. Cohen, *The Press and Foreign Policy*, esp. Chap. 5. For a slightly different view, see William O. Chittick, "State Department–Press Antagonism: Opinion versus Policy-Making Needs?" *The Journal of Politics*, Vol. 31, No. 3, August 1969, pp. 756–771.

25. An ambiguous formulation; see Chap. 4 below.

26. See Nathan Leites, *A Study of Bolshevism*, Glencoe: Free Press, 1953, which is an effort to get underneath the ideological and doctrinal elements of communism to an understanding of the operating norms of the Bolshevik leadership.

27. Yarmolinsky, "Confessions of a Non-User," p. 543.

28. For similar views on the part of Department officials who were involved in China policy during an even earlier period, see Frederick B. Hoyt, "Americans in China and the Formation of American Policy, 1925–1937," unpubl. Ph.D. dissertation, Department of History, University of Wisconsin — Madison, 1971.

29. See Chittick, "The Domestic Information Activities of the Department of State." Chittick defines the Department's "quest for constituency" in terms of public approval, acceptance, active support.

30. See Roberta S. Sigel and H. Paul Friesema, "Urban Community Leaders' Knowledge of Public Opinion," *Western Political Quarterly*, Vol. 18, No. 4, December 1965, pp. 881–895. Sigel and Friesema compare the preferences of parents in a given school district with the estimates of these preferences on the part of leaders chosen to draw up plans for a new community school for that area. And they find that there is little accurate leadership perception of public preferences. Their conclusion: "The comparison of parental preferences with community leaders' estimates of these preferences shows that community leaders are not the accurate judges of public opinion which democratic representative theory presumes them to be. And this even when the community leaders have occasion to be in close contact with their public" (p. 894).

31. See Leon D. Epstein, "Democracy and Foreign Policy," in W. N. Chambers and R. H. Salisbury, eds., *Democracy in the Mid-Twentieth Century*, St. Louis: Washington University Press, 1960, p. 133.

32. Cf. Regis Walther, *Orientations and Behavioral Styles of Foreign Service Officers*, Foreign Affairs Personnel Study No. 5, New York: Carnegie Endowment for International Peace, 1965: "[The Foreign Service Officer's] style for analyzing information tends to be impressionistic and intuitive rather than formal, methodological, and statistical" (p. 16).

33. William O. Chittick, *State Department, Press, and Pressure Groups*, New York: Wiley-Interscience, 1970, pp. 43–48; John S. Dickey, "The Secretary and the American Public," in Don K. Price, ed., *The Secretary of State*, an American Assembly book, Englewood Cliffs: Prentice-Hall, 1960, p. 160.

34. In a study of policy making on the Japanese peace settlement in the early 1950's, when polls were still being contracted, I noted that "the policy-makers themselves did not seem to be interested in the polls as a means of discovering anything about public opinion. There is no evidence to suggest that they made any use of these few opinion surveys [which were circulated through the State Department by the Public Studies Division at that time], or that they even initiated any requests for information about the findings of other polls." Bernard C. Cohen, *The*

Political Process and Foreign Policy, Princeton: Princeton University Press, 1957, p. 212.

35. In 1949 Lester Markel noted the same thing. "A high officer of the Department and a wise observer of men and events has said: 'We read the [Department's] digests [of opinion], we ponder the polls, and then we are likely to be influenced by our favorite columnist.'" Lester Markel, "Opinion — A Neglected Instrument," in Markel, ed., *Public Opinion and Foreign Policy*, New York: Harper & Bros., 1949, p. 31. See also Yarmolinsky, "Confession of a Non-User," for a fuller statement of the irrelevance of public opinion research to government decision makers. His remarks, written with Defense Department problems in mind, are fully applicable to the State Department.

36. Cf. V. O. Key's observation that "In their appraisal of public response to actions and proposals, officials proceed by impressionistic or systematic means, although hunch, intuition, impression are by far the more widely used." *Public Opinion and American Democracy*, pp. 420–421. Raymond A. Bauer, Ithiel de Sola Pool, and Lewis A. Dexter, *American Business and Public Policy*, New York: Atherton Press, 1963, report (p. 438) a Congressional preference for the mail, an unrepresentative source of opinion, as against public opinion polls, a representative source, on reciprocal-trade questions. It is more difficult to generalize about the Presidency, with regard to which samples are small and information scarce. We may note *The New York Times* story about President Johnson keeping a "sharp eye on the state of American public opinion with respect to the war, as reflected in widely published polls and private surveys taken at . . . [his] instigation." On the other hand, "No tabulation based on letters to the President has been made, because they are not considered an accurate reflection of public sentiment, a White House source said." John D. Pomfret, *The New York Times*, February 18, 1966. President Truman's reaction was quite the opposite: "The President tended to have little confidence in polling results after his 1948 experiences . . . and there is little evidence either that the polls were brought to the attention of the President and his advisers or of what their reactions to them were." Glenn D. Paige, *The Korean Decision: June 24–30, 1950*, New York: Free Press, 1968, pp. 44–45. Selig Adler, in *The Isolationist Impulse*, London and New York: Abelard-Schuman, 1957, says of Franklin Roosevelt, "He had certain new instruments [of opinion evaluation] at his command and he knew how to use them. The public opinion surveys of Elmo Roper and Dr. George Gallup (of the American Institute of Public Opinion), both dating from 1935, were carefully evaluated" (p. 279).

37. See Bill D. Moyers, "One Thing We Learned," *Foreign Affairs*, Vol. 46, No. 4, July 1968.

38. Robert Browder, *The Origins of Soviet-American Diplomacy*, Princeton: Princeton University Press, 1953.

39. *Ibid.*, pp. 85–86.

40. *Ibid.*, p. 121.

41. See, e.g., Frank Freidel, *America in the Twentieth Century,* New York: Knopf, 1960, pp. 372–373.

42. See Dorothy Borg, *The United States and the Far Eastern Crisis of 1933–1938,* Cambridge, Mass.: Harvard University Press, 1964, esp. Chap. 13. David H. Culbert, in "Tantalus' Dilemma: Public Opinion, Six Radio Commentators, and Foreign Affairs, 1935–1941," unpubl. Ph.D. dissertation, Northwestern University, 1970, p. 72, cites Travis B. Jacobs, "Roosevelt's 'Quarantine' Speech," *Historian,* Vol. 24, August 1962, pp. 483–502, as agreeing with Dorothy Borg: "His examination of additional magazines and newspapers convinced him that press opinion had been surprisingly favorable to the speech."

43. Borg, *The United States and the Far Eastern Crisis,* p. 392. Culbert, however, wonders whether the letters that Borg saw were representative of those the President saw and whether they were representative of those he received ("Tantalus' Dilemma," pp. 85–86). On the possibilities of "misreading" the mail, see Leila Sussman, "Mass Political Letter Writing in America," *Public Opinion Quarterly,* Vol. 23, No. 2, Summer 1959, p. 210.

44. Norman Graebner, ed., *Ideas and Diplomacy: Readings in the Intellectual Tradition of American Foreign Policy,* New York: Oxford University Press, 1964, p. 562.

45. Borg's account, cited above, is the best; see also Graebner, *Ideas and Diplomacy.* Manfred Landecker stresses the negative responses to Roosevelt's speech, but he seems to be saying that FDR was not overwhelmed by them. *The President and Public Opinion,* Washington, D.C.: Public Affairs Press, 1968, pp. 15–18.

46. Robert A. Divine, *Roosevelt and World War II,* Baltimore: Johns Hopkins Press, 1969, p. 42.

47. *Ibid.,* p. 43.

T ῑ﹍ ⅃E **The Many Shapes of Public Opinion**

Public opinion presents itself to foreign policy officials in a multitude of shapes. At its simplest, it may be one or two long-established and "reliable" voices: a given newspaper, perhaps, and a few people with business connections in a given part of the world. For others, it may be a formless and perhaps unexpected surge, like a tidal wave: "We get exposed to the public from all possible angles and sources, when something stirs them up — a Nasser, an Ayub. Then you hear from your mother, from your Congressman, from the whole pack." If in the process of examining the variety of public contacts I impose a certain order on them, I would enjoin the reader never to forget the often confused quality of the original. In the very confusion of voices arises the need for officials to pick and choose those whose timbre they like — to "order" them ultimately according to their *own* preferences, as they seek to define and implement what they believe to be the public or national interest.

It is not only my mode of organizing and presenting the forms of public opinion that is a synthetic act. The larger construct itself, the over-all structure of opinion shapes and sources, is a creation which — I think it is fair to say — no single foreign affairs official ever experiences. As the sum-total (or a reasonable approximation thereto) of the varied perceptions and exposures of a broad sample of foreign policy makers, the construct may be regarded as an attempt to specify the foreign policy "opinion elite" in practical terms.[1] But, to repeat the burden of the paragraph above, it is important to remember that what we call the opinion elite is only a summation, an abstraction. In reality this opinion elite has no unitary character or even existence. Few of its component parts interact in any way; rather, they participate in discrete and discontinuous realms. In short, in its public opinion aspects, the foreign policy process is riddled with pluralism.[2] And the initiative in what to listen to, or what to hear, or even whom to call on remains most of the time, as we shall see, with the official.

For discussion purposes, the first and major distinction to be made with regard to public opinion is between those sources — people and groups — which are known or are identifiable to officials and those sources which are impersonal and faceless. The crucial difference here is whether the sources carry recognizable personal or political identification marks, with all that these imply for psychic or political leverage, and not whether the relationships are face-to-face. For example, I include in the first group the press, even where officials may never see the reporters or editorial writers involved; and I include in the second group the face-to-face meetings with strangers that officials have whenever they go on the lecture circuit.

The "Identifiable" sources may be combined into three major groupings: "Intimates," "Specialists," and "Institutions." The category of "Intimates" includes figures not ordinarily understood to be significant bearers of opinion — (1) members of one's family, primary or extended; (2) close friends; (3) colleagues within the State Department who are not involved in one's own policy problems. "Specialists" have in common a knowledge, experience, or skill in policy areas that not only sets them apart from all other opinion sources but qualifies them to be treated as "equals" by officials. Among them will be found (4) notables, or "important people," many of whom have in fact served in the Department in the past; (5) experts, men of skill or other resource in particular policy areas, many of whom are currently qualified to serve in the Department; (6) advisory boards, composed both of notables and experts who are currently serving the Department in advisory capacities. "Institutions" comprise the groups, organizations, and enterprises that are so commonly thought to be the significant bearers of public opinion that they are often treated as unofficial branches of government — (7) interest groups and (8) the press.

This category also includes an official branch of government, (9) the Congress, for reasons that will be made clear in the discussion below.

The "Faceless" or "Impersonal" sources are fewer in number, but much larger in the number of people whose opinions they encompass. The sources include: (10) the mail that comes to the government on foreign policy questions, most of it ending up in the State Department; (11) audiences which officials see from time to time over the top of a lectern; (12) demonstrative behavior of one sort or another; and (13) public opinion polls.

This listing does not exhaust the sources of public opinion on foreign policy, nor is it the only way these sources can be combined; but it does include the sources of opinion most in evidence in the Department and most salient in the minds of Department officials.[3]

INTIMATES

Sociology and social psychology have told us enough about the importance of the primary group, and of close and continuing associations of a secondary kind, in shaping and sustaining attitudes so that we should not be surprised to find that foreign policy officials identify *family* and *friends* as sources of opinion on foreign affairs. What *is* surprising, in fact, given a little time to get used to the idea, is that these sources have been almost completely overlooked in the literature in favor of more formal and visible relationships. Nearly one-third of the respondents spontaneously and voluntarily cited family and/or friends in and out of the Department as public opinion sources. Sometimes this is expressed in passing references to "personal discussion," or "personal mail," or "family, neighbors, personal friends," with no attempt to describe in greater detail the tone or the context of the relationship. Others are more explicit, like a Deputy Assistant Secretary who referred to "all the professional people I know — a couple dozen friends who are tough-minded, shrewd. And my brother is a social worker, and when he comes to visit he tells me what people are saying." Still others define the content in sharp emotional terms: "I was recently at a Bar Mitzvah in ——, where I ended up arguing about Vietnam with everyone there. I was astounded at the unanimity of the criticism directed at our policy. All of this gets brought into our discussions here; we are not hermetically sealed." "If I go up to New York and visit my friends, they will batter me on Vietnam." "Whenever I go up to —— to see my family, we get into hot discussions; they ask me questions all over the map."

Family and friends serve not only as direct sources registering opinion on officials but also as indirect sources, as silent reference groups against whose known or presumed judgment an official has to measure his own position and behavior. An Office Director, describing a recent contretemps in his domain, put this opinion standard very clearly: "So, there is an embarrassment to my own personal position, among friends who follow my career. Just picture what the reader gets from his newspaper. . . . What do you think my friends will think about this kind of a thing?" This fear of "looking foolish" in the eyes of people whom one respects and whose respect is valued is, I believe, one of the greatest external constraints on the behavior of officials; we shall meet up with it again, in varying guises. And as in this instance, we have to ask each time *whose* respect is it that matters so much?

In this connection, we have to look carefully at one's *colleagues* in the State Department as a special kind of intimate association transmitting policy opinion. In the normal course the tendency of scholars is to treat all government officials as "insiders" whose participation in policy discussion is (by definition) part of the governmental process and therefore excluded from consideration as public opinion, which is (also by definition) nongovernmental in nature. By conceiving of public opinion as opinion which is *external* to the arena of policy responsibility, however, we can treat the opinion of, say, the desk officer for Australia–New Zealand on, say, the politico-military aspects of the Nigerian-Biafran war as analytically indistinguishable from the opinion of a staff member of the Council on Foreign Relations on the same subject. But the opinions of the uninvolved insider have not only propinquity to recommend them; they have the advantage of shared perspectives on policy matters, shared understandings of the constraints under which a Department official operates, shared trust in the reliability and discretion of the principals.[4]

One's colleagues in fact serve not in just one but in three different ways as guides to or sources of policy opinion. They serve, in the first instance, as "outsiders" in highly specific, individualized contexts. A Deputy Assistant Secretary refers to "knowledgeable friends within the State Department" carrying as much weight as "knowledgeable correspondents." A desk officer who was not married remarked that "my social contacts are almost exclusively with officials. But remember that we discuss issues with lots of colleagues, some of them . . . outside my area of specialization. I will discuss my problems with a friend in Near East Affairs, for example, who is without any special competence in —— Affairs. Sure, he's a Foreign Service Officer, but he is also a U.S. citizen, and when he talks to me about [my area], he talks as a citizen. When I talk to someone here about Latin America I speak as a citizen too." Exposure to the "civic" views of others in the State Department may in fact be built into the social norms of the Department in a way that the outsider does not ordinarily see (and not least because the Department does not really want him to see it). The core of the Department's work and the heart of its interests remain in political relations with individual countries, despite the efforts of successive postwar reorganizations and reorientations designed to raise the status of nonpolitical, functional aspects of the "new diplomacy." [5] The Officer-in-Charge (now the Country Director), the desk officer primarily responsible for relations with a particular country, refers privately to that country as his "parish." This close identification between the desk officer and his country gives the officer an informal as well as a formal role representing that country within the State Department. In his informal capacity as representative, he inescapably becomes aware of the attitudes and opinions of disinterested — or at least uninvolved — officials in the Department who are at the same time moderately knowledgeable about that country's policies and about United States positions regarding them. Since all this takes place, as I said above, in an atmosphere of shared perspectives (not to speak of shared fates), the byplay is for the most part good-natured and sympathetic, lacking the sharp edges of outside criticism. Nonetheless, the man to whom it is happening can hardly avoid getting the message. It does work both ways, however: "In his dealings around the Department the desk officer [for a country with whose policies there is some disagreement in the United States] is subjected to a considerable amount of condescension — friendly of course — and sneers. . . .

But when you are . . . [on the —— desk], the authority of the country rubs off on the person who deals on it with third parties." This desk officer went on to note explicitly that the same kinds of reactions — the sneers and the respect — attach to the desk officers for these countries in their relations with the public.

Second, for some Department officials their colleagues serve as guides to public opinion not by occasionally and individually acting like outsiders but by seeming to be broadly representative of the full range of informed external opinion. In this sense Department personnel are seen as surrogates for the foreign policy public, and one does not need to look very far beyond the Department to understand the spectrum of possible opinion on any subject.[6] A Deputy Assistant Secretary: "You must never forget that with an organization like the State Department you get every opinion under the sun." Occasionally, also, a bureau or office in the Department will bring together an intergovernmental group to discuss and advise on an ad hoc matter of common interest, not necessarily to advance policy (though that can never be completely ruled out) but rather to get the thinking of a broad sample of informed, responsible people — much like an Advisory Council of informed, even professionally concerned, outsiders, but minus many of its headaches.[7]

Third, certain colleagues sometimes function as intermediaries for larger bodies of external opinion, serving to remind officials of the priorities suggested or the constraints imposed by others. This is one of the effects that the Public Affairs Adviser has on many of the officials within his bureau. When the PAA has had to call a desk officer a half-dozen times in the course of the day, for help in answering a reporter's questions or in anticipation of questions he believes will come up before the day is over, the desk officer has a pretty good idea of the momentary structure of external concerns in his area of responsibility. In a much less direct way, the officials in the Department who occupy command positions in the institution's authority structure — the men who serve as other men's bosses — perform a similar function of mediation between external opinion and internal policy. Individuals are disciplined in very subtle and informal ways by the demands and expectations they see — or imagine — emanating from their superiors. Where a man "knows his bosses cannot accept a really far-out idea," as a Deputy

Office Director put it, a great deal of his effectiveness rides on his capacity to figure out the current market in ideas *from his superior's perspective*. This is an exceedingly tenuous process, as we shall see subsequently, and one that is filled with guesswork and error. Notions about what is acceptable at the end of any particular policy-making chain are hazy indeed; herein lies one of the greatest forces for conservatism in the State Department, since one can always take safe refuge in the judgment that what will be acceptable today is the same thing that was acceptable yesterday. Granting all that, there is still much incentive for the more imaginative official at any level in the Department to try to "read" the way his superior, and his superior's superior, understand and interpret (no matter how implicitly) their environment of policy choice.

SPECIALISTS

One cannot spend a day in the company of foreign policy officials, or read very far into the stories of foreign policy formulation, without becoming aware of the very great importance which officialdom attaches to men whom I am calling *notables* — private men of public standing with prior experience in foreign affairs, usually governmental experience since that is where most foreign affairs take place (although substantial international business experience counts also). [8] This is not simply a class of ex-officials; whatever it is that these men bring into governmental discussions, they bring it as individuals, as a personal property rather than as a collective attribute. There are far too few of them, considering the size of the class of ex-officials, for this to be merely the formality of consultation with the *ancien régime*. Who are they? Let me mention just a few whose names recurred so often in discussions in the Department that one would think they were in fact government officials: Dean Acheson, John McCloy, the Rockefeller brothers, George Kennan, Christian Herter, Walter Reuther.[9] These are men whose stature is based substantially on prior performance under fire, so to speak, so that they are regarded not only as men of ability and judgment but as experienced men of action who know what it means to get and to give realistic and meaningful policy advice. This is a point of fundamental importance, oddly embedded in what looks like some petty establishment-encrusted cronyism. As with current colleagues within the Department, these men all share a policy-oriented perspective: the need for a decision *today*, on the information available *now*, in the context of assumptions that cannot be easily or quickly changed and in a form that can be accepted by the many people with whom one will still have to do business tomorrow. They are on the same wavelength as the policy makers, to use a banal but accurate metaphor, and in this respect they are quite different from the vast majority of the outsiders who have something they want to say about foreign policy but are not often able to persuade policy officials that they have anything useful to say about real-life decisions.[10] Officials turn to these notables for outside views that are assimilable to inside needs — public opinion of a very special sort. Several officials have described the relationship with unusual clarity: "I came to this job [a Special Assistant on the Seventh Floor] with the belief that public opinion really means the 'significant elites.' My experience here tends to confirm that belief. Policy makers here listen to those people who are respected public figures — men like McCloy, Acheson, the Rockefellers — men who have status, stature, men who have themselves been in and out of government. Now these men are not listened to in any sense as representative of public opinion but because they are respected for their know-how, their intelligence, their previous experience in government. The Secretary will bring McCloy in, and will give him access to information that he might not have on the outside, and then get his judgment." A Foreign Service Officer serving as a Public Affairs Adviser: "The view that registers is the well-articulated thought from the guy you have respect for. The ones with the intelligence, whom you can understand because you are talking the same language, are the ones who get through to you." Another official, claiming that no new ideas had come into his office from the press in the five years he had been there, went on to say, "*Fragments* will come in, however, from experienced people, those in whom you have some personal confidence."

Occasionally someone will suggest that a given individual has greater influence on policy as a notable than he ever did as an official. In the mid-1950's, for instance, a Special Assistant to a high official said that a number of people believed this to be the case with Sumner Welles. And another official who had left office with the Democrats in 1953 and had subsequently published an article in a national magazine was told that the article "was effective and as helpful as any memorandum I ever wrote in the government." Such a discrepant voice in policy formation can, on the face of it, be had by only a few people at any one time: there are not very many notables at any given time to begin with, and most of them were men of substantial power while they were still in office. Looking at the possibility of such "deviant cases" is useful, however, in focusing our attention on some of the deeper roots of external influence characteristic of all notables. It cannot be argued that this influence flowers as the person is *removed* from the arid constraints of official circumstance, when it seems so clear that it is precisely his understanding of these constraints and his need to work effectively within them that makes him useful to the policy maker. Nor, as officials so consistently and pungently put it, is the outsider likely to come up with policy inventions that are new to the bureaucracy as a whole, especially when he stays within its constraints. What the ex-official may have, however, which takes on new significance and which amplifies his voice in policy circles, is a following, a group (small, of course) of knowledgeable people who share his way of interpreting the world and its exigencies and who find it worthwhile to exchange their ideas for his access to officials. So that when he lends his weight to one of the possible alternatives in the mill, he sharply increases the likelihood that it will get particular kinds of support, and diminishes the likelihood that it will get particular kinds of opposition, in any ensuing public debate. To this extent — our prior respondent to the contrary notwithstanding — the notable, whatever his very considerable personal contributions, is *also* representative of a segment of public opinion, or at least of a point of view.

Ernest R. May has suggested that our *fin de siècle* notables were closely watched by politicians "for indications of the directions in which opinion was likely to move." [11] I would argue a little differently, both for his period of colonial expansion and for our own era. Politicians (and policy officials) consort with notables — in part, to be sure — for indications not so much of the direction in which opinion is likely to move but rather of the whole tenor of the way in which it has *already* moved. To assume that a few men of great public stature and experience, or even family background,

are also bellwethers, leaders of national opinion, is to assume more
than either evidence or logic supports. These men are much more
likely, in their advocacy of positions, to be giving legitimacy to
views which they in turn have found politically or intellectually
persuasive than to be originating such ideas and then persuading
others of their merit.[12] (I say "more likely" because in fact they do
give even as they receive, though I would suggest as a hypothesis
that the higher the policy position once held, the less likely is the
person subsequently to be an originator.) To put the matter differently, what notables may bring to policy makers (if indeed they
bring anything) more often represents the end of a chain of influence *of* opinion, or — in the case of issues that are not yet in the
public domain — the current state of generalized opinion which
seems to them to be relevant to a subject, than it does the start of a
chain of influence *on* opinion. A vivid if unusual illustration from
our day is contained in Townsend Hoopes's account of the circumstances surrounding President Johnson's change of policy toward
Vietnam at the end of March 1968. According to Hoopes, the President came around only after most of his trusted notables, but especially McGeorge Bundy and Cyrus Vance, had finally been converted to the view that military escalation in Vietnam was
counterproductive.[13] All this suggests the very great importance of
such men as one of the devices or political structures through
which external opinion gets aggregated, refined, and focused, and
brought to bear on high officials. I shall return to this point in my
conclusion, when we will be in a better position to evaluate its significance and its implications for democratic theory and practice.

A final word or two on notables, before we leave them for a
while. It may be irreverent but not too wide of the mark to suggest
that their access to policy makers rests not only on their wisdom,
experience, and judgment but also on some less noble if more common attributes of personality. There is a strong self-consciousness
of position among men in power, which is both manifested and
nourished by association with great names of earlier times or other
realms of power. Such association is a visible measure of one's own
status and importance, all the more meaningful when one has
climbed a painfully long ladder from obscure beginnings. There
are probably more inscribed photographs exchanged annually in
Washington, D.C., than in half the high schools in the land. To

paraphrase the Cunard advertisement, *being* there is most of the fun. But if socially valuable consequences grow out of common clay, it would not be the first time; consider where most of our food comes from. Nor does it hurt high officials to be able to make a public display of support by eminent elder statesmen; that is the stuff of which consensus is, hopefully, made.

A second group of "specialists" is composed of *experts*. Whereas notables are people whose special qualifications — policy-making experience, good judgment — are related to policy *process*, experts are people whose special skills are related to policy *substance* — detailed knowledge of foreign areas and of specific problems in foreign policy.[14] Experts are, in the eyes of foreign policy officials, of two kinds: scholars, most of whom are in universities, and action- or program-oriented practitioners, in foundations or nongovernmental organizations.

Foreign policy officials have very mixed feelings about academicians — an observation that will raise no dust in the redoubts of either side. To begin with, only half of my respondents in the mid-1960's mentioned academicians as being among the people outside of government with whom they were in some form of contact. The most significant point of difference between those officials whose horizon included scholars and those who seemed unaware of them lies in departmental rank: among respondents at the level of Assistant Secretary or above, including Special Assistants working for the Secretary, only 20 percent (to be precise, two out of ten) referred to academicians as one of their public contacts. Among respondents from the level of Deputy Assistant Secretary down to and including desk officers, 59 percent (twenty out of thirty-four) mentioned academicians. Obviously, and not surprisingly, the outside expert in substantive matters makes himself known more at the level of particular substantive responsibility in the State Department than at the higher and more general levels of responsibility.

The twenty-four respondents (i.e., the twenty-two accounted for above, plus two Special Assistants not classifiable by departmental rank) who include scholars among their contacts on the outside are divided almost evenly into three groups: those who cherish the contact (nine), those who are neutral or perfunctory in their observations about it (eight), and those who for various reasons are uncomfortable with it (seven). For the first of these groups, those who are favorably disposed, the academician is seen as an extension of the government's resource capabilities in specific policy areas. Contacts with scholars are a means of tapping a larger field of expertise. This is not always seen as a search for informed opinion, but it nevertheless amounts to that. Discussions among experts at this level and on these questions are concerned less with information per se (where the government has the edge anyway) than with its interpretation and analysis and its significance for the future; and on these matters judgment and opinion are inescapably involved. At the same time an exchange is necessarily made; scholars, like notables, have to be informed about the Department's problems before their views can be solicited. An Office Director described this process as it had evolved for his corner of the world: "—— specialists are a large group in U.S. academic circles. We have continuous and close contact with them. . . . We have a continuous consultation. Professor ——, for example, has some committee business in the Department every two or three months, and when he comes he drops by, and we chat and exchange our views. When we go to university towns on our speechmaking tours, we talk with [regional] specialists. We are now instituting a system whereby an officer will make regular visits to universities, not for explicit consultations, not to sense opinion, but rather to discuss changes in the —— situation and the implications for policy. In other words, we want to talk to specific professors on substantive questions; there would be no agenda, just a mutual exchange. I will go to the [professional society] meetings in the spring, and I will do the same thing there. If time permits, I will make a visit to the Ivy League schools and later a trip to schools in the Middle West. This is essentially for contact, to see how *they* understand developments, and we are ready to be frank in our exchange of views." A Deputy Assistant Secretary for a different part of the world said much the same thing, only more briefly: "A second area of public contact grows out of our desire to be in touch with people outside of the government who are professionally competent in the areas we are interested in. . . . The benefit or value in this case is about fifty-fifty; that is, the benefit to each side is about equal. Here the value of meeting people at conferences or talking to them as consultants is great. They will suggest things to us; we in turn will say, 'Here are the problems as we see them.' This is very valuable from our point of view." [15]

The neutral or perfunctory references to academic contacts need not detain us; they acknowledge the academic community or particular scholars as a part of the outside world with which they deal, but without any elaboration or specification as to the quality or value of the contact.

The unfavorable views toward academicians expressed by my respondents in the State Department were not as widespread, diverse, or fundamental as those which have been attributed to foreign policy officials by other observers; if they are unrepresentative in this respect, it may well be due to a kind forebearance on their part in the presence of a live scholar plying his trade. Others have said — speaking of the gap between the short-term, policy-oriented, responsibility-centered needs of officials for information, ideas, and analyses and the scholar's devotion to theory-oriented research that recognizes neither deadlines for decision nor responsibility for action — that it is so wide as to be essentially unbridgeable. The Department is said to be inhospitable, if not actively hostile, to outside scholarly research, which it regards as "irrelevant," "amazingly redundant," "misinformed and inept," "unwelcome meddling," "subversive ploys." [16] Most of these evaluations did not surface in my discussions; for the most part I heard low-keyed criticisms that academicians do not get very involved in particular policy areas — a muted form, perhaps, of the "irrelevance" argument. Mixed up with this, however, is a defensiveness seemingly born of an inability to keep up with the academic community or to maintain one's own credentials as a scholar. A desk officer with an advanced degree expressed anger at the scholarly community apparently because it did not "recognize" him and include him in the network of scholarly communication and interaction. An Office Director who had done some graduate work repeatedly brought up his academic connections, each time with some ambivalence, and finally said, "But I do have to confess that my contacts, after a ten-hour day here, are rather limited; I don't mind confessing that at my age — I am fifty-three — I am tired when I go home at night, and I am not interested in rousing discussions with academicians or anyone else."

I do not have enough information on the extent of graduate-level work to be able to relate it adequately to attitudes toward outside scholars; those officials whom I know to have had academic credentials at some time, however, ended up mostly in the neutral or negative columns on this question rather than in the favorable column. A related bit of data is also suggestive of this apparent inverse correlation between scholarly achievements and attitudes toward scholars: the proportion of Foreign Service Officers is higher among those who are favorably disposed toward academicians than among those who are negatively disposed. Some of the Foreign Service Officers have also had graduate training, to be sure, necessitating a much more careful analysis before a clear relationship can be said to exist. Nevertheless it is striking that a commitment to a professional career in the Foreign Service as an action-oriented practitioner is associated with favorable attitudes toward theory-oriented scholars: four out of the seven negatively disposed officials (57 percent), five out of eight "neutral" (62.5 percent), and seven out of nine favorably disposed (78 percent) were Foreign Service Officers. A more detailed study of this question would have to distinguish not only among the academic achievements of careerists in the State Department; it would have also to distinguish among the policy achievements of academicians who are favorably regarded by officials. In other words, the concept of "scholar" or "academician" is rather broad, covering varying types and qualities of scholarship (some more policy relevant than others), and varying commitments to the academic world as distinct from the practical world of public policy. The first-hand experiences that many officials have with the academic world may consist chiefly of relationships with those people whom Richard Neustadt calls "in-and-outers," men (like himself) who move freely between universities and government assignments.[17] To the extent that academic experts as a class constitute a substantial link between the official and the outside public, the "in-and-outer" may play a more important role in the public opinion–foreign policy nexus than we have thus far understood.

To State Department officials, the classification of "experts" includes men who are program-oriented in specific substantive areas, as well as those who study area-related questions in university settings. One-third (seventeen) of the officials whom I interviewed defined the "professionally concerned" people in private foundations and in nongovernmental organizations as more or less expert specialists among the public with whom contact was important to officialdom. "We deal with the large foundations, Ford, Rockefeller, the African Institute, and so on." "We have extensive contacts with foundations, especially with Ford and the Asia Foundation, both of which are heavily involved in the area." "There are the foundations, like the Carnegie Endowment and Joseph Johnson, the Johnson Foundation and Leslie Paffrath; these people are experts and help us out a bit. The Ford Foundation also. These are all important groups with direct operational interests in the things we are interested in; so we would give them more detailed consideration than we give to the average piece of public correspondence."

A third group of "Specialists" takes the form of *advisory groups* — formally constituted groups of outside consultants who meet periodically with the officers of certain bureaus in the State Department for policy discussions. The analytical distinctiveness of advisory groups as a third variety of specialist activity is subject to some question, but I think a case can be made for it. The problem arises because, in one sense, the advisory group may be viewed as little more than a collection of notables and experts who happen to meet together. But in another and, I believe, more important sense, the advisory group has an independent and regularized existence, takes on its own shapes and procedures, and can develop to include persons and activities that would not otherwise be comprehended in either of the other categories of "Specialists." The advisory group takes people of standing and of knowledge and experience and makes them an accessory of sorts to decision makers. It thus institutionalizes the informal roles haphazardly exercised by notables and experts; it turns these people into a different kind of in-and-outer, one who moves back and forth freely in an advisory capacity, not an employment capacity.

Advisory groups come in different sizes and shapes and in response to different kinds of pressures to keep in touch with the outside public. When the European Cooperation Administration (ECA) was established in 1948 as the first major peacetime foreign aid agency, it was endowed with a Public Advisory Board of twelve members, representing major national organizations, who were directed to meet monthly. The board was so much a part of the ECA that it quickly became bureaucratized; it had an executive secretary, a senior staff assistance panel, internal conflicts, public resignations, and other appurtenances of competitive political organization. The advisory groups that one finds in the State Department today are considerably less prominent and less involved in the work of the agencies. Several of them date back to the early 1960's and were established by officials in their bureaus to meet their own felt needs for external contacts. An Office Director described the purposes of the group in his bureau in these terms: "The idea behind the Advisory Council is correctly ambivalent. It is, on the one hand, a way for us to solicit ideas and views and advice on problems from people who are not bound by our sources of information; and on the other hand it gives us an off-the-record opportunity to explain, describe, and defend our present problems in —— policy. It is a two-way street. . . . It is so rare that I cannot think of a specific case in which a point of view expressed in the Advisory Council was directly or immediately translated into a policy decision. It is not that simple. What these views do . . . is form part of a background of what public opinion stands for and stands on. I suppose one might argue that it is a more concentrated form of public opinion, and perhaps it is. . . . We look on the Advisory Council as a good way to open up new doors. We don't expect these people to know more than we know; it is rather the stimulus of the critical but not hostile mind that we are after. It is good to stretch our minds this way." A Deputy Assistant Secretary in a different bureau described the purposes of his advisory group more briefly: "It was established out of a sense of our need to have a sounding board of knowledgeable people, with whom we could bat ideas back and forth."

The "critical but not hostile mind," "knowledgeable people" — these definitions of the membership of advisory councils make clear their similarity to the notable "who speaks the same language" and the expert with whom officials can talk shop. The membership rosters include college presidents and chancellors, professors with national reputations, foundation people, bankers, prominent civil rights people, newspaper publishers, business men, former officials — men whose likes we met earlier in this section. The groups range in size from about one dozen to about three dozen members, and it is generally the case that not all the members are equally active at all times on all questions.[18]

Small numbers of highly placed people, whose access to policy makers is built into the situation — this is on its face a recipe for an important channel of public contact. It is particularly necessary, therefore, to look at the procedures that are followed by the Department in respect of these advisory groups. For the way that they are used severely constrains their effects, and as the usefulness of the channel is limited, so the willingness to enlarge it is correspondingly restricted. Typically the advisory group meets only two or three times a year, for a single day each time. Sometimes a single topic will be discussed, with a paper distributed beforehand; other times a number of topics will be covered, and a briefing will take the place of a paper. In either case, at most only a few hours can be devoted to the discussions, and often there is no opportunity (as well as no incentive) for the members of the group to prepare themselves in advance. No one is really happy with the results; a lot of the time of Department officers is invested in an effort to secure advice which "often adds little if anything to the conclusions already reached by those officers." [19] The enterprise is saved from cynicism only by the *sense* of officials that they are keeping in touch with a broader body of opinion and not by any concrete experiences of value to which they point.

Not all bureaus in the Department moved on their own to establish advisory councils; their reasons for not doing so were variants of the argument that, given the peculiarities of their areas of responsibilities, there were more efficient ways to ascertain informed opinion. In one bureau, for example, it was argued that every issue of *Foreign Affairs* and other journals of analysis and opinion contained articles pertaining to their problems, that those problems got "so much intellectual treatment in publicly available form" that an advisory council was not necessary. In another the officials met periodically with the officials of outside organizations interested in their area anyway, and they argued that this served the same purpose as a formally constituted advisory group. In still another, the practice of continuous consultation with outside area specialists on an individual basis was given as the reason why group consultation was deemed unnecessary.

In 1966 the Johnson Administration made an effort to extend the advisory council system throughout the State Department. In view of the lack of excitement which these earlier efforts had generated, it is not surprising that its proposed extension met little enthusiasm. On May 3, 1966, in the aftermath of Senate Foreign Relations Committee hearings on China policy, Senators Edward Kennedy and George McGovern publicly proposed that the President appoint a "blue-ribbon" committee of outsiders to reappraise United States policy toward Communist China. The Department's immediate response, issued by its press officer, was that such a commission was unnecessary because the Administration was already seeking "the advice of distinguished and informed Americans outside the Government." [20] Within a week, however, the Administration reversed its position; on May 8 Secretary of State Rusk "announced that the Administration was planning to set up advisory boards of experts outside the Government to provide counsel to State Department bureaus that deal with the Far East, Latin America, Africa, and other areas." [21] In the ensuing months these boards were formally constituted and members appointed to them. But a directive from above to establish an advisory council does not ensure any effort from below to make use of it once established. In one case the council had not held a meeting two years after it was set up; instead the members were periodically assured, by mail, of the Department's continued interest in their views and ideas. This does not mean that all advisory councils were systematically ignored after they were created; but it looks like reasonable evidence that the Administration attached no great priority to their actual functioning as public advisory bodies.[22]

INSTITUTIONS

The sources of public contact which I call "institutional" — interest groups, the press, the Congress — are based in continuing organizations in American society: unlike the other kinds of public contact we have been looking at, these rest not so much on the personal characteristics of given individuals or their professional achievements as upon the formal positions individuals currently occupy in the organizations for which or in which they currently speak. In terms of the number of people formally "represented" in these contacts, and the social, financial, technical, and political resources they wield, they are generally regarded as having massive and fundamental significance as voices of public opinion in the foreign policy process. Significant they are, to be sure, but not always and not uniformly; indeed, it is only by putting them in the context of all other sources and kinds of external opinion that we can get a long-needed perspective on their significance.

State Department officials interact with (a neutral phrase) a wide but quite conventional range of external interests — conventional in the sense that officials perceive and describe *interest groups* in the foreign policy field in much the same way that outside observers have customarily defined them.[23] Business interests and ethnic groups are mentioned most frequently, for reasons which I will explore subsequently. Frequent reference is also made to church groups and religious organizations; to community organizations, such as service and civic clubs and study groups, and to their national counterparts; to veterans' organizations, labor unions, civil rights groups (something new in the foreign policy field); and to radical or fringe groups on both the left and the right. The modes of contact with these groups are equally wide-ranging, including voluntary efforts by Department people to go out into the community to explain policies and the involuntary suffering of slings and arrows thrown (or mailed) by groups that are opposed to the present policy.

Organizations of the extreme right loom larger on the horizon of State Department officials than one would expect to be the case, given the whole tenor of American foreign policy since World War II, and especially given the large space occupied by organizations of the political center. Almost 20 percent of the respondents mentioned "right-wing organizations" either generally or in particular as groups with which they had had contact or of whose presence they were acutely and uncomfortably aware. An Assistant Secretary took the position that if officials do not have "the public" with them when they try to make an important shift in policy, "right-wing groups will find a large and legitimate area in which to work. If we took the initiative toward the public, we would hold down to narrow proportions the area in which the right wing could get allies."

One of the right-wing organizations mentioned by officials was the Committee of One Million, which had militantly opposed the recognition of Communist China and had gotten many members of Congress to join and to let their names be used on letterheads during the 1950's when opposition to recognition was the conventional political position. By the mid-1960's the consensus in the Department was that the Committee was no longer of any importance, but the implication was strong that in the late 1950's and early 1960's any organization that could maintain the membership of over half the United States Congress had extraordinary political "clout." [24] What remains uncertain, however, even in the musings of those who attributed great power and influence to the Committee of One Million, is to what extent the influence was properly that of the organization, either directly or indirectly, or to what extent the view that really mattered was the one shared by many of the most powerful members of Congress and shaped by the international political environment.[25] But whatever the true facts of the matter may be, the attribution of great influence to the Committee has already become the conventional interpretation; and State Department personnel who never even came close to China policy cite it as an example of the kind of impact the "right wing" can have on foreign policy. Two years ago the Committee of One Million; who knows — next year it may be the Friends of Rhodesia!

In the eyes of the more committed liberals in the State Department, the specter of the extreme right wing has greater force than this; to them it haunts the institution, paralyzing the initiatives of the moderates and leading them in conservative directions in an attempt to keep the ghost of public opinion appeased.[26] And in the process, the hand of the traditionalists and conservatives in the Department is strengthened — leading the liberals to speculate about the role the conservatives play in raising the specter of the right-wing groups in the first place. I would not want to dismiss this *in toto* as simply paranoia; a more balanced view, on the other hand, would have to acknowledge that, here as elsewhere, specters give rise to exorcisers and therefore that exorcisers, too, have an interest in specters: the fear of the fringe groups on the right, while it may paralyze some, galvanizes others into making and keeping friends on the outside. This continual cultivation serves to make the State Department quite accessible to a vast array of organizations of the center. The contact the Department has with the large number of nongovernmental organizations is thus as often the result of Departmental initiative as it is of demands from these groups for consultation. We will take up this circumstance once again in a later chapter, where we will develop more fully its implications; I mention it here just to keep us from automatically assuming a "pressure group model" in which aggressive interest groups do all the pushing and shoving and the Department all the stumbling and falling.[27]

A closer look here at the way economic interests and ethnic interests are perceived in the State Department sheds additional light on the complexities of the Departmental encounter with interest groups. These particular groups are among the most prominent organizations on the Department's horizon; they are also presumed by many critics of American foreign policy to be the most effective influences on the Department's decisions. While I am trying to defer questions about the impacts or effects of public opinion on policy making until Chapter 4, an attempt here to sort out the varied contacts that Department officials have with economic and ethnic groups cannot avoid speaking to this sensitive issue. I will treat them separately: economic groups first and ethnic interests later.

I must introduce the subject of Department contacts with economic organizations with a cautionary note: my sample of Department officials did not include any from the Bureau of Economic Affairs. Certainly this means that I have missed a number of economic contacts which take that route. In mitigation I would argue that I have picked up those economic contacts that were significant enough politically to go through political rather than economic channels. Nevertheless, the data and the generalizations that follow should be understood as referring to my group of respondents and not necessarily to the Department as a whole. But since the evidence here sustains the conclusions reached in a study that concentrated on economic organizations and foreign economic policy (though not on the State Department), I am encouraged to believe that my findings do in fact have a wider relevance.[28]

As I said above, economic organizations were the most prominent among the contacts which the Department officials whom I interviewed had with private interest groups — but these contacts were far from being overwhelming, and they were far from being the most prominent among external contacts of all types. Exactly one-half (twenty-five) of my respondents mentioned having contacts with economic interests — individual firms or associations. The half that was in such contact came disproportionately more from the levels between the desk officer and the Deputy Assistant Secretary, and disproportionately less from the higher levels and from the ranks of the Special Assistants and advisers. Eighty-eight percent of those having contacts with economic groups were in these working-level and lower policy-level ranks, 4 percent (one person) was at the Assistant Secretary level or higher; and 8 percent (two people) were Special Assistants. On the other side, only 42 percent of those who did not mention having such contacts were in the working-level and lower policy-level ranks, 27 percent were Assistant Secretary or higher, and 31 percent were Special Assistants or advisers. Seventy-two percent of those having such contacts were Foreign Service Officers, as against 52 percent of those not mentioning such contacts.[29] This latter difference, such as it is, is due to the concentration of career officers in the politically oriented working-level positions in the Department. Overall, these data indicate that the bulk of the contacts between economic interest groups and the State Department (exclusive of Economic Affairs) is at this working level, at the heart of the Department where things are done, not at the higher political levels (where presumably "influence" is more easily exerted) and not through the agency of Special Assistants and advisers who are often outside the regular channels of organizational power.

The great majority of the remarks which State Department officers made about economic interest groups and about their contact with them fall quite evenly into two categories, which are quite distinct but certainly not mutually inconsistent; in fact, four respondents are found in both categories. The first of these stresses the appropriateness and legitimacy of economic interests in developments abroad; and twelve respondents talk explicitly about it. It is not a matter of people who speak for economic interests having special access to policy makers by virtue of who they are; rather, it is a particular application of the more general position that individuals or organizations that are themselves directly involved in international relations have a normative as well as a legal right to make representations to government officials concerning those relations.[30] A Deputy Assistant Secretary stated the general position as follows: "If you are dealing with a question of commercial policy, it is the National Association of Manufacturers, the Chamber of Commerce, the Foreign Trade Council, and the like that you are interested in; the Quakers, on the other hand, are less compelling when they talk on this subject. . . . It is important to see judgment of political muscle in society as being related to specific policy areas." Economic relations between companies in the United States and enterprises abroad (public or private) constitute an important part of the package of relationships that the United States has with other countries in the world; and those people in the United States who are involved in those relations are accorded the rights of principals to be heard, at least. An Assistant Administrator in AID: "In this job the public comes at me in the form of those who have business interests in our operations. These are guys doing business in ———, people who are having trouble getting their product along, people who are trying to get a contract, or who want in some other way to help their business out. This is all quite direct; it is the business community." A desk officer for a country in Southeast Asia described the various "lobbies," chiefly economic, to which he was subjected. He concluded: "These people are mostly concerned with questions like whether we join the [commodity] Agreement, for example, or on the disposal of their stocks — in other words, economic rather than ideological or political issues." Another desk officer: "In ———, for example, there are large American investments, and the desk people are interested in the opinions of those who have those investments."

But to say that economic interests have perhaps even a special right to be heard on questions affecting their interests is not at all to say that they have the last word. Thirteen officials expressed in one way or another the primacy of the public interest in these contacts with private economic interests. Implicitly or explicitly, they view the government as a competitor of the private business community on the world politico-economic stage rather than its ally — and most certainly not as its stooge. The primacy of the public interest is put forward in three different postures toward economic interests.

1. Cooperation with economic interests in order to serve State Department policy interests. In these instances Departmental officials work closely with business or labor groups because to do so advances the Department's position directly or indirectly. An example of the indirect advantage is provided by the AID official whom I quoted earlier, who was justifying the practice of tying for-

eign aid funds to purchases in the United States: "My economist friends think this is despicable. We started it for balance of payments reasons, but we have kept it going because it has created a real constituency for us — a sizable collection of groups of people in this country who have an economic interest in keeping the program going as it stands." In other words, a foreign aid program is thought to serve American political interests better than no foreign aid program, and the price of a foreign aid program is thought to be cooperation with business interests in a share of the market thus created.

A good example of the direct advantage of cooperation is provided by the Department's relations with labor organizations. In one bureau an official said of labor groups: "Their point of interest is in our support of labor overseas, and they are our chosen instrument for implementing our labor programs overseas." In another bureau, another official elaborated the same train of thought: "In certain areas American labor organizations can do certain things as a result of their prior record and their current international affiliations which we cannot do very effectively. They can present our point of view, in the spirit of their concern for U.S. foreign policy, in circumstances where we cannot deal with labor groups in foreign countries because as official representatives we are limited to contacts with foreign governments themselves." This posture of cooperation is the most ambiguous, to be sure, because under the guise of a marriage of convenience between interests in the economic community and interests of State Department officials lurks the possibility that the real convenience consists in officials adopting the interests of the economic groups. For example, an Office Director discussed the consequences of a law, passed by a country in his purview, which regulated foreign investment and the remittance of profits therefrom. American companies having investments in that country sought the help of the State Department in getting the law modified. "I had, as a result, a number of contacts with businessmen; these contacts influenced me and others in formulating a policy. We were guided by the American business community to a large extent. Companies like ——— . . . would come to me and ask for our support; we were guided almost wholly by their interests. We might have taken action on this case anyway, because that country *needs* private foreign investment.

And a law which discourages it is not in our conception of their interests. So, we and the U.S. firms were on the same side."

2. The bending of economic interests to serve State Department policy interests. The primacy of the public interest is asserted, secondly, in efforts to induce private economic interests to alter *their* policies or practices, in order to bring them into line with important Departmental policies. It is, unhappily, not easy to document instances where this has been done: neither the Department nor the economic enterprises themselves, for their separate reasons, has any interest in publicizing the occasions when the Department has, by persuasion or by half-nelson, secured the cooperation of business or labor. Since the point is of some importance, however, I will cite two examples, taking care to obliterate all identification marks even though it means sacrificing the details. In one case, a labor strike at home had international ramifications, making it impossible for the United States government to meet certain obligations it had undertaken abroad. "We had to get the union to understand that we have these international responsibilities and that they were their responsibilities also. I was on the phone to their negotiators in —— all hours of the night, and it was not until two in the morning, at the very edge of the strike deadline, that they let me know that they would . . . [enable us to honor our commitments] despite the strike." In another case, the State Department was attempting to bring pressure to bear on a foreign government for political ends and in the process sought the cooperation of a small number of American companies whose trade was particularly important to the country in question. One by one the Department took on these firms, using whatever elements of persuasion and *force majeure* were necessary in order to get the companies to cooperate in a policy that meant an important and calculable financial loss to each of them. With respect to one set of these "negotiations": "We would have loved to announce the cooperation of the —— people immediately, but we weren't able to. So, you can see that they do have some power. We have not won this one yet. They might make us look foolish before it is over, but I think they will fall into line. We do have a certain leverage over them; they don't come into this business with very clean hands. They have bought some Soviet [material], and we know it."

3. The subordination of economic interests to Department policy

or to the "national interest." A third stance toward economic interests, both business and labor, involves their substantial subordination to political or strategic considerations when there is any conflict between them.[31] This is most often expressed in specific terms,
since that is how conflict is likely to manifest itself. In the labor
field, for instance: "Suppose you have violations of the free association principle as contained in ILO conventions. That is when U.S.
labor would get into the act. They would want the government to
support ILO action taken against [country A] or [country B], for
example. The government, on the other hand, has political reasons
and military reasons that it believes may supersede the labor interests in such a case involving [country A]. And in such a case the
government is simply not willing to shift its priorities in such matters." In a retrospective on the Congo, an official recalled that
"business interests, those who supported the Union Minière in Ka-
tanga, were in opposition to us. We felt their lobby campaigns
very strongly. We kept getting letters asking 'Why do we not support Tshombe?' The stakes were very high, and the decision was
made to support the central government in the Congo. We felt that
a majority of Americans was on our side. We felt that the United
States' interests should be aligned with the people of Africa." A
desk officer in the Bureau of European Affairs: "I cannot think of a
single case where United States economic interests were considered in our decisions — where someone said, 'Hey, have you
thought about what —— will say?' We have economic problems,
of course, but we do not consider them from the point of view of
any particular interest except for that of security."

It looks, I admit, like a one-sided and institutionally self-serving
picture that argues the legitimacy of economic representations but
the primacy of the public interest in responding to them. I cannot
claim that, with time and diligence and a finer net, one could not
uncover situations where private economic interests have had primacy over the public interest — where policy has been modified to
protect American business or where policy has been subordinated
to the interests of American business. It remains significant, nonetheless, that in the major areas of Department political policy in
which I interviewed, the prevailing judgment was the opposite.
Where private economic interests do prevail, it would appear at
least that they prevail in contravention of very strong beliefs

among officials about what is proper and about where their institutional interests lie. Whether these beliefs are so strong that they color officials' perceptions of what has actually happened is beyond the reach of my evidence.

Ethnic groups, like economic interest groups, loom relatively large on the horizon of State Department officials. One-third of the officials whom I interviewed mentioned them in one context or another as important points of contact with the outside public. Yet it is hard to discover in these broad contacts much contemporary support for the view that ethnic groups exert a significant impact on American foreign policy.[32] Vocal, to be sure; consequential, less often. The ethnic groups that were most in evidence at this point in time were Jews, East Europeans, and Negroes; and the geographic or substantive scope of their involvement was limited, respectively, to the Near East, Eastern Europe, and Africa. Other ethnic or nationality groups were mentioned in passing, as visible landmarks, but not as important topographical features.

Of these three groups, Jews and Jewish organizations stand out both in the number of officials who are aware of and sensitive to them and in the political respect accorded them.[33] The sources of this respect are varied, however, suggesting that the notion of "ethnic groups" as political actors is greatly oversimplified. One official talked about his contacts with Zionist organizations, but he summed up their impact not in terms of pressure-group politics but as a more generalized political fear of the electoral reactions of Jews in big cities, likening the situation to that of the Irish and United States policy toward Great Britain in the nineteenth century. Another, who had current responsibilities in the Near East, saw the Zionist groups as, in the crunch, merely typical of broader currents of American opinion: "Jewish leaders like you to think that they speak for all Jews everywhere, but they usually do not; some of them are uninterested, others take opposed views, and so on, just like anybody else. Yet if you get involved with Nasser in some way, you cannot dismiss them as a Zionist lobby, because lots of Americans are fed to the teeth with Nasser." Still another, who also had responsibilities in the Near East, stressed the organizational dimension: "The Jewish community is, of course, interested in Israel, and it is very well organized and vocal. They go out of their way to make their views known, through personal contact at almost all levels in the Department. They have their publications, also, both regular and irregular. They hold meetings; they adopt resolutions concerning Israel, all of which are made known to us. . . . The Jews like political organization."

In a different historical period, however, a quite different set of contacts and impacts were reported. Interviews in the mid-1950's with former officials of the Truman Administration in the State Department, Department of Defense, and White House portray a picture of intense, unremitting, and effective political action by Jewish groups in policy toward Israel from 1948 to 1952. One Department official cited this as a special exception to his generalization that "pressure groups have little influence on top security problems." Another reported a very high Administration official as thinking "that on the Israel issue the pressure from the Jewish side was just terrible." And a member of the White House staff reflected that that issue "didn't do credit to anyone, the Democrats, the Republicans or the Zionists. . . . However, I can't think of any other comparable case in our [foreign] policy." [34] Nor did the interviews of either the 1950 or 1960 periods suggest anything remotely comparable in the way of ethnic-group — or other interest-group — impact.

Department officials who handled Eastern European problems in the 1960's often encountered émigré organizations, as I have had occasion to say once before; but the political fragmentation of these groups and the political (as opposed to ethnic or nationality) character of their concerns left their mark on the officials, who spoke about these groups with little of the broad political respect that marked the discussion of Jewish groups. The Poles were noted several times as the most important and effective, more for their apparent support in the Congress than for anything else: "While the Poles have lots of organizations, I have a feeling that they exist more on paper than anywhere else. . . . These people are numerous in key Midwest and Northeast industrial areas; they are a sought-after political group. But when it comes to anything other than elections, as for example to the bringing of influence to bear on a particular issue, it all gets rather amorphous." In the African area, much was said about the interest and participation of blacks representing civil rights organizations; and much effort was expended to solicit their involvement. But their active participation as organizations representing portions of the black community was nonetheless regarded as potential rather than actual.

Other ethnic groups besides these three were noticed by State Department personnel; but these others were perceived quite differently, and their impact was much less. The desk officer could tell me the American cities where large ethnic populations from his "parish" live; but they were variously described as "not going for political action" or as having "very little interest in what is going on in ——." One desk officer said that the ambassador from "his" country was under much more scrutiny from the ethnic community in the United States than he and his colleagues in the Department were; but he reported also that ethnic "labor and commerce organizations keep up with what we do, and they express their views on what is going on in ——. These are mostly personal views, and they reflect changing attitudes; so we regard it as useful feedback on what we are doing." Finally, if evidence is needed that the State Department is not "enslaved" by ethnic groups, there is the comment of one official that "we have managed to preserve relations with the Arab states, when there are damned few Arabs in the United States." And the Department is quite able to use ethnic groups for policy purposes of its own: to get its major reform Immigration Bill through in the early 1960's, the Department "needed to get a broader base of support than merely the professional ethnic groups who have never really been good supporters"; thus began an intensive cultivation and mobilization of ethnic, minority, nationality, and religious groups behind a reform measure that was ultimately successful.

The most extensive and pervasive contact State Department officials have with the external public is with *the press*. The fact that I "bury" this discussion in the middle of the haystack, so to speak, instead of leading off with it, is not meant to suggest that I think it is unimportant; chalk it up rather to my slavish adherence to a pre-set structure of organization. The "press" is a vast institution; in its broadest working definition it includes all the media of mass communication and their operating personnel. In a practical sense, however, it is most often used by Department officials to refer to the printed media — newspapers and newsmagazines. Eighty percent of the respondents in my sample discussed their contacts with and exposure to the press at some length; although the others were silent on this point, I think it is safe to assume that they at least read a daily newspaper and thus that they, too, had some kind of contact with the press. Having earlier written a book on the pervasive relationship between the press and foreign policy officials, I tried especially hard at all stages of this research to avoid simply transferring the conclusions of that book to the present context.[35] In my interviews I handled the subject of the press no differently than any other of the possible sources of contact with external opinion, to avoid prejudging the matter, and I will present the findings here in the same manner. For the benefit of the curious, however, I will add that the correspondence between my present and my earlier findings cheered me enormously; but perhaps, if they are really curious, they will want to see for themselves.

To repeat, the press is the leading point of contact between State Department officials and the external public. Almost all officials have daily experience with it in one form or another. And though some of them are — like ordinary citizens — not fully conscious of the ways in which the press shapes their perceptions and evaluations of political opinion, others are very explicit about the press as the central vehicle in their understanding of external opinion. A Deputy Assistant Secretary: "We watch the press carefully, for example on an issue like Chinese representation in the UN . . . to see if we can detect legitimate trends in public thinking." And a remark by an Office Director, quoted earlier in a different context, makes the same point: "We all read the press carefully; not only *The Washington Post,* but *The New York Times, The Baltimore Sun,* the Louisville papers. So we know pretty well what the country is thinking. These newspapers, plus the stuff that comes from the Congress, tells us all we need to know."

The press functions as an opinion source for Department officials in two different ways: directly, as an expression of the views of a significant proportion of the political-opinion-bearing population (namely, political journalists); indirectly, as a mechanism transmitting the opinions of others, which it may or may not have had a hand in creating. Let us look first at the *press as public opinion* and then at the press as a transmission belt for the opinions of others.

The equation of the press with public opinion is very common among Department officials and among scholars, especially historians. It is standard for historians to turn to the public prints as the voice of public opinion during the period under their examination, since the press is often the only extant remnant of nongovernmental expressions of opinion. Yet contemporary chroniclers, who have more varied data at hand, also talk about the press in rather special ways as the really relevant voice of the people. Roger Hilsman, former Assistant Secretary for Far Eastern Affairs, argues, "Major changes in policy about continuing problems can usually be made only when a number of the participants in Congress, the press, and the various agencies and Departments in the Executive have abandoned hope that current policy will succeed and the rest of the participants have at least come to have doubts." [36] And Joseph Jones, who wrote from first-hand participation in the events of the famous fifteen weeks between the Truman Doctrine and the Marshall Plan in 1947, repeatedly and consistently lets the press stand for the public.[37] When we find former officials writing this way, we begin to see it as a pattern of institutional perception, and we can expect that men who are currently in official positions will share it too.

And share it they do, in highly specific ways. Officials see four different forms or channels through which the press performs its public opinion role.

First, of major importance is the manifest news content of the press. Over a third of the respondents singled out the substantive coverage of issues and events in the press as a prime source — often their chief source — of information on what others think are the important questions of the day. An Assistant Secretary talked about reporters as the "makers of issues" for policy makers. An Office Director said that seeing the major articles on his area "in seven or eight of the major metropolitan newspapers" gives one "a sense of what is being said in the country." A Deputy Office Director said: "At the desk and office level here in the State Department you do not get public opinion directly. We all read newspapers. . . . We have to worry about the Congress." Another Assistant Secretary said that looking at press coverage was one of the leading ways by which men at his level could discover "a growing feeling in this country of a certain kind." [38]

Second, of equal significance as a source of public opinion are the journalists themselves, as human beings, in a range of personal interactions from social contact to informal interview to formal press conference. Although exposure to reporters varies considerably from official to official, over a third of the respondents in this study had sufficient experience, direct or indirect, with correspondents to regard them as external sources of — as a Deputy Assistant Secretary put it — "valid policy judgments," as representatives of "informed American opinion." Reporters convey these judgments or opinions in two different ways. The process of developing and maintaining reliable contacts in the State Department is, for an experienced and knowledgeable reporter, a complex situation involving personal and professional factors. Trust and reliability and confidence are necessary parts of it on both sides (which limits the number who are interested in playing the game), but so also is a sense of mutual worth. In exchange for news items of professional advantage to himself, the reporter leaves behind him information and informed appraisal which are of professional interest to the official. The reporter, thus, joins the rather select list of outsiders with whom some few officials discuss developing policy on a candid and confidential basis; the reporter understands the official's problem and his perspective, but he is professionally motivated to stay independent of it, and even slightly critical of it, and so he sharpens his value as a source of external opinion.

A more common way in which the reporter conveys opinion and judgment to officials is by the routine exercise of his craft: he asks questions of officials and in that very process signals to them what is on *his* mind. A desk officer reported "a lot of contact with the press, in terms of the correspondents in this building who are seeking information. You have to make distinctions here; the [wire service] man is a lot better than the [wire service] stories that go out nationally. The questions he is interested in have an alerting effect on us; they tell us what is up." A Public Affairs Adviser rated "the reporters that you see" very high among the "inputs" into the Department's "intuition" concerning public opinion: "You are always getting stuff from them, both from the way in which they ask a question and from the things they tell you." The reporters are asking questions all day long: they will call officials directly; they will ask the Office of Press Relations, which will pass it on to the appropriate bureau; they will ask the Public Affairs Adviser in the bureau directly; they will ask at the Department's noon briefing for the press. The practice is so pervasive that the officials read their newspapers each morning with an eye to the possible questions that might be asked. For example, a Deputy Assistant Secretary: "We look at all the [regional] stories every morning, and if we think there will be questions growing out of them at our noon briefing here in the Department . . . we will then work out possible answers." And in this fashion the interests and concerns of newspaper correspondents are transformed into the interests and concerns of State Department officials. But it is not quite the same thing. The official is trying to "satisfy the reporter," which may be freely translated as answering his question in such a way that the reporter will either drop the subject or treat it routinely. In the process, however, he has gotten the reporter's views with unmistakable clarity — and, to the extent that he can successfully anticipate the questions that will be asked, he may even have internalized some of those views or the ways of thinking from which they derive.[39]

Of minor importance, compared with the above, are the third and fourth manifestations of the press-as-public-opinion: the editorials, and the noted columnists. This is a finding worth noting, since the conventional approach to the press puts it just the opposite, seeing the editorials and the interpretive columns as the major and the legitimate locus of the newspaper as an expression of opinion. Each of these items is explicitly mentioned by an astonishingly few officials — four in each instance. In the case of editorials, the four ranged in their attitudes from a mild depreciation (an Assistant Secretary: "I watch the editorials, but I do not consider them as reflections of anyone's opinions other than the man who writes them"); to routine affirmations of interest and appreciation (an Office Director: "We are all interested all the time in getting editorial reactions. . . . When the Secretary is abroad and is involved in something big like NATO negotiations, we like to get summaries of opinion to him on how those negotiations are being viewed in the American press"); to outright pleasure (a Deputy Assistant Secretary: "We have welcomed criticism from *The New York Times*' editorial page . . . that we were not doing enough in this field"). I have no satisfactory explanations for this treatment of editorial opinion — only a variety of conjectures, the most interesting being that editorial writers are predictable creatures and that officials tend to discount and thus to forget their predictable responses (except where they can be used for political purposes) since these do not register as "different" and thus as significant opinion.[40]

The low salience of columnists on the public opinion horizon is equally baffling. The very few who spoke about the columnists, or the pundits, were unanimous in their respect for their "great influence." I have no doubt that had I asked each respondent directly for his reaction to the news analysts as a form of opinion, I would have gotten substantial responses of some kind. But it is more significant of their true measure *as a form of opinion* that in free discussion of the press in this context so few officials mentioned them spontaneously. Once again, one searches for possible explanation. It can hardly lie alone in the fact that the columnist — a small class to begin with — so clearly speaks for himself; after all, officials do not hesitate to accept *other* individuals as legitimate and important voices of external opinion. Perhaps it is a matter of relative obscurity — the columnist losing out to the broader canvas of news coverage as the important picture of opinion in the press. Or perhaps it is simply a matter of competition, the columnist being seen not as a valuable source of outside opinion but merely as someone trying to second-guess the officials without really knowing what is going on.

It is conceivable, of course, that officials are simply unwilling to acknowledge, to me or to themselves, the influence of both editorials and columnists because they find it too threatening. But in the realm of psychological explanation it is at least as reasonable to hypothesize that officials reject outside influence they regard as competitive and threatening, as to hypothesize that they accept it but repress the evidence. In any event, we can never really know which is closer to the fact, since neither hypothesis is very accessible to the kinds of empirical research readily available to us.

The press also functions indirectly as an opinion source for officials, by serving as a *mechanism for the transmission of the opinions of others* and even for the creation and stimulation of that opinion. Two examples may suffice to illustrate this process in a relatively uncomplicated form. In attempting to account for the phenomenon of American imperialism at the end of the nineteenth century, Ernest R. May portrays the press as a vehicle for a new set of views on the question of colonialism; he describes the rather sudden flowering of colonialist sentiment among the public as it appeared in the press, and he treats it as a public responsiveness to a larger and more varied group of opinion leaders who emerged as a result of division and confusion within the establishment.[41] And in 1966, efforts by scholars and others to open up a discussion of American policy toward Communist China were the subject of detailed newspaper reporting, which itself served to broadcast the views that were being expressed in these discussions.[42]

Both of these instances deal with public opinion as a news item. Rather more subtle but no less important is the function of the press in stimulating other kinds of external opinions, which subsequently come back to the State Department either via the press or in some more direct way. A Deputy Office Director put it concisely: "The press has a way of generating interest, if not news, to which we have to respond. . . . After all, people who have opinions form them from reading, chiefly, and from listening and watching also." An Assistant Secretary said the same thing: "In Washington you respond to the public opinion that is generated by a small group of newspapermen. . . . What blankets the country via the press is an important source of public opinion." We know, however, that the Department does not in fact "hear" from very many people, and therefore it does not "have to respond" to very much outside interest. These officials are describing not the mobilization of mass opinion but rather the complex sorts of political reactions that develop in the wake of press disclosure — reactions from the press itself, from the Congress, from Embassy Row, from outside groups that may be affected — which by virtue of their large, extra-bureaucratic component are described by officials as manifestations of public opinion. An Office Director recounted several experiences of this kind: "*The New York Times* once printed a story about a rebel camp from X that was based in Y. Everyone knew the camp was there, and everyone looked the other way. But when *The New York Times* published the story, we all came to work knowing that the X embassy was reading the story, the people in Y were reading the story, along with everyone else, and so we had to decide whether we should continue to look the other way about the camp. Similarly, *The Los Angeles Times* got hold of a story on —— and misreported that. We had to take into account the questions that came up as a result, and we also had to try to keep the whole thing low-key in order to keep the Congressmen from using it in order to hit the program." [43]

The Congress is on a par with the press in its importance for State Department officials as a form of public opinion. It is not at all surprising, in one sense, to find that the Congress is on nearly everyone's mind in the State Department. It is, after all, a frequent political adversary, the gatekeeper for many of its policies, and the holder of the purse both as it affects policies and programs and as it affects the bureaucratic life-forms of the institution. But I am not concerned here with the importance of Congress to foreign policy in this political participant sense; that is the legislative aspect of the Congressional role in foreign affairs, in which Congress participates in the foreign policy process as a constitutionally empowered principal. It is, rather, the *representative* aspect of the Congressional role I am interested in here, in which Congress participates more or less as a politically freighted agent of the true sovereign, the people. This view, that the Congress has representative functions in the foreign policy field that stand relatively free of the process of legislation — functions that make it an imposing figure on the public opinion horizon — is one that has never received much attention in studies of Congress and foreign policy. [44] That may be a consequence of the practical difficulty in distinguishing between "pure representation," so to speak, and the more pervasive legislative function, in the sense that Congressional opinion may have inescapable legislative implications or overtones of a remote or secondary kind even when there are no primary legislative components to the foreign policy question on which Congressional opinion is being sought or offered. One can grant that the strategic political position and legislative power of the Congress give a special political meaning to the opinions of Congressmen on every subject under heaven — indeed, it is the legislative sanction that distinguishes the Congress from 535 men chosen at random — and yet one can still be impressed by the fact that Congress performs opinion functions in the foreign policy field in ways and of kinds that are often indistinguishable from their performance by wholly nongovernmental institutions. Let me elaborate.

As I said above, virtually everyone in the State Department is aware of the constitutional or legislative role of the Congress in

foreign affairs. As one person put it, "It is really the political process we are concerned about, with Congressmen as key participants." But beyond this, fully 70 percent of the Department officials who were sampled explicitly saw the Congress as having a
public opinion role. And as was the case with the press, this representative role takes two quite distinctive forms: twenty-eight respondents, or 56 percent of the total, saw the Congress as itself an
important form or manifestation of public opinion; whereas
twenty-two respondents (fifteen of whom are also in the first
group), or 44 percent of the total, saw it as a conduit or a mechanism for the transmission of the opinions of others.

Men in other places and at other times have shared the view
that the body of elected representatives was a valid manifestation
of public opinion in the body politic. In her assessment of President Monroe's attitude toward the role of public opinion in foreign
policy making, for instance, Doris Graber writes, "If political leaders are true surrogates of the people who drink from the same
fountain of truth, then their opinion represents public opinion." [45]
In Britain, Kenneth Waltz reports, Foreign Office officials gain an
important measure of their understanding of public opinion or "the
general will" "through MP's asking questions and Ministers listening to the murmurs of approval and disapproval evoked by their
answers." [46] State Department officials, lacking their British counterparts' access to the floor of Congress, nevertheless manage to
hear "murmurs of approval and disapproval" coming from that
body. An Office Director said on several occasions, "We talk about
public opinion, but in our area of the State Department we are
concerned with a few individual Congressmen." In thinking about
future possibilities, another official reported, "We 'factor in' American public opinion into our proposals; in other words, we recognize that people on the Hill may feel certain ways about things." A
Deputy Assistant Secretary discussed a breakfast meeting he had
had with fifty members of the House of Representatives during a
period of conflict and tension in "his" part of the world: "This was
useful to me, to learn what the average Congressman thinks —
someone from a rural constituency who is not on a foreign affairs
committee. You do not throw away your old policies and tactics,
but it can help to bend your thinking a bit to know what the
American people, through their Congressmen, would accept by

way of policy. And it certainly helped to shape my ideas. If their ideas are not usable, mine had better be pretty good and well justified." The careful reader will detect in this remark the same general attitude that has been displayed toward other outside groups: the Congress, being accepted as an embodiment of public opinion, is treated with the same combination of polite respect, substantive resistance, and tactical adaptation that mark the Department's reaction to other manifestations of external opinion.

A persistent refrain in Departmental discourse is one which talks about "public opinion" and then proceeds to illustrate it by reference to particular Congressmen. Some examples: "[Balance of payments] is another area of public concern. . . . Senator Javits especially is concerned with the British economic situation as a whole." "The Congo is a good case; the public had an acute interest in this matter. Senator Dodd came over there. . . . Senator Keating came on a visit." "For the past year and a half I have been heavily involved in ———, on the policy making side. This brings me right up against public opinion often in the form of Representative ——— of Wisconsin." Without trying to make too much out of these expressions, it nevertheless seems to me that an habitual identification of Congressmen with public opinion in this fashion is more than simply a conventional mode of discourse. State Department officials have a wide field of experience from which to draw, in order to illustrate their generalizations about public opinion. The fact that they so often choose to come down on the Congressional example seems to me to say a great deal about the context in which they perceive and evaluate Congressional interest in foreign policy and about the relative importance they attach to Congressmen-as-public-opinion as compared with other forms of public opinion. One might argue that I have this backward — that these officials are generalizing not about public opinion but about Congress. But if this is true, the fact that they cast their generalizations about Congressional interest in foreign policy in a public opinion context rather than a political or legislative context makes my point even more directly.

Nearly half of the officials whom I interviewed saw the Congress performing its representative functions in a non-Burkean way, as a mechanism transmitting the opinions of others. This view of the Congress has two aspects: some officials see Congressmen more or less as physical conduits, passing on to the State Department in a substantially unchanged form the messages they receive from their constituents, while others see the Congress itself more as a refractive device, bending, processing, reinterpreting external opinions before conveying them to officials. *As conduits*, Congressmen transmit to the State Department many of the letters they receive from their constituents that deal with foreign policy matters. They do this not primarily in order to let the Department know what problems look like at the grassroots but to get the Department's help in answering them; any request of this sort from a Congressman — called a "Congressional" — gets an answer from the State Department within three days. But even though the purpose is not the transmission of opinion, that is clearly an important consequence when hundreds of letters are sent over monthly and when both politics and protocol require that they get special attention. Odd as it may seem, the Department official with operating responsibilities is at least as likely to be apprised of the flow of foreign policy mail to Congressmen as he is of mail to the Department itself, even on subjects within his own bailiwick. An official in the Bureau of European Affairs: "My impression is that the bulk of public interest in the UK [United Kingdom] is followed through Congressmen. . . . Congressional interest tends to be focused on specific problems; a prime example right now is British shipping to North Vietnam. Congressmen get very bitter letters on this from their constituents, and then they write to the State Department." From the Bureau of International Organization Affairs: "The Congress is first in importance as a channel from the public. When Congressmen speak up on foreign affairs, they are reflecting the concern of their own constituents. We simply have to answer 'Congressionals' in three days. So we have to be responsive to these letters." Congressmen transmit the opinions of constituents verbally, also, although the lack of extensive personal contacts between Congressmen and State Department officials tends to limit the opportunities for verbal transmission to more or less formal occasions or channels — to hearings, for example, or to periodic press "roundups," or to official liaison functions.[47] An official in the Bureau of Public Affairs, thus: "I keep a jaded eye on the Congress and on the way they are perceiving public opinion. ——, in Congressional Liaison, will call me and tell me what Congressmen are telling him they are hearing when they are back home."

The notion of Congressmen as conduits of constituent opinion stresses the essential integrity of the opinion as it passes through the Congress. Other State Department officials use a different image to describe the Congress as an opinion-transmitting system: they see the Congress *as a prism* through which popular opinion passes, is rephrased, and acquires a politically significant voice which can then be heard. An official in AID suggested the prism image: "There is much more public influence on the State Department through the Congress than directly from the public — at least with respect to AID. You almost do not see the public outside the Congress. You see the public through the Congressional lenses, so to speak; it is prismatic. . . . For the average bureaucrat, public opinion exists only in the Congress." From Public Affairs the same viewpoint: "If a given point of view that is different from our own does not have Congressional expression, forget it. If it does have Congressional expression, it may still not be very important; but it can't be important if it has no important takers in the Congress." And from European Affairs, this mixed-metaphor summation: "Congress is what distills and focuses general public opinion."

FACELESS OR IMPERSONAL SOURCES

In terms of sheer numbers, *letters* represent one of the broadest modes of contact between officials and private citizens. I have already observed that the volume of mail on foreign policy that makes its way to the State Department either directly or through referral by other offices amounted to nearly 200,000 pieces in 1965. In fiscal year 1962, according to William O. Chittick, the Division of Public Correspondence handled over 270,000 pieces of mail, 7,000 of which had been referred to the Department by Congressmen.[48] And two out of every three respondents (thirty-three in all) in the Department took some cognizance, not of the "total picture" of public correspondence by any means, but at least of the mail in his particular area of interest coming from all sources. But the perceptions of the origins, quantity, and character of this form of public expression and the evaluations of its significance present a much different picture, considerably less expansive in its implications.

With respect to the origin or sources of these letters, nearly half (twenty-four) of the respondents saw them as coming from an undifferentiated general public, the implication being that these were people whose involvement in foreign policy was occasional and not especially well-informed. An official in the Public Affairs area who was familiar with the overall public correspondence situation attributed the mail mostly to what he called "single-issue" people.[49] Another person described the mail that was occasioned by the Secretary of State's appearance before the Senate Foreign Relations Committee as "a tremendous outpouring of correspondence from little people throughout the country." A third person, who had once worked in the Public Correspondence Branch of the State Department, said, "It is rare for us to get a reasoned letter on something. The people who could write those kinds of letters pick up the telephone instead." Nineteen respondents (38 percent) mentioned mail from Congressmen or mail forwarded by Congressmen, which as I indicated above has more than a little of the patina of Congress about it. Eight respondents (16 percent) identified special interest groups or ethnic minorities as the source of the mail they were most often exposed to. Four officials, all of whom were in the first group above who identified letter-writers as part of the general public, made the further point that only the mail from informed and knowledgeable people effectively attracted attention. A Deputy Assistant Secretary: "I should stress that our exposure to public opinion is really to the informed public opinion. These are the people who come to conferences, who write letters. . . ." A Special Assistant to an Assistant Secretary observed that letters "have to come from important people, like Kennan or McCloy," in order to get read by important people in the Department.

I said in the preceding chapter that the Public Correspondence Branch and the Bureau of Public Affairs made no effort to keep officers of the Department apprised of the flow of mail on their subject-areas, except where their help was required in the drafting of an answer. This fact undoubtedly contributes to the great disparities among Department officials in their perception of the volume of public mail, exaggerating the differences that stem in the first instance from real variations in public interest from issue to issue. Descriptions of the volume of mail coming from the general public — from "little people" — range from "a tremendous outpouring," to "a steady stream," to "not a lot." One desk officer dismissed the problem by noting that except for the crisis periods (which were frequent in his area), "it doesn't pay to find out" about the volume of mail. Mail which was referred to the Department by Congressmen was described in similar language: from "an amazing flow" to "a fair amount," to "very low," to "none."

The State Department keeps tabs on the preferential content of its mail — on the number of people who express approval or disapproval of trends in foreign policy — but it does not give wide distribution to the results. In particular, it almost never reveals negative majorities, though it sometimes "lets it be known" when the majorities are strongly favorable.[50] It is interesting, in these circumstances, to see how the preferential content of the mail registers in the minds of State Department officials, most of whom see only relatively small portions of it in any event. On the whole, it registers as negative and critical — or at least this is the aspect of the public mail that officials seem to be most aware of and talk about spontaneously. Only two officials mentioned the mail as overwhelmingly favorable to the Department's position; they were both within the immediate orbit of the Secretary of State and were discussing the mail that had been evoked by two recent televised appearances of the Secretary. Two other officials responded in ways that mixed affirmative and negative perceptions; one mentioned letter-writing campaigns against the Department's position in the Congo but added, "Our public correspondence on the whole has been favorable to . . . [our] point of view." The other official, who had worked in both the Bureau of International Organization Affairs (IO) and the Agency for International Development (AID) concluded that "the mail from the extreme right is much greater in IO than it is . . . in AID," which is "relatively free of the kind of stuff that arouses their leaders."

All the others (fourteen persons) who mentioned the content of the mail described it in varying ways and to varying degrees as critical and hostile. An official in the Bureau of Public Affairs who was familiar with the overall mail situation said, "We get a constant flow of letters from all over the country. Letters, as you know, tend to focus on people's discontents." And from all over the Department that same theme was heard. A Deputy Assistant Secretary: "Anyone sitting in a political desk in Washington has to deal with mail from people who do not like your policy." References to "the critical letters that come from the Congress" abound, some of which have been mentioned in prior discussions. Another Deputy Assistant Secretary observed: "We get two classes of letters. One set comes from students who want help writing their term papers. . . . The second set of letters are complaints which are forwarded to us from the Congress." And from AID: "Incoming mail is not an index of the state of public opinion, because most people are only spurred to write if they have something about which to complain. But it is a handy guide to the relative quantity and sometimes the quality of disapproval." [51]

In an unexpected way the *lecture* and the *"briefing session"* appear as means of public opinion contacts for a large portion of the officials in my sample. The Department itself sponsors "briefings" or conferences in Washington for what one official called "defined segments" of the population — for example, church groups, educators, editors and publishers — and regional briefings around the country open to all interested groups and individuals. Department officials conduct these sessions, giving talks and participating in discussions. The Department also sends from one to four officials to a city or an area in a "saturation" campaign — maximum exposure, on platforms, over radio and TV, in a short period of time. (An Office Director described a "typical" day on such a trip, which in his case usually lasted about a week: "I am on television at sunup; then a breakfast meeting, followed by a student assembly; there will be a luncheon with some civic group and then in the afternoon a university or college appearance; in the evening a reception by the local Foreign Policy Association group or the United Nations group, and then an evening panel with reporters.") And the Department responds to many outside requests from organizations for speakers by sending a willing official of some special competence in the subject matter requested.[52]

Two-thirds of the respondents (thirty-three officials) mentioned the lecture or briefing as a mode of contact, for a total of thirty-nine separate references. Not all of them regarded this mode of contact as a way of learning something about public opinion, however, particularly since these devices are manifestly for the purpose of shaping opinion. Indeed, of the thirty-nine references, eleven were only that — i.e., references to platform contact without elaboration as to purpose or consequence; eight referred to briefings and lectures exclusively as a means of communication outward from the Department to the public; fourteen mentioned them both as ways to "get the Department's story" to the people and as occasions to discover what was on people's minds; and six spoke about them exclusively as ways to learn something about public opinion. In other words, although two-thirds of the officials in the sample saw the lecture platform as a means of contact with the public, only two-fifths explicitly mentioned it as an opinion-sampling device. These twenty officials come disproportionately from the higher levels of the Department; whereas 60 percent of the whole sample were Office Directors or higher, 80 percent of this group were at that level, and the six officials who mentioned lectures exclusively as ways to discover public opinion were all Office Directors or above.

What do these officials get out of platform contact, and how? Unlike many of the other forms of opinion sampling, this kind is not thought by its practitioners to be in any way "representative" of opinion in the country at large. These officials understand the very selective nature of the audiences they are reaching — even though they differ among themselves on the criteria of selectivity. Nevertheless they get from this brief, impersonal, yet close human contact some further insight into the way that ordinary (interested) people perceive and evaluate United States foreign policy. The interaction between officials and audiences takes place throughout the sessions — in the applause or other reactions to portions of the talk itself; in the questions that are asked at the end; in the informal conversation in social encounters that precede or follow the talk. The most important of these interactions, however, judging from the comments of the officials, is the question period that follows the lecture.

From the reactions of officials to these events, one can discern several different kinds of knowledge — or, more properly intuitions — about external opinions that they acquire in this way. First, they get some appreciation of the degree of passion or dispassion that characterizes audiences or surrounds issues. An Office Director in a politically sensitive area reported, for example, that talking even to "selective audiences . . . has an important impact on the people here who go out into these communities. They can sense where there is a rational understanding of issues and where people come up with clear views, on one hand and, on the other, who it is who is just speaking out from prejudice or emotion." Another official discussed the Department's regional briefings, singling out for special mention one "where sixty to seventy John Birchers made all the noise out of thousands of people there." And another where "we heard a lot from the Eastern European refugee types who are violently anti-Soviet and can never be satisfied." Second, they get an appreciation of the relative priority of issues in the mind of the interested layman, or, as a Deputy Assistant Secretary put it, "some sense of what is bothering people." Another Deputy Assistant Secretary, who had recently made several talks at universities and at regional briefings, called this "one of the very impressive ways of getting exposed to public opinion. . . . You can tell the areas that are of objective concern to people, the areas in which people have no personal axe to grind. Today [March 1966] 90 percent of the questions that people ask concern Vietnam; this is the case even if you go to talk to them about ——. That would not be true of course for the semi-professional public groups concerned with ——. . . . But for the general public, however, Vietnam and China are uppermost in their mind, judging from the questions they are forever asking." Third, officials get some specific reaction to their own areas of interest and to the way they formulate problems and propose solutions. A Deputy Assistant Secretary: "This gives you a chance to hear the questions the people are asking about your operations." An Office Director: "You can get some sense of an audience's critical reactions from the line of questioning that occurs." Another Deputy Assistant Secretary: "It makes you organize your thoughts. You cannot talk clearly on a subject unless you are thinking clearly about it."

In my prior discussion of intuition vs. science in the Department's approach to public opinion, I gave my first indication that *public opinion polls* do not rank very high as a source of external opinion for State Department officials. I want to say a little more about that here, not only to be systematic about my treatment of all these sources but also because of the very perversity of the finding itself. To those of us on the outside who pay attention to public opinion on foreign policy issues, the polls are probably the most central measure of that opinion; in fact, the polls constitute the major contribution of social science to the objective and accurate study of mass opinion. The claim that they are insignificant from the perspective of the State Department official requires some support and elaboration.

To begin with, the public opinion polling agencies ask very few poll questions dealing with foreign affairs at any point in time. And for a number of years the Vietnam War preempted even this limited area. No wonder, then, that only 20 percent of the officials whom I interviewed (ten persons) made any mention whatsoever of polls in what were otherwise wide-ranging discussions of public opinion. That alone is a remarkable indicator of the low salience of opinion polls in the foreign policy field. And of these ten officials, fully one-half made a single, simple reference to polls as a source of information about public opinion, moving on to discuss at length some of the other forms of public opinion. One of these five men, a relatively senior official, even limited his awareness of polls to very special circumstances: "When you have a major issue like Vietnam, then there are public opinion polls, of course, published and unpublished." [53] Of the remaining five officials who discussed polls at greater length, four did so in depreciatory fashion. Two of these I quoted in the preceding chapter, in the discussion of intuition vs. science, and I need not repeat that here. A third official, himself involved in the Vietnam situation, said of the so-called "Stanford Poll," which in a widely publicized manner fundamentally questioned the worth of most other polling on the Vietnam War, "That poll made no very great noise here, so far as I can see. Maybe the P area people ground it into their machinery, I don't know." [54] The fourth person disposed of the polls by denying evidence that did not conform to expectation: "On the NBC Poll the other night, their evidence was that the doves were about equal in number to the hawks. We happen to believe that the hawks are much more numerous, that most Americans are kind of sublimated hawks." This official also said that the only poll that had stimulated a serious reaction in the Department, that "rocked a lot of people," was a Harris poll showing the President's support had slipped below the 50 percent level. "But other than that" — presumably including poll-data on substantive policy questions — "the polls are not terribly influential."

Only one official in my sample paid serious attention to polls and drew major public opinion implications from them: "Back during the Korean War, I analyzed all of the polls concerning the war, including some polls that the State Department had taken which were never made public. These polls showed that the country stood up well when we were winning . . . and when we were losing . . . but the country went to pieces when we were suffering casualties in an indecisive war. I see a parallel to that in Vietnam today."

Finally, a word about *demonstrations* as a perceived expression of public opinion. At the time of my interviewing, the demonstration against the Vietnam War had been part of the political scene for about a year; its forms were experimental, and its variety was being adumbrated. In the following years the mass protest developed as a nearly respectable political instrument in the foreign policy field, as the struggle against the Vietnam War spread to larger and larger segments of the population. The transformation has been such that the reactions of State Department officials in 1965 and 1966 to street or campus protest are not automatically to be extrapolated to the 1970's. It is interesting, nevertheless, to see how officials did respond to these new and different forms of public involvement after a year of experience with them, if only because it suggests how new forms of public expression are assimilated to customary institutional responses.

By mid-1966 only a half-dozen respondents included demonstrations, protest marches, and teach-ins among the relevant or salient forms of public opinion. Four of these six persons were in either the Public Affairs area or the Far Eastern area and had had to deal with these phenomena as part of their official responsibilities. Only one of the six defined the "protest march" as a way to influence the course of foreign affairs; the others regarded them as the efforts of "a small though vocal minority of the population," which had to be "handled" but not otherwise heeded. The tendency to dismiss the protests as the work of small fringe groups on the radical left, as a passing phenomenon, is exemplified by a Deputy Assistant Secretary who in January 1966 referred to the National Teach-In held in April 1965 as "the high-water mark of the Vietnam protest." Another Deputy Assistant Secretary drew a sharp distinction between operational and nonoperational considerations: "You have to *deal* with the Congress, you have to get money, and so on. All of this gets very operational, whereas public opinion simply engages in demonstrations or writes letters."

THE EMERGING PICTURE

This broad canvass of public opinion as perceived by State Department officials is only one step in the exploration of the public's impact on foreign policy; we have to go on, now, to questions of appraisal, evaluation, effects — to consider how external opinion is assimilated into the internal governmental processes of foreign policy formulation. But before we do, we should take note of the picture that is beginning to emerge: the ingredients of public opinion as they are experienced in the State Department are substantially and significantly different from the standard ingredients, or aggregations, as they are defined by political scientists and other outside observers.

We conventionally portray opinion as manifesting itself chiefly in the form of public opinion polls, organized interest-group activity, newspaper editorials, and, less often, letters to public officials and to newspapers; and sometimes we even let one or two of these forms carry the whole burden. These forms or categories of external opinion are of course the most clearly visible from the outside, and they also encompass the largest number of articulated viewpoints. But it is not much of an exaggeration to say that these categories, designed to enlarge our vision of nongovernmental participation in policy processes, have become blinders; they have come to delimit artificially the areas in which we look for the content of public opinion and thus for its consequences. From the perspective of the foreign policy official in Washington, the opinion landscape takes on rather different contours. The polls and editorials move into the background, along with most of the mail. Organized interests and particular groups are somewhat more common, although in narrow areas of specialization and with varying entrées to the front. In the foreground stand the Congress and the "working press" and all the other individual "contacts," formal and informal, that we have seen make up the private and professional worlds of the foreign policy official. The implications for both the theory and practice of representation and of reponsive government are extensive, and I shall consider them later. Simply to point the way, however, I would draw attention here to the findings of Warren Miller and Donald Stokes and others, to the effect that Congressmen themselves (despite what foreign policy officials think) may not in fact come very close to understanding, reflecting, or acting upon the foreign policy attitudes of their constituents.[55]

NOTES

1. See Gabriel A. Almond, *The American People and Foreign Policy*, 2d ed., New York: Praeger, 1960; and James N. Rosenau, *Public Opinion and Foreign Policy*, New York: Random House, 1961, for a specification of the opinion elite in categoric or definitional terms.

2. See Robert A. Dahl, *Who Governs?* New Haven: Yale University Press, 1961. James N. Rosenau seems to be arguing the contrary in *National Leadership and Foreign Policy*, Princeton: Princeton University Press, 1963, when he says, "Apparently national opinion-makers do interact frequently, and apparently they are getting to know one another" (p. 331) But his "national opinion leaders" comprise only a small portion of the opinion elite as I describe it in these pages.

3. On an earlier occasion, after studying the process of policy formation on a single foreign policy issue, I ventured some hypotheses about the nature of external opinion as it was differentially experienced at the Executive and Congressional levels. See Bernard C. Cohen, *The Political Process and Foreign Policy*, Princeton: Princeton University Press, 1957, pp. 94–109. The present study obviously does not permit direct testing of any of these hypotheses; indeed, by treating the Congress here as an opinion *source* and not as a *target* (as in the earlier study) I have made direct comparison impossible. Despite these formal inadequacies, this, current exploration of the opinion environment of the State Department is not irrelevant to those earlier concerns, since I am still talking about the way foreign policy makers perceive their opinion environment.

4. See Andrew M. Scott, "Environmental Change and Organizational Adaptation: The Problem of the State Department," *International Studies Quarterly*, Vol. 14, No. 1, March 1970: "[The Department of State] is insulated in that its members have a high level of interaction with one another and a relatively low level of interaction with significant figures in the outside environment . . ." (p. 90).

5. For the most recent of these, see the so-called Herter Committee Report: *Personnel for the New Diplomacy*, Report of the Committee on Foreign Affairs Personnel, New York: Carnegie Endowment for International Peace, December 1962; and *Diplomacy for the 70's: A Program of Management Reform for the Department of State*, Washington, D.C.: United States Government Printing Office, December 1970.

6. See Stanley Hoffmann's argument that the public "deserves to be treated as one of the forces that affect the definition and execution of foreign policy since . . . specific elements of it, as members of the bureau-

cracy, play a direct and tangible role in policy-making." *Gulliver's Troubles, or the Setting of American Foreign Policy*, New York: McGraw-Hill, 1968, p. 228.

7. See pp. 92–95.

8. At the end of the nineteenth century, governmental experience in foreign affairs was less common than private experience, and the "notables" of that day, whom Ernest R. May refers to as cosmopolites, opinion leaders, the establishment, apparently came more often from private than public life. See May, *American Imperialism: A Speculative Essay*, New York: Atheneum, 1968. Lawrence I. Radway defines contemporary "notables" explicitly in the May fashion; see his *Foreign Policy and National Defense*, Glenview, Ill.: Scott, Foresman & Co., 1969, pp. 121–123.

9. Townsend Hoopes, *The Limits of Intervention*, New York: McKay, 1969, discusses the role of the Senior Advisory Group on Vietnam in reversing President Johnson's policy of escalation in Vietnam. The Senior Advisory Group was an informal "body of distinguished former diplomats, soldiers, and public servants who had rendered great service to the country in foreign policy or in military posts of high responsibility. The Group" had counseled with the President once or twice a year since 1965." The members of the Group who were in attendance at a crucial meeting on March 25 and 26, 1968, is the above list writ large: Dean Acheson, George Ball, McGeorge Bundy, Douglas Dillon, Cyrus Vance, Arthur Dean, John J. McCloy, General Omar Bradley, General Matthew Ridgway, General Maxwell Taylor, Robert Murphy, Henry Cabot Lodge, Abe Fortas, and Arthur Goldberg (pp. 207, 214–215). Goldberg was the only participant who had current foreign policy responsibilities, and he was not a regular member of the Group, having been invited to this meeting by the President. As this list makes clear, status as a notable has more to do with prior service than with political party identification.

10. Andrew M. Scott, discussing the "informal culture" of the State Department and its inhospitality toward theory and research, summarizes the typical Department view as follows: "Since outsiders do not 'read the cables,' they cannot possibly have useful ideas about what should be done." "The Department of State: Formal Organization and Informal Culture," *International Studies Quarterly*, Vol. 13, No. 1, March 1969, p. 14. Outsiders who have been weaned on the cables, however, are something else again.

11. May, *American Imperialism*, p. 40.

12. For the view that academia is in any event the major source of new ideas, see Adam Yarmolinsky, "Ideas into Programs," *The Public Interest*, No. 2, Winter 1966, pp. 70 ff.

13. Hoopes, *The Limits of Intervention*, esp. pp. 214–224. President Johnson's own account of the circumstances surrounding his change of policy differs from Hoopes'; see Lyndon B. Johnson, *The Vantage Point: Perspectives of the Presidency, 1963–1969*, New York: Holt, Rinehart & Winston, 1971.

14. Both kinds of qualifications and skills are included in the outside

expertise discussed by Chadwick F. Alger, "The External Bureaucracy in United States Foreign Affairs," *Administrative Science Quarterly*, Vol. 7, No. 1, June 1962.

15. At a subsequent point in the interview, this official ranked academicians as the most important of his external contacts and went on to express his worry about trends he saw emerging in the academic community — trends which have become much more visible in the few years since: "Is there a fundamental change going on from a period which began with Franklin Roosevelt and seems to have ended with John Kennedy, where government was thought of as an ally, to a new situation where the academic community now thinks of government as an enemy, or at least as a group of people whom they do not want to be caught associating with? . . . This kind of situation ought to concern all of us here in the Department."

16. E. Raymond Platig, "Foreign Affairs Analysis: Some Thoughts on Expanding Competence," *International Studies Quarterly*, Vol. 13, No. 1, March 1969, pp. 23–24. See Scott, "The Department of State," pp. 1–18.

17. Richard E. Neustadt, "White House and Whitehall," *The Public Interest*, No. 2, Winter 1966, pp. 55–69.

18. William O. Chittick, *State Department, Press, and Pressure Groups*, New York: Wiley-Interscience, 1970, says that the Advisory Committee of the Bureau of African Affairs includes "some one hundred individuals who are formally consulted annually on American policies toward that continent" (p. 230). My respondents reported only thirty to thirty-five individuals.

19. Andrew Berding, *Foreign Affairs and You!* Garden City: Doubleday, 1962, p. 44.

20. Tom Wicker, *The New York Times*, May 4, 1966, p. 6.

21. Richard Eder, *The New York Times*, May 9, 1966, pp. 1, 3.

22. See R. Smith Simpson, *Anatomy of the State Department*, Boston: Beacon Press, 1967, pp. 229–230.

23. See David Truman, *The Governmental Process*, New York: Knopf, 1951; and V. O. Key, Jr., *Politics, Parties, and Pressure Groups*, 5th ed., New York: Thomas Y. Crowell, 1964.

24. A sign of the Committee's decline was Senator Jacob Javits' public withdrawal of membership, as reported in *The New York Times* by E. W. Kenworthy, December 17, 1966.

25. See A. T. Steele, *The American People and China*, New York: McGraw-Hill, 1966, pp. 119–125; and Roger Hilsman, *To Move a Nation*, Garden City: Doubleday, 1967, pp. 292–296.

26. It is not only in the State Department that one finds this liberal view. The power of "the right" as the dominant image of American public opinion among government officials, the legacy of Senator Joseph McCarthy, is one of the major themes in Daniel Ellsberg, "The Quagmire Myth and the Stalemate Machine," *Public Policy*, Vol. 19, No. 2, Spring 1971, pp. 240 ff.

27. William O. Chittick cites as apparently typical this remark by a

Department official: " 'The view of a pressure group is not of a lot of use for the Department; the chief value of such a group is in educating the public.' " *State Department, Press, and Pressure Groups*, p. 239.

28. R. Bauer, I. Pool, and L. Dexter, *American Business and Public Policy*, New York: Atherton Press, 1963.

29. The N here of those not mentioning such contacts is 25; but in the previous sentence it is 26, since one official occupied two distinct positions in the Department.

30. The general position, as applied to public policy in general, was effectively stated by Frank Bonilla, "When Is Petition 'Pressure'?" *Public Opinion Quarterly*, Vol. 20, No. 1, Spring 1956, pp. 39–48. See also Bauer, Pool, and Dexter, *American Business and Public Policy*, p. 434.

31. In his assessment of the strength of policy conviction, Roger Hilsman, a former Assistant Secretary of State, writes as follows: "Among the principal findings of a British government committee appointed to study the powers of ministers was that most men find it easier to go against their own pecuniary interests than they do to go against a deep conviction on policy. . . . in the business of Washington, the stakes are high and the issues fundamental, both to our society and to the question of war and peace for the entire world. In such circumstances it is not surprising that passions run strong and full." *To Move a Nation*, p. 10.

32. Among the writings that attribute a significant impact to ethnic groups are Louis Gerson, *The Hyphenate in Recent American Politics and Diplomacy*, Lawrence, Kans.: University of Kansas Press, 1964; and Thomas A. Bailey, *The Man in the Street*, New York: Macmillan, 1948.

33. See "Mideast Lobbies: Uneven Match," by Robert H. Phelps, *The New York Times*, April 6, 1970, pp. 1, 14. Phelps calls the pro-Israel lobby "one of the most potent in the Washington sub-government."

34. Former Secretary of State Dean Acheson denies the claim that President Truman's pro-Zionist posture was political opportunism. "From many years of talk with him I know that this represented a deep conviction." (Acheson, *Present at the Creation*, New York: W. W. Norton, 1969, p. 169).

35. Bernard C. Cohen, *The Press and Foreign Policy*, Princeton: Princeton University Press, 1963.

36. Hilsman, *To Move a Nation*, p. 263.

37. Joseph M. Jones, *The Fifteen Weeks*, New York: Viking, 1955.

38. See, in this connection, Cohen, *The Press and Foreign Policy*, pp. 208–247.

39. *Ibid.*, pp. 227–229.

40. I do not attach much importance to Glenn Paige's account of President Truman's reaction to editorial opinion on the Korean crisis. Paige reports that Truman read, on Monday morning, June 26, 1950, editorials in *The Washington Post* and *The New York Times* urging the President in strong language to be firm. "The President was interested in these expressions of editorial opinion because they paralleled his own

conclusion that the United States should make a determined positive response to the North Korean aggression." Glenn Paige, *The Korean Decision: June 24–30, 1950*, New York: Free Press, 1968, pp. 145–146. I would define Truman's "interest" in these expressions of editorial opinion as "nominal"; he had already refused to entertain discussion of the political aspects of the situation from his closest advisers in the first Blair House Conference. *Ibid.*, p. 141.

41. May, *American Imperialism*, pp. 187–191, 233.

42. E.g., "China out of the Cupboard," *The Economist* (London), March 12, 1966, pp. 1003–1004.

43. See Cohen, *The Political Process and Foreign Policy*, Princeton: Princeton University Press, 1957, in which I describe a situation of the opposite kind, where press coverage was "not sufficient to create or activate a substantial body of interest in the issue" (p. 120).

44. E.g., James A. Robinson, *Congress and Foreign Policy-Making*, rev. ed., Homewood, Ill.: Dorsey Press, 1967, Chaps. 4 and 5.

45. Doris Graber, *Public Opinion, the President, and Foreign Policy*, New York: Holt, Rinehart & Winston, 1968, p. 247.

46. Kenneth Waltz, *Foreign Policy and Democratic Politics*, Boston: Little, Brown & Co., 1967, pp. 172–173, citing Kenneth Younger, "Public Opinion and Foreign Policy," *British Journal of Sociology*, Vol. 6, June 1955, and Lord Strang, "The Formation and Control of Foreign Policy," *Durham University Journal*, Vol. 49, June 1957.

47. E.g., "Congressmen Find Public Disturbed," *The New York Times*, April 18, 1966.

48. William O. Chittick, "The Domestic Information Activities of the Department of State," unpubl. Ph.D. dissertation, Johns Hopkins University, 1964, pp. 191–192.

49. Chittick writes: "According to the officers interviewed on this aspect of the public affairs operation, most of the Department's mail reflects the 'newspaper headlines,' and so it may be assumed that a large portion of the incoming mail is stimulated by the mass media." *Ibid.*, p. 192.

50. In September 1958 a State Department official gave a reporter some figures on a negative majority, and before the brouhaha ended, it had involved the Vice President and the top editors of *The New York Times*. See Marian D. Irish, "Public Opinion and American Foreign Policy: The Quemoy Crisis of 1958," *The Political Quarterly*, Vol. 31, No. 2, April–June 1960, p. 157.

51. Cf. Chittick, *State Department, Press, and Pressure Groups*, p. 164. Letters written to the editors of newspapers tend also to be negative or critical; see David L. Grey and Trevor R. Brown, "Letters to the Editor: Hazy Reflections of Public Opinion," *Journalism Quarterly*, Vol. 47, No. 3, Autumn 1970, pp. 450–456, 471.

52. Chittick concludes from House Appropriations Subcommittee hearings that Department officers made nearly 1,000 speeches to nongovernmental organizations in 1967. *State Department, Press, and Pressure Groups*, pp. 225–226.

53. It is unclear whether he was responding to the preemption of the polls by the Vietnam War question or to the fact that the President was at that time publicly brandishing the polls that supported him on the war. See "President Finds Backing on War" by John D. Pomfret, *The New York Times*, February 18, 1966.

54. On the Stanford Poll, see "Public Opinion and the War in Vietnam," Stanford University: Institute of Political Studies, March 15, 1966; a more formal analysis of the findings is contained in Sidney Verba *et al.*, "Public Opinion and the War in Vietnam," *American Political Science Review*, Vol. 61, No. 2, June 1967, pp. 317–333.

55. See Warren E. Miller and Donald E. Stokes, "Constituency Influence in Congress," *American Political Science Review*, Vol. 57, No. 1, March 1963, pp. 45–56; the summary of roll-call voting studies in Cleo H. Cherryholmes and Michael J. Shapiro, *Representatives and Roll Calls*, Indianapolis: Bobbs-Merrill, 1969, Chap. 7; and Cohen, *The Press and Foreign Policy*, pp. 238–241.

We come closer now to the core of our concern with the impact of public opinion on foreign policy: what happens to the tiger when he goes through the gate? We have a better idea now whom foreign policy officials regard as the important bearers of public opinion. But what about the opinions themselves? How are they perceived or interpreted in a political sense? And what kinds of responses or reactions do they stimulate among officials? Are there any discernible patterns in the assimilation of opinion or in its rejection? What do they tell us about the impact of opinion on policy and/or on policy makers?

Let me make a broad and very important distinction at the very start. When I talk about the responses or the reactions to public opinion, I want to distinguish those affecting substantive foreign policy from those that affect information policy. The former deal with efforts to do something about substantive policy in the light of opinion. The latter deal with efforts to do something about opinion in the light of policy. I will take up the first of these responses in this chapter — the range of effects that opinion has on substantive foreign policy matters — and in the following chapter I will consider the reactions of officials that involve information policy, or the manipulation of opinion. To give an overall perspective to the problem, however, I will simply say here that policy makers' responses to public opinion fall as often into the information policy range as they do into the substantive policy range. For starters, then, the response of officials half the time is to want to or to try to reshape opinion into something more congenial. What are the responses like the rest of the time? And what clues do they provide for our better understanding of the aspiration to reshape opinion?

VARIETIES AND EFFECTS OF OPINION

At any given point in time, there are a number of dialogues taking place throughout the State Department between officials and bearers of public opinion, on an array of substantive questions. I have not been able to make an independent investigation of these dialogues, in order to make any independent judgments about the accuracy with which officials perceive or interpret the points of view being expressed to them. The evidence available to us from other sources, however, suggests that large doubts may well be in order. Two major studies of the Congress indicate that the legislators' perceptions of constituency opinions on foreign policy matters are highly selective and inaccurate.[1] It would be unrealistic to assume that foreign policy officials were immune to these same mechanisms of distortion, especially when they operate in an environment equally highly charged with political competition and personal motivation and ambition. More particularly, why should nonelected officials be expected to do a better job than elected ones of interpreting the foreign policy preferences of constituents, when they are less experienced politically, have fewer interactions with constituents, and are at the same time more closely identified with policy choices? The possible gap between the views that are actually expressed to Department officials and the officials' perceptions of those views is of no small importance; the fact that it is not being studied directly here is not meant to depreciate its significance. Nonetheless we confront, and have to deal with, the perceptions themselves — the prevailing modes of interpreting the thrust of the opinions they hear.

I have said before, and it bears repeating here, that foreign policy officials are *engagé*. They are not neutral agents of a national, or presidential, or institutional will, carrying out policies with a mindless bureaucratic efficiency; rather, they are very intensely involved in the issues of the moment and deeply committed to particular views or proposals bearing on those issues. They start, thus, with strongly held conceptions of desirable goals and means in foreign policy, and they look warily at external opinion (as they do in fact at internal opinion also) from the perspective of how it fits with what they are doing or would like to do. In my interviews with State Department officials I have recorded 143 discrete references to external opinions, references which emerge from this reflexive, nondeliberative process of coping with others as they seek to advance their own policy preferences. These opinions fall into a neat array on a continuum that defines their relationship to the officials' or the Department's own positions. At one end of the continuum are opinions *supportive* of the positions being taken by Departmental officials. Next to support stands *indifference,* which in a practical sense means the absence of significantly observable support or opposition. In the middle is *countervailing opinion,* which consists of substantially equal measures of opinion on all sides of an issue, effectively balancing or offsetting the impact of any one segment of it. Moving on to the far side, one finds *advocacy,* or the urging onto the Department of views or proposals that are not currently being entertained or that are active alternatives to those currently in vogue. And at the far end are opinions in *opposition* to prevailing positions or policies of the Department. Off the continuum I have one additional and residual class of opinions I shall call *unspecified;* they may be any of the above, but their precise content was not sufficiently clarified by officials to enable me to locate them on this continuum. The distribution of these 143 references to public opinion by type is shown in Table I.

Cutting across these perceived varieties of public opinion are differences in the perceived *effects* of opinion. Once again, I am unable to report any independent investigation of the actual dispo-

TABLE I Varieties of Opinion as Seen by
State Department Officials

Supportive	16%
Indifferent	6
Countervailing	10
Advocacy	16
Opposition	29
Unspecified	22
Total (less than 100% due to rounding)	99%

sition of opinion-laden issues and the reasons therefor, so that I cannot personally testify to the presence or absence of any discrepancy between the reported consequences that public opinion has on foreign policy and the "real" consequences. The distressing aspect of this problem is that — unlike the gap between the expression of opinion and its perception by officials — the possible gap between the perceived impact of opinion and some more-or-less objective reality is impossible to ascertain without the active help of officials at every stage; in other words, we cannot escape some dependence on the officials' own perception of what is happening, when, and to whom. It is quite conceivable that there is bias in the reporting of the effects of opinion; but which way the bias may run is not so clear. Let us examine the range of perceived effects of opinion, and then I will return to this question of possible bias in the reporting of specific instances.

Just as officials evaluate external opinion according to how it fits with their own positions, they look at the impacts or effects of that opinion from the perspective of what it means for their own freedom to "put the pieces together," to "fashion initiatives," to determine the national interest in particular cases. And in similar fashion, the varieties of impacts as discerned in the same 143 references may be arrayed along a line that defines degrees of constraint. At one end are opinions or opinion-circumstances that we may describe as *effective constraints*, since they direct officials into policies which run counter to their own preferences. Included here are opinion interventions that are described by officials as effective in restraining them from proceeding along some policy lines, or in persuading them to move in other directions, or in generally exerting some influence over their preferred behavior. Next to these stands a class of impacts which I call *nominal constraints;* these are simple asseverations by officials of constraint at the hands of the public, without any substantive explanation — no detail or even identification of circumstances to support the claim. Beyond this are opinions we may describe as *ineffective constraints*, efforts which have tried but have not succeeded either in restraining officials from some courses of action, or in inducing them to pursue others, or in generally exerting some influence over their choices. And lastly there are opinions we may call *positive nonconstraints:* those which are described as encouraging officials to proceed along policy lines they have already measured and staked out and those which are permissive in their effects, granting officials an apparent free hand in choosing any course of action they wish or confirming their long-suspected possession of such freedom. The distribution of these effects by type is shown in Table II.

Reflect for a moment on the problem of possible bias in the way officials perceive or report the effects of public opinion on their own actions or those of their colleagues. The possibility of bias seems to me to reside much more in the first three classes of effects, those involving the success or failure of intended constraints, than it does in the last class, which involves the substantial absence of intended constraint. If the reasons for this first conclusion are less than obvious now, I think they will become clearer as the analysis of these effects unfolds. Within the first three classes of effects, however, the possible sources of bias point in both directions, with the net balance in some doubt. It will be recalled that the prevailing informal doctrine among State Department officials stressed the importance to them of the exercise of their professional judgment, independent of any pressures of public opinion. In conformity with that doctrine or outlook, one would expect Department officials to brush aside external opinion whenever possible — and even to claim with exaggerated frequency that it *was* possible. The fact that references to the ineffectuality of public opinion are almost matched by references to the effectiveness of the public constraints suggests that the informal doctrine represents an unfulfilled wish as much as it does an operational reality; and unfulfilled wishes might further conduce to exaggerated claims. On the other hand, matching the logic that suggests an exaggeration of "ineffective constraints" is some internal evidence suggesting the opposite, a

TABLE II   Varieties of Opinion Effects as Seen
by State Department Officials

Effective Constraints	25%
Nominal Constraints	15
Ineffective Constraints	38
Positive Nonconstraints	22
Total	100%

temptation to claim more external constraint than actually existed. The evidence for this lies in my interviews themselves — in the tendency of officials to assert an influence for opinion that is flat and unsupported and unconvincing; the classification of "nominal constraints" was in fact designed to include all such assertions that had some major shred of illusion about them. The frequency of these claims (even assuming that some of them may be genuine) suggests that the *formal* doctrine of popular control in democratic policy making is alive and well and living just beneath the surface in the State Department. The net balance of these uncertainties seems to me to favor, by a slight margin, the "ineffective constraints." That is to say, I am inclined to believe that Department officials have on the whole exaggerated the impact that external opinion has had on their policy considerations and conclusions. But I lack what I myself consider convincing evidence of this, both in degree and in kind, and so I propose to regard the distributions of constraint, as claimed, to stand as a reasonably accurate representation of the way things are in the State Department.

So far we have looked separately at the varieties of public opinion as they are perceived and evaluated by State Department officials and at the varieties of impacts which officials claim for these opinions. It remains now to put these two things together in order to tell what kinds of opinions seem to have what kinds of effects. As Table III shows (see page 138), a large number of combinations require our attention. As we examine the most important of these more closely, we will see the immense and conflicting varieties of political circumstance that are too often obscured as a single phenomenon — "public opinion" — for which a single effect is sought.

SUPPORTIVE OPINIONS

Perhaps the best reason for starting off with opinions that are supportive of prevailing policy is that, because they are so very obvious, they underline the diversity of the possibilities inherent in the public opinion–foreign policy relationship. Not all opinions are negative, in other words; and not all possibilities reduce to the one most commonly talked about — i.e., how can "we, the people" get the foreign policy establishment to change its ways? We

TABLE III   The Effects of Different Varieties of External Opinion
(in number of references)

Varieties of Opinion	Effective Constraint (N = 36)	Nominal Constraint (N = 21)	Ineffective Constraint (N = 55)	Positive Nonconstraint (N = 31)
Supportive (N = 23)	1	0	1	21
Indifferent (N = 9)	5	0	4	0
Countervailing (N = 14)	0	0	4	10
Advocacy (N = 23)	10	3	10	0
Opposition (N = 42)	17	5	20	0
Unspecified (N = 32)	3	13	16	0

often seem to overlook the fact that "support" is itself a variety of opinion that has some consequences in policy; instead we tend to look at those policies as if they were a product only of bureaucratic life, which public opinion is challenged to alter.

Sixteen percent of the references to characteristics of public opinion noted its actual or potentially supportive nature. I am not saying that 16 percent of the opinions transmitted to the Department were affirmative; rather, I am saying 16 percent of the references by Departmental officials to their public opinion context were concerned with circumstances where opinion was seen to be supportive. That proportion seems reasonable enough, given the general view within the Department that it hears mostly from people with complaints or dissatisfactions. Yet it is worth pointing out that officials have some freedom in the way they perceive and interpret expressions of opinion and that they have some incentive (in an ambiguous circumstance, particularly) to interpret them as supportive.[2] That they do not do more of this suggests the strength of their preoccupation with less congenial sorts of opinion.

In the vast majority of the references to supportive opinions (twenty-one out of twenty-three), such opinions are interpreted as having *nonconstraining* effects, of two different kinds. The major effect is to *encourage* State Department officials to persist in their chosen policies and even to give them a boost in that direction.[3] A Deputy Assistant Secretary: "Any guy who is working on a policy or a program is out of his mind if he fails to look at a degree of public support as a kind of insurance policy; it will not by itself get him where he wants to be, but it certainly helps." Another Deputy Assistant Secretary: "We watch public opinion to get allies." A Special Assistant: "Most people here are interested in public opinion not in the sense of being shaped by it but rather in gaining support for something they want to undertake or measuring support that may already exist for what they want to do." A lesser effect, especially of predictable support, is substantially to *free* officials to do almost anything they want. From the Public Affairs area, this observation from experience: "Whatever the President wants, the public will support him on." And from the higher reaches of the State Department: "[Public opinion] is in support of NATO, and we assume that anything we do in support of NATO will be accepted."

At the risk of laboring the obvious, I want to stress this finding that opinions which are interpreted as supportive have specific instrumental consequences that are advantageous from the perspective of foreign policy officials. These officials, both in informal conversations and in their customary public rhetoric, pay great attention to "the need for public support," a phrase so common that it begins to look like one of the pillars on which the whole structure of public decision making rests — as well it might. But whenever I asked officials what they *meant* in a practical way by "public support," they were nonplussed, unable to answer without reflection. One highly placed official, when I asked him that question, looked at me for a moment and then said, "I have never really thought about this before." The rhetoric has usually seemed to mean only that in a democracy foreign policy has to move hand-in-hand with the popular will or else some unspecified but evil consequences will overtake us. But in practice these terms are very difficult to define and measure in any generally acceptable way. What does it mean "to move hand-in-hand"? What is "the popular will," especially in a policy area where so few people have knowledge or opinions? What consequences will in fact ensue? Officials cannot begin to answer these questions, and they do not cus-

tomarily think in these terms, for they are attuned instead to questions of immediate policy advantage. What "public support" does
mean to them in practice is something very concrete and palpable:
do we have friends, or have we at least neutralized our enemies,
in strategic places — in and out of the government — so that we
can carry out our plans at what is, for us, worthwhile cost? [4] (And
if the answer should be no, minds immediately turn, as we shall
see in the next chapter, not to the revision of plans or to the recal-
culus of costs but to the problem of creating or mobilizing the necessary friends.)

Because one might assume that supportive opinion could have
only nonconstraining effects on officials, it is instructive to look
briefly at the two instances where support was understood to have
different kinds of consequences, at least potentially. An Assistant
Secretary saw the support the Administration was currently receiving on the Vietnam War as ultimately *constraining* — as a bear
hug from which it would eventually be struggling to escape: "We
are stuck with a group of enthusiasts on Vietnam whom we would
never have chosen. How to unload the right-wing baggage from
our Vietnam policy will be a major political problem some day."
And on the opposite side of the fence, an official argued that even
strong support for a position was *not an effective constraint,* that it
did not limit officials to that position or prevent them from doing
the very opposite. "There is general public support for German
reunification, and we would think twice before we came out with a
dismissal of the whole problem. But if we wanted to say, 'Let's
drop all this nonsense about unification and live with what we
have,' we could make that stick, and we would get a lot of support
for it also." [5]

INDIFFERENCE

By "indifference" here I mean not only active opinions that are
genuinely indifferent toward or uncertain about alternative policy
outcomes but also the more common absence of any discernible
opinion whatever. "Apathy" or "uncaring" are the terms that more
fairly describe the opinion states of most of the people being referred to here, but from the policy maker's point of view it is widespread public indifference to the problems and choices before him

that constitutes the operative perception. The Vietnam War resulted in the mobilization of mass opinion to such an extent that it effectively obscured the many foreign policy questions on which there continued to be only very low levels of public interest. It also obscured, at least for a while, the experience of many years during which vast individual and organizational efforts were made to stir up popular interest and participation in foreign affairs. That whole endeavor to create an aware and informed public opinion in the foreign policy field grew out of the World War I experience — its antecedents in secret diplomacy and its consequences in the American retreat into isolationism. And it rested on the assumption that public indifference would sooner or later lead to catastrophe — that the United States government would be restrained, by the lack of positive evidence of public support, from making the kinds of firm and enduring foreign policy commitments conducive to a stable and responsible world order.[6] Though the assumption that indifference means effective constraint has been part of the public mythology for two generations, it does have competitors on the contemporary scene. Bill Moyers, a former assistant to President Johnson, gave it a rather narrow construction when he argued that "there are questions on which governments dare not act without evidence of genuine support" and then added, "War is clearly one of those questions."[7] V. O. Key, on the other hand, saw indifference as an ineffective constraint: "Non-participators, it should be fair to assume, have little role in shaping the dikes of opinion within which the day-to-day policy of government flows. To the extent that persons at this level have opinions, those opinions probably carry relatively little weight."[8] James N. Rosenau went even further, claiming that indifference was a positive nonconstraint: "Whenever governmental responses to situations do *not* provoke debate among opinion-makers . . . the lack of controversy among leadership segments constitutes, in effect, passive support for the decisions and actions of officials."[9] And in my earlier study of the Japanese peace settlement of 1951, I concluded that the perceived indifference of public opinion gave the policy makers very substantial freedom of action.[10]

The reactions of State Department officials to public indifference, although not very numerous, were divided almost evenly between those who felt it was an effective constraint and those who thought it was an ineffective one. Those who felt it was an *effective constraint* (five) argued quite simply that without "public support," i.e., without some allies on the outside testifying to the merits of one's position, it was very difficult to make a winning case for a policy in the governmental process. Several persons attributed the failure to get the multilateral force proposal (MLF) for nuclear sharing in the NATO alliance off the drawing board in part to the fact that the idea attracted no enthusiasm outside its small circle of proponents within the government. A desk officer's comments on it: "I hope I do not give you the impression that public opinion has no effect on us. I think the MLF is a good case of the opposite. It generated no public support, and that was a factor in why it died." [11] Another official who was even more closely involved with the MLF spoke to the same effect and generalized this way: "If you are on some line of public policy, and you lack a degree of at least elite support and understanding, you are in constant trouble. People at the higher levels in the State Department, who are advocating something before a Congressional committee, for instance, that has little or no public support that they can show that committee — these people are carrying another burden on their backs." The same point was made by an official in the Policy Planning Council, where ideas are likely to involve future possibilities or contingencies and for which there is, almost by definition, no current body of knowledgeable supporters: "These things [that we are doing] have almost *nothing* to do with public opinion. It is hard to sell things to our basic audience here in Washington, I assure you, especially when there is no public opinion to point to. But we do our job anyway."

The opposite position was taken by respondents (four) who claimed, with V. O. Key, that those who did not make themselves heard had no consequences for foreign policy, either as a drag on potential initiatives or as an impetus for action — i.e., they were an *ineffective constraint*. This position argues, in effect, that if the majority is really silent, one has no way of knowing how it divides on issues or whether it is concerned and informed enough to divide at all. A Deputy Assistant Secretary: "We do not have to address ourselves to those who take no part in any of this. . . . In other words, the uninformed American citizen has no impact in terms of whatever views he has; how could he have, if he does not have a defensible view?" A Deputy Office Director: "The safest thing to say about American public opinion vis-à-vis —— is that it is tolerant and almost completely uninformed. . . . We are not pushed by U.S. public opinion on our policy towards ——."

It is worth noting that neither of these two positions gives any support to the notion of "the silent majority" as it has come to be understood — that is, as a large body of people holding a particular and predetermined set of opinions. Nowhere in my interviews with State Department officials was there expressed any fear that if larger portions of the general public were mobilized into foreign policy activity, they would either force the government into action of some particular kind or keep the government from undertaking certain ventures. Those who see public indifference as a constraint do not argue, in President Nixon's terms, that the silent majority of Americans is committed to America's interventionary role in the world or at least to an international politics of power and prestige; nor do they argue, in the more conventional terms of the last half century, that the silent majority is isolationist at heart, unwilling to make any lasting commitments to an international political order. Rather, they are bemoaning the simple lack of ready allies for their own policy stances, and they readily believe — as we shall see in the next chapter — that efforts to create and/or mobilize those allies from among the public will have a substantial payoff *no matter what the policy question may be.*

COUNTERVAILING OPINION

In a speech in New York City in November 1925, Secretary of State Hughes "complained of the telegrams that fell like snowflakes in a thick storm, clouding each issue with diverse opinions." [12] What Hughes saw fit to complain about, others have rejoiced in. [13] Recent literature suggests three different sets of consequences stemming from a shower of opinions on all sides of a foreign policy question, each of which may be true under different conditions or circumstances. One view is that the balance of pressure created by the nearly equal distribution of opinions on both or all sides of an issue has a liberating effect on the policy maker, by freeing him from any compulsion to respond favorably to strong pressure on only one side. He does not automatically retain, or regain, his freedom of maneuver; he may in fact simply be subject to other constraints from within the policy making system. But at a minimum, it is argued, "conflicting positions by groups . . . serve as systemic checks on group influence," thus moderating or weakening their impact.[14] A second, and opposed, view is that it is the unity of outside opinion that frees officials, liberating their imagination and creativity, and conversely that the absence or the breakdown of consensus among the nation's opinion leaders brings confusion, inadequacy, or worse to American foreign policy.[15] And still a third view — advanced in the context of Congress but having a wider relevance — is that a substantial divergence of opinion opens up for more serious study the question of the constituency's interest in the matter at hand.[16]

The weight of the evidence from interviews with State Department officials strongly supports the first of these three hypotheses about the impact of countervailing opinions. Ten out of fourteen references to balanced opinion of this kind saw it as *positively nonconstraining* in its effects, as permissive in the freedom it affords officials to make their choices. For example, a Deputy Assistant Secretary: "There was the greatest public interest in the ——— question. But there were such conflicting streams in American public thought on that one that public opinion made little difference. . . . These expressions of public opinion and public thought confirmed us in our conviction that we could do what we wanted, without any long-term effects on the stability of our commitment to ———." Another Deputy Assistant Secretary: "Where you get conflicting points of view represented in the Congress — for example, on the ———, where there are strong voices on both sides — we do what we ourselves think is right, which in this case happens to be working with ———." And an Office Director: "The press is so divided that you can find support for almost anything you want to do."

Four officials defined the impact of countervailing opinion as an *ineffective constraint.* An Office Director, commenting on a potentially troublesome development: "There are such divisions in the country on the whole Far Eastern question, as evidenced by these hearings and university statements on China, that I think this question of ——— won't have too much effect. I don't expect any major noise." And an Assistant Secretary observed: "If sentiment is mixed, you can operate; if it is mobilized against you, you cannot." Still another official argued that where the "lobbies" on both sides were of a modest order, they were themselves not an important policy consideration; in his view, however, that circumstance simply delivered his particular program into the hands of the Congress, where "the least significant member . . . is of the greatest importance to us."

The fact that there is no echo from State Department officials of the second viewpoint sketched above — that "disunity" of opinion leads to confusion, errors of judgment, and so forth — calls for some further comment on that hypothesis. It seems to me that what Rosenau and May are describing are differences in degree so great as to constitute differences in kind, and these are rare and exceptional rather than normal circumstances. A unity of external opinion liberates officials only when it is unusually large and extensive *and* when they share in it — i.e., when it is seen as "supportive." I do not believe, for instance, that President Nixon found "liberating" the public reaction to his Cambodian venture — a reaction that by all conventional standards one would have to say represented an unusual degree of unity among normally disparate external sources. Similarly, a breakdown in the external consensus leads to confusion and uncertainty in policy only when it too is unusually large or extensive *and* when it too is matched by important divergences in opinion among officials. President Johnson confronted a wide divergence of external opinion on his Vietnam policy throughout his full term of office. In 1966, a State Department official remarked to me: "There are two opposing opinions on Vietnam to begin with, which helps to neutralize their influence." But it was only toward the end of his term, when his advisers began to split on the Vietnam question, that anything even approaching "confusion and uncertainty" began to develop.[17] But where opinion is not held very strongly or extensively to begin with, disagreement on the outside has no great impact on officials. In fact, words like "disunity" or "division" or "dissension" make sense in a foreign policy setting only when applied to a context where diverging opinions *are* held very strongly and by unusually large numbers of people.

ADVOCACY

I have made a distinction here between advocacy and opposition, though they are only slightly different manifestations of the same opinion phenomenon — namely, dissent. Advocacy registers dissatisfaction with existing or projected policy by the device of recommending alternative policies, whereas opposition is simply the overt expression of dissatisfaction with or disapproval of current or planned policy. Advocacy is *specific*, in the sense that it is generally organized around concrete proposals; by contrast, both support and opposition tend to be much more diffuse in their policy referents.

The effects of dissent in both its forms resemble those of indifference, oddly enough, and are quite unlike either supportive or countervailing opinions. Both advocacy and opposition have multiple consequences, rather evenly divided between effective constraints and ineffective constraints, with a smaller cluster of indeterminacy or nominal constraint in between. In neither case are dissenting foreign policy opinions seen as having any clearly nonconstraining effects. That is, on the face of it, no great surprise. What *is* unexpected — especially in view of the explicit discounting of opinion that one encounters at nearly every turn in the State Department — is the fact that dissenting opinions of both types should be seen as imposing effective constraints quite as often as they are held to be ineffective constraints. Looking now at those alternative policies being urged on officials by outsiders, there are some differences we can observe between those that are effective and those that are ineffective in changing the direction of policy.

Advocacy which is seen as *effectively constraining* by State Department officials tends to be associated with policies that have a broad political significance and even some moral overtones. Eight out of the ten references to advocacy as effective constraint concerned policies of this kind. These are policies which State Department officials generally have no great difficulty describing as fully consonant with their prevailing conceptions of what is right or appropriate or in the national interest. One official said, "When the Germans first refused to extend their statute of limitations on war crimes, there was a lot of noise in this country. I argued with Germans all over on this question. I told them they just had to . . .

[extend] it. [If they did not,] there would have been a boycott of German goods. . . . There would have been hostile editorials in the newspapers. There would have been an increasing number of letters. . . . I would certainly rather take on the chore of arguing with the [German] diplomats to do the sensible thing than to agree to something with them and then look like an ass in the public eye." An official in AID: "A couple of other relevant groups are the —— and the ——, which are both interested in what we are doing abroad. They have persuaded us that they are right, and we have followed their advice and their recommendations for that reason, and not for any kudos we might earn." In another case, a Deputy Assistant Secretary did have trouble accepting a broad policy that was being pushed on him as in the national interest, though most of his colleagues felt otherwise: "It is also possible to have an active public opinion drive you into policies that make no sense. A good example of this is the current pressure for an anti-proliferation treaty. Here we are going firmly down that road with no good thoughts having been given to the consequences all around of such a treaty, or any thought as to whether the whole trip is worth it." [18]

Advocacy which is seen as presenting *ineffective constraints* tends to be associated with policies which for one reason or another can be easily dismissed or sidetracked by officials as not in the national interest. In some cases this is because the policies being pushed on the Department are patently special-interest measures of narrow advantage. A desk officer: "We certainly weigh all the views of the —— groups; but if a man comes in here with a specific proposition, he is going to get nowhere." Another official reviewed what had happened after the Indonesians began their policy of "confrontation" with Malaysia in the fall of 1963: "The United States immediately interrupted the aid program, making no new commitments and permitting the existing commitments to peter out until finally, when they were fulfilled, the program came to an end. There were lots of external pressures [to resume the program]; there were the commercial interests of American exporting industries — planes, food, clothing, even military supplies. Our position was that we would not provide any items which the Indonesians could use against Malaysia." In other cases it is because the policies being advocated are so far out of line with current policy or current thinking in the Administration that ordinary incremental change could not begin to accommodate them. For example, an Office Director: "The Quaker audience is a one-attitude audience. . . . The Friends think that foreign policy should be conducted on a higher moral level; that the United States should make certain accommodations to China, it should remedy the indignities which have been heaped upon China over the centuries." And a Deputy Assistant Secretary: "We can't do anything about the ideas these people propose in their letters — for example, their ideas to settle the ——— dispute — but you don't want to act as if you are not welcoming those ideas."

In still other cases policies being pushed on the Department from the outside are rejected for reasons that reduce to the now-familiar argument that the Department is charged with the determination of the national interest in foreign policy matters, and no single outside group is competent — in all senses — to do the job instead. Since this argument has been made before, I shall give only one further illustration of it here. A desk officer: "It is simply *not* the case that we make policy as the result of interest group or public opinion pressures. Sure, we know what the [interest group] thinks, but when we make choices, we make them on the basis of what we think the national interest requires. Public opinion establishes a range of possibilities, but choices have to be made by men who deal with the problems from a position of knowledge and responsibility."

There remain a few respondents who referred to advocacy as a *nominal constraint,* suggesting that the Department was moved by these pressures but leaving quite ambiguous the true extent and direction of the movement. A very experienced diplomat was also experienced at clouding the issue: "If a [Congressman] has a special public in his district, the opinions of that small group in that district will, in some situations, have a great impact on policy. We have to take that kind of situation into account." Responses of officials in the Department to the hundreds of recommendations that came out of the International Cooperation Year panels were also characteristically ambiguous about the extent of innovation in the recommendations and about the impact of these proposals on the Department. One man at the Deputy Assistant Secretary level said the panel he was involved in as an adviser had made some "fair proposals" which were taken seriously, but he subsequently added, "In many respects it was an artificial exercise; we contrived to come up with a report that would go beyond where we are now, at the same time keeping 'the art of the possible' in mind. The report suggested a number of things that were already in the wind here." Another official reported that "the recommendations that came from ———'s panel were damn good — and they were not in line with government policy. And so the government people argued intensely with ———, with people flying to ——— to talk with him and with others. It made us look intensely at our policy. To be sure, we came out at the same place that we had been before."

OPPOSITION

Opposition, relatively pure and simple, is the second and "classic" form of dissent. It is by all apparent measures the external response to foreign policy which is most often perceived by officials — or at least it is the one that so concerns them that it lingers longer at the forefront of their awareness. It is also the response that serves as the central organizing theme for much of the historical and political concern with American foreign policy. If I pay more attention to it here than to the other varieties of opinion, it is precisely because opposition has so bemused all and sundry that it has virtually become synonymous with "public opinion and foreign policy"; those who want to organize it and those who want to overcome it have, between them, shaped the broad approaches to the field. Those who want to study "public opinion and foreign policy" have often found, in these confrontations between foreign policy officials and hostile nongovernmental opinion, the promise of significant findings about the process of foreign policy making in the American democracy.

Let me point out right away, however, that though both literature and conversation tend to treat opposition to foreign policy as an unambiguous phenomenon, it is not quite that clear-cut. I have used the phrase "relatively pure and simple" as a way of evading a problem of definition which, if one speculates on it long enough, can boggle the mind. Foreign policy is a congeries of current stances and commitments, alternative possibilities for new ones which may or may not alter present ones, and a variety of aspirations which have not (yet) acquired the status of either an official posture or commitment. "Opposition" to any single worm in this bucket may generally be construed as "support" for another one; it may also be construed as the establishment of "countervailing opinion" and even as "indifference" to all other possibilities. (This point, obviously, could have been made earlier in this chapter — for example, support for any policy may be interpreted as opposition to its competitors. I have elected to raise it here because its complexities are clearer after one has become familiar with the different varieties of opinion.) One example may reveal some of these complexities: the Committee of One Million, which I have mentioned before, was at one time a very active lobby against the recognition of Communist China by the United States and against its admission to the United Nations. But during the years in which the Committee was most involved in the effort to get annual commitments from Congressmen in favor of resolutions opposing admission to the United Nations, official United States policy — its stance and its commitments — was likewise opposed to recognition and to admission, and for reasons which were substantially independent of pressures from the Committee of One Million.[19] In other words, opposition to a *change* in policy which the Administration had no present intention of proposing could also be defined as support for the policy which the Administration was actually pursuing. This problem of definition is, happily, rather easy to overcome, and not simply by making an arbitrary judgment on the matter. Since an official's perception of the constraint he faces seems to be affected to an important degree by the way he defines his political environment in the light of his own objectives, it is important that we be guided in our judgment of these things by *his* definition. And most of the time officials categorize outside groups or individuals, and/or the positions that they take, in a singular fashion; they interpret these views in the light of their own commitments and aspirations and have no difficulty in deciding unambiguously what they think of them. In the case of the Committee of One Million, to return to my example, officials from 1961 on almost uniformly saw it as being among the opposition, despite the apparent congruence of the two positions. Without our exploring here the varied reasons why this was so, it is nevertheless clear that a different set of possible impacts — a different range of perceived constraints — accompanied that evaluation than was the case during the Eisenhower Administration, when most of the higher State Department officials interpreted the Committee's position as essentially supportive.

References to foreign policy opinions of an opposition nature in the literature of foreign policy making very often treat them as *effective constraints* on policy.[20] We have to remember, however, that the evidence for conclusions of this kind is quite uneven and that constraints are frequently attributed to public opinion in the absence of convincing evidence.[21] General theoretical statements, which are even more remote from the factual data of foreign policy making, seem especially to reflect the position popularized some years ago by Walter Lippmann, who argued that Western liberal democracies were a declining factor in world politics because their leaders, fearful of public opinion, were not willing to make difficult and costly decisions.[22] V. O Key, in fact, sounds like a social science echo of Lippmann: "The techniques employed by government for the appraisal of the response in public opinion to governmental actions and to changing circumstances are relatively crude. Perhaps the most serious consequence of inadequate opinion appraisal is that officials often fear to act on matters of conceded urgency lest the public response be hostile." [23] The theme is a common one. In their comparison of the Soviet and American political systems, Brzezinski and Huntington maintain that nonexecutive groups in the United States do not normally participate in foreign policy decisions; rather, they debate and criticize after the fact. "These outspoken attacks in the United States can produce modifications of policy in practice. They certainly shape the Administration's anticipations of the reactions to its next decision in the same area and thereby also presumably affect the content of that decision. Anticipated reaction is thus a restraint in both the British and American cases." [24] James N. Rosenau posits a model of the role of national nongovernmental leaders in the foreign policy process in which he too assigns an effective veto power to negative opinion; unlike Key or Brzezinski and Huntington, however, Rosenau's is not a "latent" veto effective by means of anticipation but is presented as an actual veto exercised in decision making: "National leaders have an informal authority which the ordinary citizen does not possess, which officialdom cannot ignore, and which thus enables them to prevent or permit the selection of alternatives that are formulated, modified, and proposed by government leaders." 25

These claims seem illogical — for example, if anticipated reactions, based on criticism of the last decision, are *really* a restraint on the next decision, effectively keeping officials in line, then what gives rise to the criticism that presumably sustains the anticipated reactions? They also seem exaggerated, especially in the absence of evidence. Officials often *do* "act on matters of conceded urgency," and they are not often visibly prevented from selecting the alternatives that they have put forward. Yet such claims cannot be dismissed out of hand: they are inexact formulations, to be sure, but they derive from a sense that public opposition interferes in some fashion with the formulation of foreign policy, and that sense of interference is shared by a large number of State Department officials who do not hesitate to label opposition as an effective constraint on their freedom to choose.

There were seventeen clear references to such constraint in my interviews, ten of which referred to specific cases and seven of which were general statements. The general statements followed two distinct lines: an amorphous sense of amorphous limits on policy choice, with varying degrees of constraint involved; and a sharper sense that the limits all derive from Congressional reaction. Those in the first group ranged from the Deputy Office Director who claimed that "public opinion is much more a negative constraint than it is a positive force," to the official in Public Affairs who saw the negative constraints as extremely few. Public opinion, he argued, operates by the mechanism of creating "a real furor, with everyone asking questions, and lots of explanations required," and the kinds of questions that can set such a train in motion are quite limited: "Public opinion keeps you away from the extreme choices. . . . It keeps you from making abrupt changes in policy directions. . . . [But they are] not absolutely ruled out, of course." Those in the second group were substantially agreed that fear of Congressional reaction — strong opposition, the demand for explanation — was a major restraint on the State Department. An Office Director: "Many of the higher-ups in the Department are sensitive to Congressional opinion, and they are very reluctant to press sensitive issues onto the President. . . . They hesitate to recommend [a policy proposal] if they themselves think that it will go sour."

The references to specific cases of effective constraint deriving from the opposition of external groups are more interesting and instructive, but a word of caution is in order: the cases make it clear, as have some of the "case studies" mentioned above, that nongovernmental opinion does at times limit governmental behavior in foreign policy in highly specific ways. Of course, no one has really doubted *that*. But the extent of such constraint, and its circumstances, *are* in question; and the specific cases cited here reinforce the judgment that it is quite limited in extent and perhaps special in the circumstance. The cases mentioned — and I repeat my earlier point that officials were chary about getting deeply involved in detailed discussions of these matters — were the following: recognition of the Vatican; family planning in underdeveloped countries; the U.S.–U.S.S.R. Consular Convention and other "bridge-building" measures; the Vietnam War; the Korean War; the MLF; sanctions against Rhodesia; and the Indian-Pakistani conflict of the middle 1960's. Some of these are major issues, others are not; in any event, they are a small part of the foreign policy business carried on in the State Department even by or within the purview of the people with whom I discussed these matters. My subsequent discussion of public opposition as an ineffective constraint will put this in further perspective. I simply want at this point to enter a cautionary note against reading too much too soon into these particular cases.

Eight cases or issues are too few, furthermore, to provide any reliable clues as to the kinds of issues or the circumstances that are likely to result in effective public constraints. But a little speculation in that direction may be warranted as a tentative basis for further investigation. Four of these issues dealt, though in different ways, with wars or war-related military policy: the Vietnam War, the Korean War, the Indian-Pakistani war, and the MLF. And two of them involved religious questions: first, the diplomatic recognition of the Vatican and second, family planning. The Consular Convention raised questions of anti-communism and involved ethnic groups and also ultra-conservative organizations; and sanctions against Rhodesia posed substantially an economic problem. Let us look at two of these a bit closer.

In the case of the U.S.-U.S.S.R. Consular Convention, which had been signed in June 1964, State Department officials were saying privately in 1966 what the press was reporting openly in 1967, namely, that opposition chiefly from right-wing groups in the country, apparently inspired by FBI Director J. Edgar Hoover, had been instrumental in holding up Senate consideration of the Convention.[26] The treaty was finally approved in March 1967, but a year earlier its fate, as an Office Director described it, was quite problematic: "My impression is that President Johnson does not want to be pushed into legislative adventures that will seriously aggravate his own relations on the Hill, unless those adventures are really vital. It is *not* vital that the Consular Convention be ratified." A similar reasoning was advanced with respect to the family planning question in AID: "We stay a step behind, in order to avoid getting a violent reaction, especially from the right wing of the Catholic Church. We did not want to lose Catholic support for the whole AID bill just because we are doing something on family planning. After all, the family planning item is a mere ten million dollars out of an AID budget for next year of about two and a half billion dollars. So it would be wrong for us to jeopardize the whole for the part, to lose Catholic support for the two and a half billion by going out on a limb for the ten million." The same factors were apparently at work here that were involved in the decision not to include aid to the Soviet Union as part of Lend-Lease in the summer and fall of 1941.[27]

In addition to these perceptions of effective policy constraint, five officials talked about the impact of opposition in a much more ambiguous and less convincing way — what I have been calling *nominal constraint*. The implication in their remarks is that the State Department is aware of and receptive to criticism, that opposition views are carefully considered and treated as an "input," an important factor in decision making on substantive policy. To repeat a comment I quoted in an earlier chapter: "I was recently at a Bar Mitzvah in ——— where I ended up arguing about Vietnam with everyone there. I was astounded at the unanimity of the criticism directed at our policy. All of this gets brought into our discussions here; we are not hermetically sealed." But in the absence of information specifying policy impact, one is entitled to skepticism or at least to suspended judgment. It is also possible that the impact to which the officials allude so vaguely concerns not policy but packaging, presentation, public relations, as the following remarks by a desk officer suggest: "There was a lot of criticism, back in 1962–1964, of our policy of continuing aid to —— when things were getting tough for us there. This criticism came from the Congress and the press. . . . The people here were certainly aware of the criticism, but I can't say what the consequences were. It is really what the people on the Seventh Floor [the Secretariat] feel that matters; and it affects the style of foreign affairs more than the substance." This is so characteristic a mode of response among State Department officials, in fact, as we shall see in the next chapter, that it is even more reasonable to interpret ambiguous remarks as meaning impact on information policy than to assume they refer to substantive policy.

One does not find a large literature concerned directly with the question of opposition opinion as an *ineffective constraint* on foreign policy; but that may well be a function of the way scholars define the questions they ask and present their findings. They are usually interested in exploring the processes of foreign policy making, and thus their attention is captured by external opinion only when it is a "significant factor" — i.e., an effective constraint — in decision making. Given that predilection, however, we are probably entitled to regard most studies of foreign policy making in which public opinion plays no visible role as examples of cases where opposition opinion — assuming there will always be some — was not a significant factor, was without any constraining effect. To study the role of public opinion more directly in cases such as these requires a conceptual scheme that treats nongovernmental groups as constituent elements of the foreign policy process, so that one's attention is directed to them without fail, no matter what their position and no matter what their impact.[28] Lacking systematic efforts of this kind, we lean heavily on the passing remarks of historians and participants, such as this one by former Secretary of State Dean Acheson: "It is not strange . . . that the [China] White Paper . . . should have evoked bellows of pain and rage from the China bloc in Congress and the China Lobby in the country, and enlisted the full efforts of their combined propaganda apparatus. Since, however, these did not affect the course of Administration policy or the strong support given it by the Foreign Relations Committee . . . we shall pass on to other crowding developments of this eventful year."[29]

The view expressed by Acheson, that foreign policy officials can ignore or discount public opinion that is opposed to them, is by my reckoning the most widely expressed view in the State Department concerning the impact of opinion. Although Acheson is generally thought to have been a uniquely independent, perhaps even arrogant, spirit in American foreign policy circles, in this particular respect he was quite typical of the Department he served and led for many years. Twenty references to the ineffectiveness — or ineffectuality — of critical opinion were made by eighteen people, just over a third of the respondents. These officials give or suggest three different lines of reasoning as they explain why it is all right for them to dismiss opinion that is opposed to what they are doing. I may exaggerate when I say "three *different* lines of reasoning;" though they are different in the sense that they are both analytically and practically distinctive, there is another sense in which they are simply different sides of the same flash-cube, very closely related to each other both structurally and functionally.

First, there is a reason which should be familiar to the reader at this point: we know best (an official will say); our job is to determine the national interest in particular circumstances, and we should not be talked or pushed out of our best judgments.[30] If I may repeat here a comment I quoted earlier, by an Office Director: "But even though you know how some of these things are going to look, you cannot pander necessarily to the popular reaction. The executive has to *lead* — it has often to take unpopular stands. This is where you pay off, where you do what you are supposed to do." Another Office Director: "The cry was then taken up by others. It took courage and vigor on the part of authorities here to continue the policy of economic support for the ——— government, but it was done." A Public Affairs Adviser: "But even when Congress is in opposition, as it is now on the Vietnam question, our policies still go on. We are always asking 'Are we doing the right thing?' especially when there are public outbursts." His implied answer, of course, was "Of course."

A second reason may be summarized, though at the risk of caricature, as: we officials have the effective power of decision; we can do pretty much as we like, and it all comes out in the wash. The literature on foreign policy making seems to me to reflect this viewpoint both in what it chooses to pay attention to and in what it says.[31] Some expressions of this line of argument seem as brash

as my summary of it. In the Public Affairs Bureau an official repeatedly dismissed the influence of any outside opinion on policy.
"Even on Vietnam no significant public opinion enters U.S. policy
as far as the State Department is concerned." And a desk officer:
"In a crunch, leaving the Congress aside, no outside force can keep
us from doing what we want to do." But others, like this experienced senior official, are more subtle (if, in the outcome, no more
correct): "My judgment is that we are going to do what we set out
to do in Vietnam, and not five years from now or three years from
now but in the reasonably near future. And then a lot of criticism
will disappear when it looks like we are on top of the situation."

The third reason given for the dismissal of opposition opinion is
also familiar: we officials can't pay serious attention to the offbeat
opinions of fringe groups — those whose views are so alien to what
we are doing that to accept them means giving up everything we
stand for. Typically, the John Birch Society and other unspecified
"right-wing elements" are named in this context, along with organizations such as SDS from the militant or pacifist left. The Department is leary of any groups whatsoever that are outside the "consensus" or the "mainstream." [32] An Assistant Secretary: "All the
right-wing groups were against us, and they have all attacked us.
If one were to tabulate all of that, the ratio of correspondence was
very greatly against us.[33] But the overwhelming majority of American people, I am sure, could be mobilized to support us, as they
did on the ——— Bill." Similarly, in 1966 the Vietnam protesters
were regarded as a small if vocal minority of left-wing radicals, op-
portunists, "political virgins," whom officials could not take very
seriously even when the officials themselves had doubts about the
wisdom of the war (as some of them clearly did even then). For
the most part the problem was defined chiefly as learning how to
deal with them. For example: "We make a point now of insisting
that our speakers be politely treated, or else we will not let them
speak. . . . Throughout all this, U.S. policy has not changed; only
the manner of its presentation has changed."

The importance of this third justification for paying no heed to
outside opposition is that it is easily expanded to include people
whose "fringe" position is a matter of dispute. Thus any kind of opposition can be put beyond the pale precisely because it *is* opposition, "fringe" or "respectable," and because there are powerful po-

litical or ideological obstacles in the way of accommodating it. This was long true, for example, of anti-Vietnam War opinion coming from otherwise respectable establishment sources and for opinion coming from equally eminent authorities favoring the normalization of relations with Communist China. In other words, opinions are readily dismissable if they are not operational or politically acceptable to officials, given their bundle of preferences and commitments, personal and political, private and public. Accommodation or change of this order is implicitly seen as a function of the electoral process, when new men come in with new orthodoxies, rather than of work-a-day influence processes.

UNSPECIFIED OPINION

By unspecified opinions I mean ambiguous references to opinion which obscure its evaluative character, though not necessarily its source. In a way this is a residual category; surprisingly, however, it is second in size only to the references to hostile and opposed opinion. It is hard to say whether this represents a lot of generalizations about opinion of all kinds, or whether a lot of opinions which officials "hear" is not seriously evaluated for political content, or whether it is mostly presumed to be in opposition. I incline to the latter two views, because most of this opinion, as Table III shows, is perceived by officials as posing either nominal or ineffective constraints — a pattern of impact unlike that of any other specific variety of opinion and one that is consonant with superficial interest in opinion or with negative appraisal of it.

The three references to opinion in the abstract as an *effective constraint* are a distinct minority, and of course an exception to the immediately preceding remark. In one case, an official expressed the view that American policy in the Near East was quite different from what the State Department would make of it in the absence of United States public opinion, which he defined not as Zionist organizations but as a concern for the electoral reactions of Jewish voters in metropolitan areas. Another attributed great influence to the public "which is represented by the Congress. Once a significant Congressional point of view is made known to us, we do what they want." And the third attributed great power to the press, but "only if there is a concerted press approach which is reflective of U.S. public concerns."

A much larger group of references (thirteen) fall into the category of *nominal constraint* — claims of impact that are cast in doubt by the very language of the claim. The remarks of a Deputy Assistant Secretary suggest how empty the formalism really is; speaking of contacts with professors and notables, he said: "They are not very up-to-date on the state of the play, but they do have a perspective that is fresh even though it is simple. You haven't had a chance to refashion these views, so they are useful." It is difficult to imagine how they could possibly be "useful" in a substantive policy sense, given this condescending view of them. Other claims of constraint have a familiar vagueness: "It is bound to enter your calculations . . . it must make a difference." "Everyone is sensitive to" public reactions to his decisions. "My boss . . . is conscious of" what he hears. "This has some effect." "On Vietnam, general public opinion is a major factor, of course." The public has "an indirect punch" on my work. "People here in the Department *are* listening to people on the outside. . . . It does make a difference." "All of this has an impact on me." Six of the thirteen references of this kind were to an undifferentiated public opinion; three were to notables; two to specialists and scholars; and one each to correspondents and to ethnic groups. I do not rule out that these remarks were meant seriously, but I do not quite know what they mean.

References to unspecified opinion as *ineffective constraints* are larger still (sixteen) and quite clear in their import. Here officials are dismissing the relevance of opinions of unspecified content in the same fashion and with some of the same sharpness as they dismissed dissenting opinions. There is no doubt that some of these opinions are known or assumed to be negative; this would probably be the case with respect to the mail (five references), which, it will be recalled, was earlier described as focusing on people's complaints. A desk officer: "Constituent mail is easily disposable; we have usually already answered it some eighteen months before." An Office Director: "The letters that come to the Public Affairs area do not affect us at all. When there are a few of them, they do not matter; and when the letters are numerous enough to be answered by boilerplate [i.e., tape-fed automatic typewriters producing uniform letters], then that is all handled by Public Affairs, and we never hear from them." But other officials dismiss the press (three references) and polls (one reference) as institutions irrelevant to policy makers without regard to the positions they take. From the Secretariat, for example: "I don't think policy makers pay much attention to [the working press and the pundits] in their role of attempting to shape policy. They do not have the necessary information." And still others dismiss opinion in general (five references), on both empirical grounds ("Opinion does come to the State Department, but by the time it gets to decision making places it is rather effectively neutralized") and normative grounds ("The leadership in the State Department . . . [doesn't] want our recommendations based on what I think public opinion will accept, but rather on what will advance our interests in the area"), also without regard to its policy content.[34]

CONCLUSION

We have seen, in these pages, the different ways in which public opinion is perceived and interpreted, made more manageable both psychologically and politically, and finally assimilated or digested with limited impact on the policy preferences of State Department officials. As several officials have argued, support or at least acquiescence is the preferred condition of opinion. But if the bulk of opinion simply cannot be read in either of these ways, the next best thing from the officials' point of view is a structure of countervailing opinions, since it can be made to yield substantial freedom of action. A State Department brochure of some years back put its case for countervailing opinion quite transparently: "Your opinion counts even if you neglect to express it, because, in failing to say what you think, you lessen the likelihood of the course you favor being adopted and pursued. Too often it happens that those who endorse a policy merely nod to themselves, while those who oppose it raise their voices." [35] And President Nixon reiterated the case in his plea in November 1969 for the "silent majority" to express itself on his side, as a counterweight to the anti-war movement. Even at a high level of public interest and involvement, President Nixon — like President Johnson before him — was able in this manner to enlarge his area of initiative in dealing with specific foreign policy issues.

Up until this latter point, however, we have more or less treated the conditions of public opinion as something the State Department simply lived with and adapted to, in one way or another. But that is an incomplete view of the matter. Of course the Department has to live and work with opinion as it exists — or appears — at any given moment; but the Department also has some freedom, some scope, to try to change that opinion, to create a more congenial or permissive environment for the succeeding moments. This is the response to opinion which affects information policy rather than substantive political policy, as I mentioned at the start of this chapter. Let us turn now to this aspect of the impact of opinion, to gain a better perspective on the way the State Department treats the opinion of the moment.

NOTES

1. Raymond Bauer, Ithiel de Sola Pool and Lewis A. Dexter, *American Business and Public Policy*, New York: Atherton Press, 1963; Warren E. Miller and Donald E. Stokes, "Constituency Influence in Congress," *American Political Science Review*, Vol. 57, No. 1, March 1963.

2. A good example is suggested by Ernest R. May, who points out that at the moment of decision on the Philippine Islands, the United States government perceived an imperialist public opinion that was supportive of United States action in taking the islands. But May also argues that elite opinion was divided and confused at the time, which leads me to conclude that, if May is right, officials actually had considerable freedom in the way they chose to "read" opinion. See May, *American Imperialism: A Speculative Essay*, New York: Atheneum, 1968.

3. See Joseph M. Jones, a former State Department official: "To those interested in how foreign policy is made, it may be pointed out here that no atmosphere is more conducive to official action than that created when public figures on the Right and on the Left happen to agree, even though for different reasons, that a daring, even 'visionary' course of action should be taken. The effect upon government officials is almost tangible: it raises their sights; it opens the psychological and political doors to action and invites them to pass through." *The Fifteen Weeks*, New York: Viking, 1955, p. 234.

4. See Max Frankel, "Issues of China Policy," in *The New York Times*, June 9, 1966: "Some officials who came to Washington five years ago with hopes of altering China policy have been sufficiently encouraged to defer their planned resignation from Government. Those who have wanted to make a modest start on the problem at the United Nations believe they now have their best chance in years if they can demonstrate enough public support to win the President's backing in a politically rough year for all Asian policies."

5. James N. Rosenau describes a similar situation involving public

support for foreign aid: "[Our] model does not presently account for a . . . situation in which officialdom [i.e., the Congress] vetoes a consensus widely shared by diverse groups of national leaders. Yet, our inquiry would appear to have uncovered a situation precisely of this kind." *National Leadership and Foreign Policy*, Princeton: Princeton University Press, 1963, p. 335. For a further view that "support" gives an administration flexibility on policy, see John E. Mueller, "Trends in Popular Support for the Wars in Korea and Vietnam," *American Political Science Review*, Vol. 65, No. 2, June 1971, pp. 368–369.

6. See Bernard C. Cohen, *Citizen Education in World Affairs*, Princeton University: Center of International Studies, 1953.

7. Bill D. Moyers, "One Thing We Learned," *Foreign Affairs*, Vol. 46, No. 4, July 1968, pp. 661, 662.

8. V. O. Key, Jr., *Public Opinion and American Democracy*, New York: Knopf, 1961, pp. 199–200.

9. Rosenau, *National Leadership and Foreign Policy*, p. 20. In another place Rosenau argues that the public is only rarely "activated by questions of foreign policy" and that this gap in motivation between public and officials "normally has the consequence of freeing officialdom from the restraints that the citizenry imposes in the domestic [policy] area." James N. Rosenau, ed., *Domestic Sources of Foreign Policy*, New York: Free Press, 1967, p. 34.

10. Bernard C. Cohen, *The Political Process and Foreign Policy: The Making of the Japanese Peace Settlement*, Princeton: Princeton University Press, 1957, pp. 215–216.

11. I think it is fair to add, however, that it attracted little enthusiasm among the NATO countries also, and that may have been a more important factor in its being shelved. See John D. Steinbruner, "The Mind and Milieu of Policy-makers: A Case Study of the MLF," unpubl. Ph.D. dissertation, Massachusetts Institute of Technology, 1968.

12. As quoted by Selig Adler, *The Isolationist Impulse*, London and New York: Abelard-Schuman, 1957, p. 120.

13. E.g., John Kenneth Galbraith: "Incidentally, I would urge that the radical right be kept in perspective. I have a feeling that at any given time about three million Americans can be had for any militant reaction against law, decency, the Constitution, the Supreme Court, compassion and the rule of reason . . . this fringe is an inescapable aspect of our polity. The singular feature of liberals is their ability to become aroused over each new threat as though it were the first. Perhaps this is good for it becomes the countervailing force." *Ambassador's Journal*, Boston: Houghton Mifflin, 1969, p. 268.

14. Lester Milbrath, "Interest Groups and Foreign Policy," in Rosenau, ed., *Domestic Sources of Foreign Policy*, p. 250. For the same view, argued explicitly, see Cohen, *The Political Process and Foreign Policy*, p. 209; and for the implicit argument see Manfred Landecker, *The President and Public Opinion*, Washington, D.C.: Public Affairs Press, 1968, pp. 74–75, and Robert P. Browder, *The Origins of Soviet-*

American Diplomacy, Princeton: Princeton University Press, 1953, pp. 37–39.

15. See Rosenau, *National Leadership and Foreign Policy,* pp. 26–27; and May, *American Imperialism* (who attributes the emergence of an imperialist policy to division and confusion within the ranks of establishment public opinion).

16. Bauer, Pool, and Dexter, *American Business and Public Policy,* p. 316.

17. See *The Pentagon Papers,* New York: Bantam Books, 1971; and Townsend Hoopes, *The Limits of Intervention,* New York: McKay, 1969.

18. And sometimes officials patiently cultivate an external advocacy that "forces" them to do things they are anxious to do; e.g., Robert A. Divine cites President Franklin D. Roosevelt as looking for a buildup of interventionist sentiment that would push him into a policy of convoying British ships across the Atlantic, in the spring of 1941. *Roosevelt and World War II,* Baltimore: Johns Hopkins Press, 1969, p. 42.

19. See A. T. Steele, *The American People and China,* New York: McGraw-Hill, 1966, pp. 119, 249.

20. E.g., Raymond H. Dawson, *The Decision to Aid Russia, 1941,* Chapel Hill: University of North Carolina Press, 1959, pp. 218, 233–234, 238; Dorothy Borg, *The United States and the Far Eastern Crisis of 1933–1938,* Cambridge, Mass.: Harvard University Press, 1964, p. 398; Doris Graber, *Public Opinion, the President, and Foreign Policy,* New York: Holt, Rinehart & Winston, 1968, p. 192; Cohen, *The Political Process and Foreign Policy,* Chap. 12; and for a case involving the Congress, see Bauer, Pool, and Dexter, *American Business and Public Policy,* p. 293.

21. See Chap. 1 above.

22. Walter Lippmann, *Essays in the Public Philosophy,* Boston: Atlantic-Little, Brown, 1955.

23. Key, *Public Opinion and American Democracy,* p. 422. And on p. 286: "Governments that listen most respectfully to the attentive public . . . thus may be driven to paralysis."

24. Zbigniew Brzezinski and Samuel P. Huntington, *Political Power: USA/USSR,* New York: Viking Press Compass Books, 1965, p. 217.

25. Rosenau, *National Leadership and Foreign Policy,* p. 17.

26. See *The Milwaukee Journal,* February 19, 1967, p. 8.

27. Cf. Dawson, *The Decision to Aid Russia, 1941.*

28. I employed such a scheme in my study of the Japanese peace settlement some years ago, and I emerged with a complex picture of public opinion at the policy-making level, including opposition opinion which had no constraining effects whatsoever. See my *Political Process and Foreign Policy.* See also Graber, *Public Opinion, the President, and Foreign Policy:* "The bulk of the research effort which has gone into this book has yielded negative data — an absence of specific concern with public opinion" (p. vi).

29. Dean Acheson, *Present at the Creation,* New York: W. W. Nor-

ton, 1969, p. 307. Notice the suggestion here that the existence of a countervailing opinion made it easier to "pass on." At a later point Acheson expanded his comment: "A good deal of nonsense has been written about the effect of the attack of the primitives, before and during McCarthy's reign, on the China policy of the Truman Administration. Whatever effect it had on our successors, it had little on us" (p. 369).

30. Browder describes aspects of the decision to recognize the Soviet Union in terms such as these; see *The Origins of Soviet-American Diplomacy*, Princeton: Princeton University Press, 1953, p. 107.

31. E.g., Glenn D. Paige, *The Korean Decision: June 24–30, 1950*, New York: Free Press, 1968; Kenneth M. Waltz, *Foreign Policy and Democratic Politics*, Boston: Little, Brown & Co., 1967. In a recent and sensitive textbook, Sheldon Appleton has written: "An American President confident that his policy actions will bear conspicuous fruit before the next election can conduct foreign relations pretty much as he pleases, despite sizable immediate elite and mass opposition. But he had better be right if he wants to continue to be President." *United States Foreign Policy*, Boston: Little, Brown & Co., 1968, p. 307. And Warren Miller has reminded us that even being "wrong" is not necessarily of great consequence: "Voting behavior today is not acutely responsive to the issues of foreign policy." "Voting and Foreign Policy," in Rosenau, ed., *Domestic Sources of Foreign Policy*, p. 230.

32. But of course what is on the fringe and what is in the mainstream will vary historically. Selig Adler writes that "by 1923 . . . the isolationist front had broadened and deepened. The isolationist coalition now represented more than a pooling of groups who hated Wilson for diverse reasons. It had become a genuine groundswell of public opinion." *The Isolationist Impulse*, p. 164. Dorothy Borg concludes that the President and other officials were influenced on the quarantine question in the last analysis by "the same sensitivity to isolationist and pacifist criticism that they had shown earlier." *The United States and the Far Eastern Crisis of 1933–1938*, p. 398. We should keep in mind, however, that in 1937 "isolationist and pacifist criticism" was probably still in the mainstream; at any event, it was hardly on the fringe, as it became after World War II.

33. Note, incidentally, the condition-contrary-to-fact in this remark about the systematic treatment of correspondence.

34. Cf. Bauer, Pool, and Dexter's comment on the Congress: "On the simplest level, communications [with constituents] with respect to foreign-trade policy had to compete with, and frequently were lost in, the welter of other communications. This was particularly true of conversations which Congressmen and their assistants had with other people. . . . The communications they received were poorly remembered and ill-understood." *American Business and Public Policy*, p. 413. And note Theodore C. Sorensen's comment on President Kennedy: "The final difference in the Kennedy treatment of foreign and domestic affairs was the relative influence of Congressional and public opinion. His foreign policy actions were still constrained within bounds set by those forces, but they

operated more indirectly, and his own powers of initiative and decision were much wider." *Kennedy*, New York: Harper & Row, 1965, p. 509.

35. "Your Opinion Counts," U.S. Department of State Publication 5606, General Foreign Policy Series 93, November 1954, p. 12.

FIVE

Opinion at the Gate—II

I suggested in passing in the preceding chapter that when the tiger is at the gate, it is a normal reaction not to let him in but to try to divert him. When State Department officials talk about the public opinion–foreign policy relationship, they are as likely as not to have in mind a relationship in which they are the actors or initiators, and the public the object of their attention, which is the reverse of the situation that has occupied us thus far. In fact, the State Department is pervaded with an orientation toward political public relations. I am going to run the risk of being misunderstood and call this instrumental attitude toward public opinion a manipulative orientation. One of Webster's definitions of manipulation is "to change by artful or unfair means so as to serve one's purpose." The Department does not, in my view, use "unfair means"; it *does* try very hard to be artful in the pursuit of its purposes, which are to organize and mobilize and if necessary alter the public opinions that it and others involved in foreign policy making hear, so that they are favorable to the Department's political or policy interests. This manipulative attitude toward external opinion is among the most widely shared views in the Department. By conservative count, forty out of my fifty respondents made 109 clear references to the appropriateness or desirability or necessity of actions designed to modify external opinion.[1]

I repeat that I regard this as normal institutional political behavior in a democratic environment. The Department has vast and important policy responsibilities, which like all other policy responsibilities require something akin to "the consent of the governed" in order to be exercised. And it is simplistic to assume either that such consent can be attained without any effort at explanation, persuasion, or mobilization or that the Department will make no such efforts on its own behalf in order to carry out its responsibilities as it defines them. We all recognize this and accept it, particularly when it is made explicit. But so much of the time we look at the problem from the other end, seeking ways to secure the consent of the *governors* as the means of narrowing the gap between public opinion and foreign policy, that it begins to seem somehow inappropriate for foreign policy officials to attempt to build a political base for their policies. It is interesting and revealing that Roger Hilsman found it necessary to stress the point that foreign policy making is, throughout, an exercise in politics, and that he is widely applauded for reminding us of this fact.[2]

What is the manipulative orientation in the State Department like? How does it manifest itself? Is it really as pervasive as these numbers suggest? And what are we to make of this? What is its import?

PUBLIC RELATIONS PERSPECTIVE

The public relations perspective runs through almost everything that the Department does and that its officials say. Often, in fact, it is the *basic* public opinion response, in the sense that all the standard phrases about "taking account of" public opinion or being "sensitive to" it refer not to adaptations in substantive policy but to appropriate adjustments in information policy or procedures. An Office Director: "Since I have been in the Department, the trend has been steadily upward, in the direction of more conscious efforts to take account of public opinion in the big sense. We have better facilities now, better programs in terms of going to the public."[3] A desk officer, discussing the Vietnam controversy and its effect on the Department (this was in 1966): "We do have a problem domestically. The Secretary of State as a consequence has increased his public appearances, our community program has expanded, our speaking tours have increased, and so on. The whole episode [*sic*] has led to greater efforts on the part of the Department to explain and defend American foreign policy to the American people." Another official close to the Vietnam situation: "The Administration is very sensitive to public — public and Congressional — opinion on Vietnam; and it tries to respond to it by sending out speakers, trying to answer the mail, having press conferences." And a Deputy Assistant Secretary: "We worry about our public relations because we worry about the 'heat' that these groups can put on us. You get dissent. You can sense the reservations that people have, and as a result you have to sharpen your rationale in support of your policy." Considering that none of the above officials had Public Affairs posts or responsibilities, one can hardly dispute the observation of an official in the Secretariat, which I quoted earlier in a different context: "Most people here are interested in public opinion not in the sense of being shaped by it, but rather in gaining support for something they want to undertake, or measuring support that may already exist for what they want to do."

It is clear from the tenor of the above remarks that officials are not in the least embarrassed or apologetic about the public relations function and make no effort whatever to conceal it or underplay it as something distasteful or inappropriate even though necessary. There is, in fact, an obvious tone of pride in the way the Department has risen to the occasion, as it were. Going beyond this, however, there are officials who argue in principle that the government has legitimate leadership functions in respect both of policy *and* opinion and that the State Department has to shoulder the obligation to lead, to inform, to educate in the foreign policy field. A desk officer: "The important thing is that someone gets out ahead and clarifies the situation for the public. . . . Someone has to lead." A Deputy Assistant Secretary: "If there is a tendency in public opinion quarters to concentrate on the adverse side of issues or situations, we want to try to see that our own side of the story is being told. This is a legitimate part of the business of the State Department." Another Deputy Assistant Secretary: "There is an obligation to detail the way you are doing it." And an Assistant Secretary: "Any government officer has to deal with public opinion as it is, but he also has to try to inform public opinion, to argue his case, to try to persuade people."

I stress this point precisely because it may ring false in the 1970's, when the tenets of the preceding third-of-a-century of

American foreign policy are under sharp attack and efforts to "inform" and "persuade" are greeted with skepticism, if they are not shouted down altogether. It may be well to remind ourselves, however, that throughout the past generation, in a period of substantial internationalist consensus, men who shared in that consensus routinely expected — even urged — the State Department to exercise its leadership so as to nail down that consensus, to minimize the temptation to nibble on the apple of isolationism periodically offered to the American people by such unlikely serpents as former President Hoover and Senator Robert A. Taft, Sr. Officials who were prominent in foreign policy in a succession of administrations during this period are particularly eloquent on the obligation to take the lead in the formation of opinion. Former Secretary of State Dean Acheson, discussing the famous National Security Council Paper NSC-68, has written: "It was not enough to give the President wise, though tough, advice and expect him to create acceptance in Congress and the country for the resulting action. We also had a duty to explain and persuade." [4] According to Andrew Berding, who was Assistant Secretary of State for Public Affairs under Secretary of State John Foster Dulles, Dulles "believed that the President and the Secretary of State had the duty to take the leadership in foreign affairs. . . . However . . . the Administration had a responsibility to inform the people adequately and bring public opinion along with it." [5] And Theodore Sorensen writes that President Kennedy "recognized his obligation to 'lead, inform, correct and sometimes even ignore constituent opinion, if we are to exercise fully that judgment for which we were elected.' And no problem of the Presidency concerned him more than that of public communication — educating, persuading, and mobilizing that opinion through continued use of the political machinery, continued traveling and speaking, and, above all, continued attention to the mass media: radio, television, and the press." [6]

If some officials accept *in principle* an obligation to shape public opinion, many more accept it *in practice*, with or without any specific justification. The obligation to inform and persuade has been institutionalized in the State Department, both in its bureaucratic structure and in the attitudes and doctrines of officials governing their everyday behavior in the conduct of foreign policy. In Chapter 2 I noted the main organizational features of the Bureau of

Public Affairs, and I pointed out the transformation of that bureau over the last twenty years into an institution almost wholly concerned with public relations. Public Affairs is not a large factor in the State Department and not an especially popular field of work for foreign policy careerists.[7] But that is not an adequate measure of the importance of the public relations function in the Department. A more substantial measure is the acceptance of the public relations doctrines, and the prevalence of supporting attitudes, at all levels and in all parts of the Department. Few officers work — or want to work — *in* Public Affairs; many more work *at* public affairs. The facilities and resources that are available to a President, and which so fascinated President Kennedy, are not available to ordinary State Department officials, to be sure; still, they do what they can, in ways that are congenial and reasonable. They contribute to the process of feeding the press and correcting its "mistakes." "Daily, we have very much in mind giving the Department spokesman the material that will help mold opinion." "The press is full of distortions. . . . And so we have to correct misinformation, even from responsible news sources." "We spend a lot of time trying to set the press straight. . . . This is very routine; it is a standard function." They participate in the Department's conferences, symposia, and briefings for nongovernmental organizations, for editors and publishers, for educators; and they give lectures all over the country. "I have done far more than my share of public speaking for the Department, on speaking assignments which range from boring through the acceptable to the exciting. . . . It is important and necessary to explain your policies in a democratic society." "I have felt a responsibility to help explain to the people of the United States the policies and realities of foreign relations." "We are encouraged to give speeches, and I give a major one about once a month."

Performance of public relations work is one measure of its acceptability among State Department officials. Another measure is the frequent criticism one encounters that the Department's public relations activities are so rudimentary. By way of contrast, not one official criticized the Department for *engaging* in such activities — only for not engaging in them very actively or intelligently, for not doing a very good job! A desk officer: "We are still in a primitive state of public relations here in the State Department." An Assistant Secretary: "We have got to learn how to unlock frozen attitudes." Another Assistant Secretary: "When historians of the future look back at this period and ask what we did that was worthwhile, the most important and significant development is this effort we are engaged in to produce a better world. Now how the hell do you get that across?"

Almost all of these officials — those who justify or accept present practices and those who criticize them as inadequate — seem surprisingly insensitive to what I had thought might be an important question in the Department: in view of the well-advertised Congressional antipathy toward any activities in the State Department that might be interpreted as "propaganda" directed toward domestic audiences, what is the dividing line between "education" and "propaganda"? Several officials were more than insensitive; they were plainly outspoken in their view of public relations activities as instrumental efforts to bring the right kinds of pressure to bear on Congress. "We want to keep down the level of hostility, which may get to Congressmen if it gets too high." "We should be analyzing those parts of the country whose Congressmen are causing us the greatest difficulty, and then try to work on the public in those areas. We don't do anything like that, or at least I don't think we do. Our speechmaking is a contribution to public education, nothing more." "Congressmen look to the mass media, so we support mass media information programs." "There was a limited amount of pressure [on Congress] from the public until we here did a job on an organized basis. We sold the —— bill just as they sell foreign aid and Vietnam. Without that effort, the so-called interest groups would never have been able to do it themselves."

The reason for the insensitivity, apparently, is that the problem is not — or is no longer — a real one. Not only is it extraordinarily difficult, both theoretically and practically, to draw a workable line between education and propaganda; the Congress in fact regularly tolerates information efforts which are explicitly designed to build public and ultimately Congressional support for Administration proposals, negating the value of any concern it might have in principle for domestic propaganda. Two younger officials, both desk officers, seemed to detect a change in this direction in the recent past: "The Conferences for Editors and for Non-Governmental Organizations are public relations efforts, of course, but we have to be careful not to step over some ill-defined boundary. But things are much looser in this respect in the last few years." Then he added, with obvious irony, "We present the facts; our role is education." The second desk officer had been describing the Department's early involvement in the campus debates on Vietnam: "It is interesting that none of our critics ever suggested that there was an impropriety in our giving out our views. . . . This is a new dimension in the manner in which the Department explains itself." But one has only to follow the loose trail of the Department's involvement in the effort to put across the Truman Doctrine in 1947 to realize that little has objectively changed in the last few years.[8] What *is* new, perhaps, is that most officials in the Department are no longer concerned even in principle about the problem.

ACTIVE AND REACTIVE MANIPULATION

The manipulative orientation toward external opinion takes two major forms, which I am calling spontaneous and reactive; and both of them are evident in the remarks I have quoted above. By spontaneous manipulation I have in mind what most of us think of as the public relations view of a problem: in the words of a Deputy Office Director, "We have to think about what we can sell." In this view, the Department has to think about the problems of public reception from the very beginning of a policy venture and at all subsequent stages in its development. "Educating the public," trying to get or maintain "public support," is a continuous, integral aspect of the Department's work. But foreign policy officials do not generally think of the products of foreign policy as being ultimately shaped by public taste in the manner of soap or automobiles. Fairy Soaps or Edsels may come and go, but to the Departmental official the world is round, the United States is an inescapable part of it, and at any one time our choices are severely circumscribed.[9] So the Department does not *really* "think about what we can sell" in the sense of putting public affairs people at the heart of the policy design process, the decision making process.[10] Rather, it is concerned most of the time with *how* to sell decisions and programs arrived at by complex political and bureaucratic processes. Notions about public opinion play a role in those processes, to be sure, but as we have noted earlier, they are most often intuitively derived and instrumentally deployed. Within the very broad and usually implicit assumption that "anything we are likely to come up with is sellable," the fundamental problem is how to merchandise it. An Assistant Secretary: "We constantly have to be concerned with matters of presentation, with the forensics of the case, and so we are trying to solve problems by speeches, words, statements that the Departmental spokesman can use."

In terms of the varieties of opinion that we explored in the preceding chapter, the purpose of spontaneous manipulation is, by adroit publicity, to move at least parts of the attentive public out of "indifference" on an issue and hopefully into passive or active support. Support, in order that officials might have maximum freedom to develop their position; but at least a dent in indifference, so that officials are not booby-trapped at a later point by the sudden and unforeseen mobilization of hostile opinion. An Assistant Secretary: "People handling the —— problem thought they could work that one out in silence. . . . But when they tried to make a major shift in silence, they found they couldn't do it; you have to move the public with you."

Reactive manipulation, on the other hand, is a more defensive, reflexive approach to public relations. In this mode, public relations are not a planned effort to nudge public opinion out of indifference and into support. Rather, they are an attempt to "put out fires," to respond to "errors," charges, criticisms of policy, programs, or institutions as they appear. An official in the Bureau of Public Affairs: "We try to spotlight for everyone in the Department the areas that we see as problems — the areas that need clarification, the areas that have not been adequately explained." An official in AID: "When anyone criticizes us in the press, we all come to a screeching halt and look very carefully around at what we are doing. This does not shape our direction. . . . Mostly what we do is simply put out the fire: we check the record of the case, we may lop off a head, we will write up our answer to the charges to save for a future contingency, and that is about it." A Deputy Office Director: "These contacts, or pressures, from the public probably influence our tactics, not our strategies. You trim your sails a bit here and there. When you write a speech, you are aware of criticisms that have been received about aspects of policy, and on the chance that the speech will be picked up and given a certain amount of publicity you want the speech — even though it may not be exactly on that subject — at least to be responsive to these criticisms."

Reactive manipulation, the reflex to put out the fire, can only take place after the fire alarm has been sounded. Information about hostile or critical public opinion is the tocsin. Officials read into such opinion some policy constraint, as we saw in the last chapter; but more often they read into it some guidelines for their public relations responses. From AID: "Mail is useful in pinpointing areas of misunderstanding and actual disagreement and has an influence in shaping the content of all informational materials." [11] An Office Director: "I am interested in reading the insertions that Congressmen put in the back of the *Congressional Record*. It is a useful way for me to anticipate critical remarks that are made about our policies, and it helps me to prepare answers to these criticisms in my own mind." A desk officer: "At the start of these teach-ins, in March of 1965, we simply did not know what the dimensions were of this protest movement. In terms of our policy orientation and our public presentation, it was necessary to know the nature of the problem. But the theme turned out always to be the same. . . . [The National Teach-in] confirmed our view on both the size and the dimensions of the movement. . . . Throughout all this U.S. policy has not changed; only the manner of its presentation has changed."

The purpose of spontaneous manipulation is, as I noted above, to "create a position" in the media and thus to engage public groups in emerging policies and hopefully to enlist their support. The objective of reactive manipulation, on the other hand, is to soften or eliminate opposition and hopefully to mobilize or if necessary create a countervailing opinion — in order to minimize the constraints to which officials feel compelled to yield and to enlarge their freedom of maneuver.

Underlying both of these types of manipulation — indeed, sustaining the rounds of activities that are necessary in each case — are some widely held beliefs in their efficacy. In both sets of circumstances officials display immense optimism that candor on their part will move the public in the way they — the officials — want the public moved. But one question they never quite address themselves to is how much candor? Or candor about what? What do they mean by "adequate information"? In one sense, adequacy is defined only in retrospect: information is adequate if there is substantial support within the public for the policy in question. But officials do seem to have something specific in mind: the persuasiveness of the truth, *their* truth, the facts and the reasoning that move *them* — at least to the extent that they can talk to outsiders in these terms.[12]

Spontaneous manipulation responds to the general faith that if people are kept informed about policies as they are being developed, support for those policies (and for the men and institutions that are developing them) will be forthcoming. Public relations, in other words, will supposedly result in public approval of policies and in accretions of political strength to the men who are responsible for them. The International Cooperation Year provided for some officials a model of what could be accomplished by being relatively open with outsiders: "Everyone was healthier as a consequence of the ICY. If the Secretary of State or the Vice-President would get 500 of those people back here in the fall, before the election, and really level with them on Vietnam, on foreign aid, and so on, everyone would be better off." In a different area, a Deputy Assistant Secretary, referring to a sensitive policy issue: "This [concern] has been the primary subject in our dialogues with citizens groups, academic groups, the press, as we explain why it is necessary to do certain things to move to our long-term objectives in ——. If you can talk off-the-record with people, I am impressed with the results you can get." Another Deputy Assistant Secretary: "If the Administration is to sustain its policy, it needs to have the support of at least a majority of the American people. We have to present cogently and forcefully what the real reasons are for our involvement in Vietnam."

Reactive manipulation rests on the same general premises as spontaneous manipulation, but with one important practical difference: it is responding to opinion which is already engaged, and negatively so. In these circumstances public relations have more limited goals — defusing some of the opposition and perhaps building or simply mobilizing a counterweight to what remains. In the service of this more modest goal, public relations activities are also thought by many officials to be quite efficacious: "We always have to be explaining, and when we do, we get good responses." A Deputy Assistant Secretary reported, "When we decided early this month to put the whole series of arms arrangements in some kind of perspective, I was amazed at how the heat went down to zero [in the Congress and the press]. . . . With this simple rationale, the critical element in the pressure against the State Department disappeared." Another official related a problem with some unions that were proposing action against countries trading with North Vietnam. "We conferred with the union leaders in ——, telling them what the facts were, since what they had told the press was inaccurate. . . . When they understood the picture, which of course we gave to them on a confidential basis, we have not heard any more about it from them." On the matter of countervailing opinion, I want to keep clear the distinction between officials taking what advantage they can of offsetting opinions where they already exist and officials using public relations efforts to create or to organize a body of opinion that can then be used to balance off a corpus of opposed opinions. Officials report successful efforts of the latter kind as well. An Office Director: "When there is a newspaper campaign involving a —— policy question, sure this affects us. We have to ask, can we build a counter position? This is sometimes difficult to do, but it can be done." A senior Department official reported such a successful venture, on a small scale but involving an active and hostile interest group: "We opened everything to them. Over a six-month period we converted five men. They were sure the State Department would not level with them, and they were surprised at our candor."

INSTITUTIONAL PROMOTION

Manipulative efforts of both the spontaneous and reactive varieties are continuous, automatic, very much a reflex action for individuals in the policy-oriented, politically charged environment of the State Department. I have suggested above that most of these efforts are policy related, that officials are trying by these means to advance particular policies. A more accurate way of putting it would be to say that officials are trying to enlarge their capacities to advance particular policies. While much of this activity is in fact limited to specific policies, some of it extends more broadly to programs, some even more broadly to institutional capacities, and some to the standing of particular individuals, to their political power — to their capacity to influence decisions, programs, policies.

We need not tarry long over the specifically policy-related use of public relations, since a large part of our discussion up to this point was concerned with this. It may be enough to repeat that at every level, from President to desk officer, officials try by artful means to develop public attitudes that favor the policies *they* favor. Sorensen describes President Kennedy's role in masterminding the public relations campaign that was designed to secure, ultimately, the widest possible margin of support in the Senate for the Nuclear Test Ban Treaty.[13] And at the desk-officer level, another illustration is provided by the man who pointed to his desk and said, "Right here on the telephone I helped *The New York Times* editor write their editorial on the selection of ——— [as President] in ———." [14]

In a real sense it is very difficult to separate policy promotion from programmatic and institutional promotion; every time an official talks publicly on a policy question, he inescapably represents the State Department as well as the policy program or area with which he is identified. If he performs well or is substantively persuasive, he scores gains on all of these fronts. At the same time there are specialized efforts in the State Department to promote both programs and the foreign policy institutions themselves and thereby to improve their policy making capabilities. At the program level, for example, this description: "Our job is to see that the program does not become the stepchild in reporting. We try to get reporters to see real . . . programs at work. The programs are not perfect, but if we can show that ——— knows what he is doing, and if we can go from two lines of indirect reference to four paragraphs of direct comment on what we are doing, then the Congressmen are more disposed to tolerate our programs." And at the institutional level the Department manages a variety of activities that are aimed at improving the public image of the State Department and the Foreign Service. One program puts diplomats in residence on university campuses for an academic year, where they give courses, public lectures, and otherwise engage in the intellectual and social life on the campus and in the surrounding communities. Another program puts young scholars in residence in the State Department for an intensive week of briefing and observation in bureaus that correspond to their own areas of expertise. The Foreign Service has public members on its promotion panels. "One of our motives, very frankly, is to have people go back to their communities and talk about us. We have done a wonderful job of convincing people that we are serious, hard-working, dedicated."

PUBLIC RELATIONS AS PUBLIC OPINION

There remains one point, and to my mind a very important one, to be made about the attempts to shape public opinion and the consequences of those attempts for policy making. James N. Rosenau has argued that the task of consensus building "whenever . . . [officials] need domestic support for their endeavors abroad" is "herculean," for the reason that the public is not ordinarily or easily "activated by questions of foreign policy." [15] I think this overstates the problem, though I recognize that we are given no specific meanings or measures for "domestic support" or "herculean." Nevertheless, when efforts to attract widespread public support take on extraordinary proportions in a range that *does* entitle them to be called "herculean" — and I do not think that this does or even can happen very often, almost by definition — we have to ask whether those efforts do not themselves constitute a significant *direct* opinion input into the policy process. The mechanism involved here is a feedback loop, in the sense that foreign policy officials dominate the public discussion of a policy, which they (and Congressmen also) then monitor and on the basis of which they draw conclusions about their freedom to take next steps. The loop may not even go any further or deeper than the media of communication; the public relations activity results in press coverage, which is then interpreted as significant public opinion. Charles Frankel has put this very graphically, metaphorically borrowing the language used by the captain of the destroyer *Maddox* to express his doubts about what had really happened to him in the Gulf of Tonkin incident in August 1964: "I didn't know about these doubts of Commander Ogier's while I was Assistant Secretary of State. But looking back on my government service, I wonder how much of what government hears is really the sound of its own screws, reflecting off its own rudder and coming up through its own highly selective sonar." [16]

Frankel is talking about ordinary circumstances in the conduct of government and the perception of opinion. I am not disposed to quarrel with the kernel of his truth: the foreign policy establishment usually does take the lead in these matters, getting prominent coverage in the media, shaping the public discussion in terms of issues, problems, orientations, priorities, and so on. But in these ordinary circumstances the public relations efforts are ordinary, or routine, too. The issues are put forth in the way the Administration and the State Department understand them, certain strategic publics are cultivated, and for the rest it is reactive manipulation, yielding opinion initiatives to outsiders and responding to them when, as, and if it seems appropriate to "keep the record straight." One does hear one's own screws, but one hears other things too, and one is left, like Frankel, "wondering" what he is really hearing. In extraordinary circumstances, however, which is to say less frequently, the foreign policy establishment is moved to more extensive measures — to public relations efforts (spontaneous manipulation) on a scale that, with the cooperation of the press, effectively dominates the discussion in nongovernmental channels. In these unusual circumstances it seems to me that the screws do come through both more loudly and clearly, that foreign policy officials hear a "public opinion" that is more an echo of their own voices than their persuasive results. Several examples may serve to illuminate these points and to suggest how vulnerable officials are to their own signals, directly as well as indirectly.

When the Roosevelt Administration moved toward diplomatic recognition of the Soviet Union in 1933, it sought public allies for its position reversing fifteen years of nonrecognition. The Administration's most powerful motives for recognition were shaped by the international political situation, by the growing imbalance of power especially in the Far East. But officials were apparently reluctant to base their appeal for support on *realpolitik,* fearing that there would be little response to such an argument among nongovernmental groups. And so administration officials stressed the trade advantages: diplomatic relationships would stimulate trade between the two countries, which would give a boost to the economy which was then in the midst of the Great Depression. Believing that the public would respond favorably to this trade argument, the policy makers emphasized these economic consequences of recognition as the public basis of their approach to the Soviets. Not surprisingly, this was the argument subsequently given back to the Administration by what Browder calls "the great majority of the American people" as the justification for United States policy. These were, in other words, the responses of people who were substantially echoing the obvious cues they were receiving — giving not "interest" responses to the situation but "attentive public" responses to the argument. Officials were thus confirmed in their belief that the public would respond to the trade argument — and by implication would not respond to the foreign policy argument.[17]

In 1947 the Soviet Union was still a problem for American foreign policy officials, and they were still constrained by what they felt was the unresponsiveness of the American people to arguments of political or strategic interest. With Communist guerrillas sapping the strength of the postwar Greek government and with the British government financially unable any longer to sustain the burden of assisting the Greek government, the larger strategic question of future access by the Western powers to the eastern Mediterranean and the Suez Canal was suddenly put at the top of the American foreign policy agenda. To gain the support of the Congress for a program of military and economic aid to Greece and Turkey and to build a broader base of support for any future measures to forestall the encroachment of Soviet power, the Truman Administration enveloped the proposal in a broad doctrine that stressed the ideological menace, the threat of communism to democracy and to "free peoples" everywhere. Once they embarked on this line, foreign policy officials developed it as a central element in their rhetoric on the new American foreign policy of active international involvement. And — again not surprisingly — it immediately came back to them as "public opinion," as the external justification of the government's foreign policy.[18] Anti-communism, which began as the Administration's way of getting domestic allies for its policy of containing the power of the Soviet Union, soon became something of a policy itself, in response to the public response.

The Nuclear Test Ban Treaty of 1963 may also have been an event in which an Administration heard a public opinion which was really the echo of its own efforts. Believing that there was a large measure of resistance to the treaty in the Senate, and that the public, largely favorable, might not make itself "heard in time," President Kennedy himself helped to organize and direct a large effort at public mobilization. The interpretation in the President's circle was that the effort was objectively effective — that public opinion grew even more favorably disposed, leading to a secure margin of victory in the Senate.[19] A closer scrutiny of the event makes it rather clear, however, that "public opinion" in any form was not a significant part of the Senate's appraisal of the Treaty or of its vote on it. Schlesinger himself seems to limit any change in opinion to the public opinion polls.[20] To the extent that Senators relied on outsiders in reaching their final judgments, it was the position of the President himself and his bargaining efforts, and the testimony of the Secretary of Defense and the Joint Chiefs of Staff, which seem to have been most important.[21] In other words, if anyone heard anything "in time," it may well have been the Administration hearing its own substantial efforts at public persuasion and drawing the conclusion that there was a new public opinion environment that had made the crucial difference.

A FUNDAMENTAL POINT

Does it make any difference, finally, that these manipulative orientations are so deeply entrenched in the State Department? And if it does, *what* difference does it make? The fact that an overwhelming proportion of foreign policy officials accepts the desirability or necessity of shaping the public opinion environment along supportive lines is, I believe, of fundamental significance to this inquiry. Without equivocation it tells us that external opinion is a matter of continuing concern to officials, even though (as we have seen) it may not often be an important direct influence or constraint on policy. Quite clearly, individuals and groups outside the State Department are given some weight in the assessments of political forces that politicians everywhere — in the Congress, in the White House, in Cabinet and agency positions — make as they try to figure out what policies will "float" and what will not. What those assessments are — which is to say, *why* officials are concerned about external opinion and *what* they are concerned about — goes to the heart of the problem in this book; and to these questions let me now turn.

NOTES

1. Cf. Doris A. Graber: "Information from the case studies indicates that support, rather than advice, is the major concern of the decision makers and that support is sought more by finding ways to make accomplished decisions acceptable to the public than by adjusting the decisions to public tastes." *Public Opinion, the President, and Foreign Policy,* New York: Holt, Rinehart & Winston, 1968, p. 363.

2. See Roger Hilsman, *To Move a Nation,* Garden City: Doubleday, 1967.

3. Cf. Andrew Berding, a former Assistant Secretary of State for Public Affairs: "Many officers think they have taken public opinion fully into account in reaching decisions, but it is surprising how often they have overlooked vital points of presentation." *Foreign Affairs and You!* Garden City: Doubleday, 1962, p. 180.

4. Dean Acheson, *Present at the Creation,* New York: W. W. Norton, 1969, p. 377.

5. Berding, *Foreign Affairs and You!* p. 169.

6. Theodore C. Sorensen, *Kennedy,* New York: Harper & Row, 1965, p. 310.

7. See John E. Harr, *The Professional Diplomat,* Princeton: Princeton University Press, 1969, pp. 159–161.

8. See Joseph M. Jones, *The Fifteen Weeks,* New York: Viking, 1955, pp. 100, 137, 150, 168; and Dean Acheson, *Present at the Creation,* p. 220.

9. William Whitworth, "A Reporter at Large," *The New Yorker,* July 4, 1970, quotes Eugene V. Rostow, Under-Secretary of State for Political Affairs from 1966 to 1969: "Foy Kohler, who was one of my colleagues in Washington, used to say that the trouble with foreign-policy work is that you have to take the world as it is"(p. 34).

10. But they sometimes think that the President does make decisions on that basis: "[President Johnson] is putting the emphasis on health, education and agriculture — a sort of extension of the Great Society overseas. But I guess there is another reason for this, also. To sell the Congress — and to sell the public — on the idea of 72 separate aid programs individually tailored to the problems of the country, with pilot projects and so on, is extraordinarily difficult; it is not very sellable, the whole notion is too complex. On the other hand, health, education, and food have a universal appeal. And I should say that this is not just a sales problem; these are real problems also."

11. Cf. William O. Chittick: "Public correspondence is invaluable as a guide for planning information policy on foreign policies since this correspondence sometimes shows how the public has misinterpreted a political event or in what way its perspective is too narrow." *State Department, Press, and Pressure Groups,* New York: Wiley-Interscience, 1970, p. 165.

12. Cf. Berding: "The support of the American people for our foreign relations can be obtained only if they are kept adequately informed of our foreign policy thinking and developments. If they understand what our foreign policy makers have in mind, they are far more likely to give their approval." *Foreign Affairs and You!* p. 168.

13. Sorensen, *Kennedy,* p. 739.

14. See the articles by Max Frankel, "Alternative in Vietnam," *The New York Times,* April 25, 1966, and "Issue of China Policy," *The New York Times,* June 9, 1966, in which he writes of efforts by officials "to encourage outside pressure to reinforce their own counsel."

15. James N. Rosenau, "Foreign Policy as an Issue-Area," in James N. Rosenau, ed., *Domestic Sources of Foreign Policy,* New York: Free Press, 1967, p. 34.

16. Charles Frankel, *High on Foggy Bottom,* New York: Harper & Row, 1969, p. 93.

17. See Robert Browder, *The Origins of Soviet-American Diplomacy,* Princeton: Princeton University Press, 1953, p. 108.

18. See Jones, *The Fifteen Weeks,* p. 143; and Acheson, *Present at the Creation,* pp. 219–225.

19. See Sorensen, *Kennedy,* p. 739; and Arthur Schlesinger, Jr., *A Thousand Days,* New York: Fawcett, 1967, pp. 830–834.

20. Schlesinger, *A Thousand Days,* p. 834.

21. See Mary Milling Lepper, *Foreign Policy Formulation: A Case Study of the Nuclear Test Ban Treaty of 1963,* Columbus: Charles E. Merrill Publishing Co., 1971.

SIX   **Toward a Greater Responsiveness**

The preceding chapters have perhaps narrowed the generality that is so characteristic of the theoretical literature concerning public opinion and foreign policy.[1] We cannot yet formulate that "reliable general theory describing how public opinion influences foreign policy" whose absence Appleton regretted, but we have perhaps a clearer understanding of the different ways that opinions are perceived and absorbed by foreign policy officials and of their diverse and limited consequences for policy making.[2] It remains now for me to draw a broader set of conclusions dealing more explicitly with questions of democratic theory, including problems of responsibility, responsiveness, and change.

THE WEAKNESS OF ELECTORAL ACCOUNTABILITY

It is still an unresolved question just how "foreign policy" issues differ from all the other kinds or classes of issues of public policy that course through the American political system.[3] But no matter how one tries to differentiate foreign policy — whether by substantive concern, or by area of major impact, or by decision making channels — the effort to comprehend the political relationships between decision making on such issues, on the one hand, and domestic, nongovernmental opinions, on the other hand, raises the basic questions of all democratic politics. How do the people rule? How do their preferences get embodied in public policy? How do the governed control the governors?

The traditional answer, of course, is that democratic control of

184

rulers and policies is exercised ultimately and definitively at election time. If the people do not like the foreign policy decisions made by their government, they can hold the administration responsible at the next election, choosing a different set of leaders. And, presumably, the inescapable day of reckoning, the prospect of electoral accountability, induces a sensitivity to public preferences between elections whenever important decisions have to be made.[4] But reality, we are learning, does not conform very closely to this description out of normative democratic theory. Democratic control of foreign policy — indeed, of any particular area of public policy — by means of electoral accountability functions weakly when it even functions at all. Let us look at this a bit more closely; for if there is no great likelihood that political responsibility will be a major and reliable instrument of democratic control of foreign policy, we have to look elsewhere for some answers to our questions.

To begin with, what I have called the foreign policy establishment consists of one elected official and a large bureaucracy of appointed and career officials. Politically appointed officials are supposed to be the President's agents, the instruments of his control over the bureaucracy; but Neustadt has pointed out the ambiguities in these relations, particularly as they involve officials outside the White House itself, who have institutional responsibilities, resources, and obligations that flow from the bureaucracy as well as a charge that flows from the President.[5] Professionalism in foreign policy, in the form chiefly of the Civil Service and the Foreign Service, further removes the bureaucracy from the President's reach. The development of a foreign policy bureaucracy in the White House in recent years is itself evidence of the intractability of the State Department bureaucracy, from the President's perspective.[6] And these career officials are of course immune to any direct electoral sanction. The era of Senator Joseph R. McCarthy demonstrates that career officials are not beyond the reach of politics, but it turns out to be caution, more than direction, that politics contributes. And the one elected official, the President, seems to share with elected officials all the way down the constitutional ladder a very attenuated electoral accountability for his decisions and for those taken in his name, whether by his administrative agents or by his own White House staff.

As Kenneth Prewitt points out, even at the city council level of American government (where electoral accountability might be expected to be concentrated because constituencies are small and reasonably homogeneous and policy areas are limited in scope) legislators find it easy to ignore public preferences. "Men enter and leave office not at the whim of the electorate, but according to self-defined schedules." [7] Adding foreign policy to the policy areas being acted upon seems to make little difference. At the Congressional level, Miller and Stokes found that among winners as well as losers, incumbents as well as challengers, there was a sizeable gap between public preferences and legislative behavior in the foreign policy area in particular.[8] And at the Presidential level, the evidence is growing that popular dissatisfaction with the direction of foreign policy (as distinct from lack of confidence in the management of those policies) is responsible for only a very small net amount of the Presidential vote. Apparently the President, like a city councilman, finds it very easy most of the time to ignore public preferences when he cannot otherwise mobilize or neutralize them.[9] The possibility that, in Milton Rosenberg's words, "important publics [will] be brought to dangerous levels of mobilized indignation [by White House-level foreign policy decisions], to levels that threaten electoral losses and legislative or financial abandonments," is very slim indeed, so slim that we cannot seriously treat it as an operative sanction.[10] Very few foreign policy questions pose *these* risks, though they may well pose others. Most of the time, as any politician, public official, or pollster can testify, the real problem is finding more than a handful of people who even know what the issues are — much less what they are *about*. And the history of the war in Indo-China makes it clear that even in those rare cases where decisions do lead to very high levels of "mobilized indignation," those levels of indignation have uncertain power to constrain the policies of a President who has a strong sense of national interest and obligation. Such decisions do not pose a clear risk of "electoral losses and legislative or financial abandonments"; rather, as I point out below, they may undermine public confidence in the political system itself, but that is much harder for a President to measure, to evaluate, and to react to. One President may conclude that he should not stand for reelection at such a price to the political system, whereas another may conclude that firmness and discipline will sustain the system while the policy is worked out.

RESPONSIVENESS AS AN ALTERNATIVE
TO RESPONSIBILITY

If political responsibility of the formal, classic sort has little bearing on the direction of foreign policy — if, in other words, the ultimate electoral sanction is not really a sanction at all — where else do we look for some answers to our questions about the relations between governors and governed? *Responsibility* as electoral accountability is for all practical purposes neutralized or supplanted by a much more subjective and less easily recognized phenomenon, *responsiveness* on the part of officials to expressions of public preference. Responsiveness is not an instrument of democratic *control;* rather, it refers to the conditions and the mechanisms whereby public preferences may get considered and possibly embodied in public policy. Francis E. Rourke's definition of responsiveness for a bureaucratic political system — "the extent to which it promotes a correspondence between the decisions of bureaucrats and the preferences of the community or the office holders who presume to speak for the public" — will serve our purposes here.[11] It is broad enough to include the adaptation of officials to public preferences and the modification of public preferences through the efforts of officials. This definition has a long way to go before it is operational, but it does make clear the dimensions of the phenomenon with which we are concerned. Since responsibility is so hard to establish and so easy to evade, even modest efforts on the part of officials to be "responsive" to public preferences — or even simply to *appear* to be responsive by a willingness to meet, talk and argue, if not yield — may be sufficient in practice to meet the pressures of those few who care. Prewitt argues that the likelihood of responsiveness is increased by the *presence* of conditions that establish accountability.[12] I am arguing, however, that responsiveness is a practical if not very effective substitute for electoral accountability and that the likelihood of responsiveness may even be increased by the *absence* of accountability, by the intuitive understanding of officials that there simply is no other way short of violent upset in which public preferences can be brought into the foreign policy arena.

"Taking public opinion into account," in all its elusive and discouraging meanings, is the operational alternative to, not the forerunner or the consequence of, being "held to account" by that same public.

Officials support this view in the way they define their own obligations in foreign policy making. Officials at all levels except the very top generally reject any formal obligation to consider public opinion as part of the definition of their role or job; and officials at the very top periodically remind their subordinates that that is the way it should be. An Office Director put it as follows: "Our thoughts about the best courses of action have to be adjusted to public opinion only at the political level — that is, on Capitol Hill and in the White House. The leadership in the State Department prefers it that way. They don't want our recommendations based on what I think public opinion will accept but rather on what will advance our interests in our area." A Deputy Assistant Secretary: "Consideration of public policy ought to be free of politics at our level, and we should let the top people decide what to do about public support. If the guy on the desk cuts a couple of inches off the cloth, and then we take another few inches off of it here, it is an unseemly garment by the time it arrives at the Seventh Floor — the Secretary's Office." And at the Assistant Secretary level an official complained that talk about public opinion and politics "drains out the professionalism in our work here." President Truman's famous reprimand to Under Secretary of State James Webb during the first Blair House Conference considering the United States response to the start of the Korean War, that he and he alone would handle the domestic political implications of the situation, is a still-living and often-repeated injunction in the Department.[13] And one of Secretary of State Dean Rusk's assistants reported: "The Secretary's instructions to us are that we should reason out what is best for the United States, and not to think about whether it is popular or unpopular, feasible or infeasible, and so on. . . . That is certainly his intention. Let someone else worry about whether it is publicly feasible. And this in turn is what the President expects of the Secretary."

But while officials routinely deny any *obligation* to pay attention to public opinion, in practice they admit — sometimes readily, sometimes reluctantly — to responsive *behavior*, of the kinds we have seen in earlier chapters. And though this behavior is uneven and underwhelming, it is found even among those officials who reject any formal job-responsibility for it: "It doesn't mean we are impervious to public opinion." A tender concern for Congressional opinion is particularly widespread in the Department; in the words of an Office Director, "President Johnson . . . is very sensitive to Congressional opinion (rather than public opinion as such), and I think he would be unhappy with his public servants if they did not reflect the same sensitivity." It seems more likely, however, that the President and/or the Secretary of State are, at the least, ambivalent about the exercise of political sensitivity at lower levels and that their periodic instructions to their subordinates to avoid questions of popularity and feasibility are reactions to what they consider *excessive* responsiveness on the part of Department officials to external opinion — particularly external opinions of a kind that they themselves do not wish to pay much attention to.[14]

Indeed, the injunctions from above not to take on the responsibility for public opinion are simultaneously injunctions not even to be responsive to it at all. Chittick notes that Secretary of State Rusk "made it clear to his subordinates early in his administration of the Department that he did not want them to take domestic political views into account in making decisions at their level."[15] Nonresponsibility for public opinion may be a noble sentiment for professional subject-matter specialists, but nonresponsiveness to it is unrealistic for most of them, especially since they are *supposed* to be — from their job standpoint — politically sensitive, "hard-nosed," practical realists! The conditions of work, including their many public contacts — some of them even arranged at the very direction of the Department — make such isolation impossible to begin with. In other words, circumstances conducive to responsiveness are very nearly built into the situation. And simple experience shows them that when things go wrong, when the hornets get stirred up, they are the ones who pay a large part of the price of inconvenience and discomfiture.

Events in 1970 illustrate the way the Department creates an environment in which "responsiveness" is permitted, without establishing it as a responsibility of the Department or even cultivating it as an important pastime. In January of that year, the Deputy Under Secretary for Administration, William B. Macomber, Jr., made a major statement on the Department's need for a new "management strategy," a "reform from within" that would enlarge the Department's leadership capacity in the foreign affairs field.[16] In that extended speech there were two short paragraphs on the subject of "outside contacts." Two weeks later the Department announced that 13 Task Forces had been established for purposes of internal study and planning for the implementation of Macomber's program, one of them (Task Force IX) dealing with "Openness." [17] In December 1970 the task force reports were published, in a massive document entitled *Diplomacy for the '70's: A Program for Management Reform in the Department of State*.[18] The report of Task Force IX makes a strong argument for a Department that is more "open" and "responsive" to others, in the government and outside it, than is currently the case.[19] "Openness," however, is defined as "essentially a state of mind" — a perspective which minimizes the need to treat it significantly as a matter of organizational structure and practice — and the intra-governmental aspects of the problem are given somewhat more emphasis than the Department's relations with the "outside." [20] Moreover, a distinction is drawn between the wish of recent Presidents "to take full responsibility for domestic reactions to political decisions" and the Departmental concern for "close contact with American public opinion." [21] The recommendations of the Task Force in the area of "Relations With the Public and the Foreign Affairs Community outside the Department of State" reduce essentially to: (1) "a more responsive speaking engagement program" for Department officers; (2) a more responsive handling of public correspondence — a recommendation which is clouded by an inconsistent concern both with the excessive use of standardized replies and with the insufficiency of automation in the handling of the correspondence; and (3) an expansion of exchanges between Departmental personnel and Congressmen, academics, youth, and businessmen.[22] The Task Force also recommended, more generally (and ambiguously), for each Assistant Secretary a deputy who would be responsible not only for "openness" but also for "public affairs" (presumably in their current meaning) and "congressional input." [23]

This is probably the most extensive plea for a more permeable diplomatic establishment that has ever come out of the State Department. Nevertheless, it would be difficult to conclude from all of this that major changes in the relations between the Department and the public or the Congress had been made or were even in the offing. In particular, it should be noted that many of the relations with outsiders which the Department wishes to extend are with organizations or classes of people who are more likely to be supportive, or at least sympathetic, than hostile to United States foreign policy.[24] But any Foreign Service Officer or State Department official could find in it, if he wished, a warrant for a moderate degree of personal contact with and responsiveness to external publics.

To the extent that the President expects his subordinates, including his Secretary of State, to "lean against the wind," to be not especially responsive — an expectation reinforced by the modern practice of not appointing politically significant figures to the post of Secretary — a greater burden of responsiveness to external opinion comes to rest on the President himself. The situation at his level is the reverse of that I just described for the lower, "working" level: there, officials disclaim any formal obligation or responsibility to external opinion, while they are in fact somewhat responsive to it in very specific, ad hoc terms. The President, on the other hand, willingly accepts the formal obligation and responsibility he denies to others (rather meaningless since he knows he is unlikely really to be "held to account"), but he can actually *be* responsive to external opinion only in the most abstract, general way. For one thing, he is directly exposed to so little of it; the very nature of his office and his position have led an astute journalist to conclude that an American President, "once in the White House, may be in worse position to judge public sentiment than most of his fellow citizens. And the worst of it is that he may never realize it." [25] And for another, he is usually too deeply involved in particular policies. That involvement develops partly as a result of the way he has chosen to present issues in public debate.[26] And partly it develops through the normal pressures of his bureaucracy, through what Charles Frankel called "a kind of rolling commitment to policy." [27] Because of this deep involvement in policy, the President cannot be very open to opinions of a different stripe or even spend enough time on them to *seem* willing to give them a fair hearing.

What we have, then, in our foreign policy process is a slight amount of responsiveness, in the form mostly of individual exposures to public preferences and of some occasional linking of these preferences to policy (leading to reinforcement as well as to adaptation). This sort of responsiveness is the stepchild of a political system and an institutional culture that give it only minimal encouragement or support at the working levels, where it is feasible, and political sanction at the top levels, where it can scarcely be exercised save in the most general ways. The difficult question, of course, is how much is enough? Or how much is desirable? What kinds and degrees of responsiveness, and at what levels, are sufficient to take the place of an impaired electoral accountability and to sustain "consent" to American foreign policy among its followers?

Merely to ask these questions is to signal the practical impossibility of answering them objectively or to everyone's satisfaction. For it is by no means universally agreed that we should *want* to improve on the present situation. There is substantial resonance outside the foreign policy establishment for the view that is general within it — that policy must be insulated from the vagaries of public opinion, that government cannot deal intelligently, imaginatively, forcefully, or consistently with its foreign relations if it has to read the cue-cards held up periodically by outside publics.[28] This view has some support, I find, even among young critics of our Vietnam policy when they can be persuaded to consider opinions other than their own and issues other than Vietnam. But there are few, it is fair to say, who think that that insulation should be complete. Even those who believe in substantial foreign policy autonomy have points at which their concern for the integrity of policy is matched by their concern for the integrity of the political system itself when large and especially active portions of the foreign policy public do not consent to a major policy and find little or no recognition of that fact among foreign policy officials. Such things do not happen very often, certainly no oftener than once a generation, but when they do, as in our own day, they reverberate throughout the political system. One may believe that "the power to govern depends on widespread acceptance and implementation of the idea that citizens ought to cooperate and acquiesce in public policies" and *still* believe that government is not without some responsibility for presenting to its citizens policies in which large majorities can be persuaded to acquiesce.[29] Responsiveness is thus, paradoxically, a condition of autonomy in foreign policy making;

and its possible improvement — without going so far as to say "How much is enough?" — is a matter worthy of our reflection. But I will restrict my observations to the problem of responsiveness at the Department level, where my attention has been focused up till now, and forego as much as I can the temptation to speculate about responsiveness in the White House — except, of course, where the two are closely related.

IMPEDIMENTS TO RESPONSIVENESS

If we want to consider whether it is possible or feasible to improve the responsiveness of State Department officials to public preferences, and in what ways or by what means, we have to start by looking explicitly at the sludge that clogs these veins in the body politic. I will look at this first from the point of view of its contents — i.e., the character and the organization of opinion itself — and second from the point of view of its treatment — the Departmental mechanisms, formal and informal, that process it.

Foreign policy opinion, to begin with, is so ambiguous and obscure by the time it enters the State Department processing plant that there is very little of a sharp or clear-cut character to which Department officials *can* respond.[30] This circumstance is not widely appreciated. There is a misleading notion abroad in the land that public opinion on foreign policy has an unmistakable clarity about it — that despite all of the problems connected with it, it nonetheless addresses itself reasonably unambiguously to specific policy matters. The public opinion polls are responsible for much of this belief, in that they generally produce artifactual majorities that support or oppose issues. In so doing, the polls reinforce the community of political activists, people who feel very strongly about issues and who cannot believe, despite compelling evidence to the point, that most people are not similarly moved by political questions.[31] In the foreign policy field in particular, the conception of a clearly delineated public opinion is strong; party divisions are less sharp in foreign policy, and poll majorities have for a long period been rather clear-cut on the broad axis of international participation. Thus one hears holistic characterizations of public opinion on foreign policy matters that one does not hear on domestic policy matters: public opinion is customarily described as being "ahead of" or "behind" the positions taken by the President or the Congress on foreign policy questions — a characterization that implies not only unity and location but also (and deterministically) direction of movement.[32]

But the fact remains that public opinion very rarely comes at foreign policy officials unambiguously or uniformly, as "public pressure"; it comes rather in small bits and pieces, on all sides of issues, on no side of them, even on nonissues; and serious, substantive, policy-related responsiveness to such a mixed and contradictory bag is often beyond the reach of mortal man. The Vietnam War, I must say once again, is not typical; indeed, it gives every evidence of misleading us not only in the presumed lessons it bears with respect to the impact of public opinion on foreign policy but also in the sense in which it is used as the surrogate for all foreign policy, the master example. War is not like other foreign policy issues; the price it asks even of the uninterested and uninformed is very high, and it usually lasts long enough for attitudes to be reshaped and specific opinions to be formulated and organized. *Even so*, even after a half-dozen years of active military involvement in the Vietnam War and a mobilization of public opinion unprecedented in this generation, opinions were still disparate both in their manifest content and in their policy implications. Officials could still find, in the dispersion of opinion coming their way, an important body of "support" for many different positions with respect to the conflict in Indo-China.[33] On other — more common, more typical — issues, the ambiguity and uncertainty of opinion are among its most salient characteristics. Its levels are low, by any conceivable measure; and the public contacts of policy officials, limited as they are to begin with, are concerned much of the time with general foreign policy subjects and with general attitudes toward them rather than with specific opinions on specific policy matters that are up for decision. These may be politically relevant opinions, in V. O. Key's sense, but they do not offer easy or convenient handles for politically relevant responses.[34]

This lack of clarity and focus in the content of foreign policy opinions often leaves little to which foreign policy officials *can* reasonably respond. Beyond that, the attenuated form in which opinion is aggregated and "represented" does not do very much to foster the nascent sense among officials that they *ought* to be responding to it. Some years ago Paul Lazarsfeld and Elihu Katz, describing the flow of communication on public questions within the body politic, formulated the "two-step flow" hypothesis; this postulated a stratum of highly involved, politically committed and informed individuals who exposed themselves to a great deal of information about government and policy in the mass media and who then, a bit like Typhoid Mary, passed it on in appropriate form to others in face-to-face encounters.[35] James N. Rosenau has correctly suggested that the process may in fact be even more complex than this — that it is a three- or a four-step flow.[36] In either case, the image here is roughly that of a slightly flat-topped pyramid, with policy communications spreading wider and wider as they get farther away from their original sources in the government and their public sources in the media. The flow of opinion on foreign policy into government may be likened to this two- (or three- or four-) step process in reverse. I do not mean to suggest that this is an organized or well developed or even conscious process of opinion aggregation and representation, any more than the flow downward is well structured; nor do I mean that it all funnels back through the media alone. Rather, there is a progressive narrowing and shortening of the political range of foreign policy opinions as they enter the necessarily restricted ambit of government officials, so that in the end, as we saw in Chapter 3, these officials draw their intuitive impressions of external opinion from relatively few sources that are close at hand. Much of the opinion that reaches officials is a long way from any identifiable base in the opinions of the larger minority that is attentive to foreign policy in this country. Organizational bureaucracies take stands, in lieu of their members; a few Congressmen summarize the way they interpret their few constituents' messages, without notable accuracy; newspapers amplify a few opinions and lend their weight to even fewer; a handful of individuals who have access to foreign policy officials give expression to views developed after varied exposures to public and specialist debate.[37] From the official's point of view, this is the bulk of "public opinion." Except for those infrequent occasions when the President or the Secretary of State can summon up a flood of public messages that temporarily overwhelms this small group, it is what he has to work with most of the time. But he recognizes it for what it is — a not particularly representative, and certainly not a deliberately representative, aggregation of opinions, a not necessarily reliable expression even of a more general or pervasive "public mood." [38] So tenuous, in fact, is the representative quality of these few voices of outside opinion that they may more accurately be said to be participating in the foreign policy debate not as agents at all but as principals, in some cases even as principals who are trying to establish a public following.[39] As principals, however, they have uncertain standing — and thus uncertain footing — in any adversary encounter with officials who are legally empowered and practically furnished to formulate and conduct foreign policy and who are usually fully preoccupied with that very task. This weak position characterizes not only private persons or institutions in this foreign policy public but members of Congress as well, many of whom hold hearings and mutter and still concede primacy to foreign policy officials in the Executive branch.[40] In these circumstances the official has substantial freedom to listen most attentively to the most congenial (i.e., the most supportive) voices within this external public — that is, to be "responsive" to those who are "on his side." And when it is inconvenient or impolitic for him even to hear other views, much less respond to them, he has no trouble either tuning them out or justifying his doing so: for the obligation to use his best policy judgment is accepted as superior to any injunction to be responsive.

The failure of external opinion to impress itself unequivocally upon State Department officials is due in large part, as I said above, to its own equivocal character; but a small part of that failure resides in the weakness of formal Departmental mechanisms to scan for and process such opinion. And beyond this, there are also informal mechanisms or processes for the treatment of opinion which — insofar as I understand them correctly — seem to attenuate it even further and thus to limit still further the possibilities of responsive behavior.

We saw in Chapter 2 that the Department has virtually abandoned the task of trying in any centralized, institutional fashion to learn anything systematic about external opinion. The reasons for that abandonment, as I pointed out there, have to do with the essential meaninglessness of the opinion information that was being provided the Department by its Office of Public Opinion Studies and with the absence of any conviction that it was possible to do better. The consequence of that abandonment is not only that each official in the Department has to rely mainly on his own individual resources for the gathering and interpretation of opinion information; in addition, it means that the Department collectively plays a predominantly passive role in the whole public opinion process, depending on external initiatives for most of its public opinion information and contacts.[41] The Department thus connives at its haphazard and unrepresentative exposure to public opinion, which then becomes a basis for an indifferent responsiveness to it.[42] Whether the Department can in fact do better than it has done in the past by way of the institutional collection and analysis of information concerning public opinion is a question I will take up later in this chapter. But to put it in better perspective, we need also to look more closely at the informal mechanisms of intuition that have been the inescapable alternative devices for opinion processing for Department officials, as they fall back on their own resources.

In the absence of any other significant possibilities, these intuitive mechanisms or processes, operating in the recesses of the minds of officials, must play an extraordinarily important part in the way these officials go about organizing their reactions to public opinion. I say "must play an important part" rather than "do play" because, though I am convinced both by logic and by evidence that "the recesses of the mind" are the locus of officials' assessment of foreign policy opinion, we obviously know very little about what goes on there. When the collection, analysis, and evaluation of opinion move from the realm of the predominantly explicit and systematic to the predominantly implicit and intuitive, our knowledge about them becomes correspondingly uncertain. Two common interpretations of the way intuitive processes impinge upon policy revolve around the notions of "anticipation" and "internalization." The common result, unhappily, is to put these mechanisms of assessment, evaluation, and political conversion of opinion somewhat beyond our reach. But I shall try to deal with them anyway, keeping constantly in mind their nebulous character. Assuming we *can* specify what we are talking about, what are the implications of these mechanisms so far as responsiveness is concerned?

The classic statement of "anticipated reaction" as a crucial mechanism by which political opinions are transformed into political influence is that of C. J. Friedrich.[43] Although we are dealing here not with elected officials, as he was, but with appointive and career officials with varying sensitivities to electoral considerations, the phenomenon is psychologically the same: officials, anxious to reduce their uncertainties and to maintain a comfortable working level of "public support," are said to anticipate in their foreign policy formulations the preferences and reactions of politically relevant outsiders.[44] Glenn Paige interprets the key decisions at the start of the Korean War in this way: "[President Truman's] anticipation of what would be popularly acceptable rather than any organized expression of popular will seems to have been crucial. . . . The same pattern of experience-based anticipation of internal setting responses rather than the existence of direct lines of influence is illustrated by the recollection of Secretary Acheson that prior to the air-sea decision on Monday, he 'needed no special notification that certain Republican Senators were constantly critical.' " [45] Similarly, Selig Adler writes that by 1923 "the isolationist coalition . . . had become a genuine groundswell of public opinion, formidable enough to give pause to even intrepid and far-sighted makers of foreign policy." [46] The pride that many State Department officials take in their own and their colleagues' political sensitivity, which I discussed in an earlier chapter, is another expression of the Department's presumed responsiveness to public opinion by anticipating its reactions.

One cannot really quarrel with the *existence* of "anticipated reaction" or with its obvious importance for the decisions of foreign policy officials. If "learning" means anything at all, it means that as human beings we reduce the universe of possibilities to an ordered set of probabilities as a result of experience and instruction. And we then proceed, in the affairs of state as in other human affairs, with a set of expectations about the way others will respond to our actions or initiatives. This much, at least, is not really in doubt. But the exact nature and identity of the reactions that are being anticipated, and thus the character of the implicit responsiveness to public opinion, are uncertain. To repeat my prior point, a great deal of this is simply inaccessible to realistic research design; the kind of inquiry that is necessary asks too much — practically, politically, and psychologically — of officials. What is accessible, however, suggests very strongly that the preferences and reactions which officials anticipate in their ordinary policy rounds, to the extent that they are even at the conscious level, are much more those of *insiders* than of outsiders, those whose hands cannot be kept off the clay that is being molded. In any event these anticipations, vague and usually implicit to begin with, are all mixed together in varying judgments about who and what are in fact "politically relevant." Only in the most general, definitional (or normative) way can one say that officials are thus being responsive to public opinion; in truth, the connections between unknown opinions thus anticipated and specific Department behaviors are so obscured that it hardly seems appropriate even to consider them in the context of responsiveness.

The situation is hardly better with respect to "internalization." The anticipation of reactions is at least a quasi-conscious process of matching expected reactions to alternative possibilities, even if the expected reactions themselves are not wholly explicit or consciously formulated. But "internalization" — the sharing by officials in policy attitudes or preferences that are so widely held and deeply felt that they may be said to permeate the culture — is by definition a less-than-conscious phenomenon: officials are said to reflect public opinion on foreign policy matters because as members of the society they have been subject to the same social and cultural factors that shape public opinion. "Political leaders incorporate the views of the public into their decisions because they themselves are members of the public." [47] The common notion of "the climate of opinion" is sometimes couched in this language of "internalization." [48] At other times the "climate" is used in the opposite sense of an externally sited constraint. [49] Responsiveness is as abstract and remote a notion in this context as it is in the case of "anticipated reaction." For internalization as a conversion mechanism is essentially mystical; it assumes a spiritual or sociocultural identity of all relevant (though unspecified) opinions and excludes the possibility of significant political differentiation. And if we want to take the mechanism apart to see *how* it works — whose views, on what aspects of foreign policy, are in fact incorporated, and by what channels — we find we cannot do it, for internalization as a psychological process is even less accessible to practical research than is anticipation. [50]

In sum, then, responsiveness further eludes us in situations where largely unexpressed opinion is said to be impressionistically registered and intuitively evaluated by psychological processes that are obscure to us. We have been content to assume that there is a meaningful or at least tangible political responsiveness in these mechanisms, and we have invented attractive concepts and language to explain the processes involved. But the truth is, we do not know! And careful, logical inquiry suggests even that "responsiveness" may be an inappropriate concept to describe whatever it is that happens in this "black box" that sits between unarticulated external opinions and governmental decision making on foreign policy. What looks like a convergence of preferences taking place there may have less to do with the insights or intuitions of officials than with the indifference of the public or its ordinary practice of taking cues from governmental stimuli. Indeed, the mechanisms — and in part the motivations — of both "anticipated reaction" and "internalization" are so imprecise and general that they may be applied, with little change, in order to explain how totalitarian regimes stay in power.[51]

These impediments to observable, measurable responsiveness are impressive; and yet they do not come anywhere near to constituting a full catalogue of the things that clutter up the channels between officials and outside publics. In particular, I have omitted any discussion of the institutional pressures and of the international policy commitments that generally constitute higher orders of obligation for foreign policy officials, taking precedence over the (dimly) perceived preferences of people on the "outside." [52]

But even this sketchy review of the obstacles yields considerable insight into the problem and suggests some lines of effort that might — just might — increase the opportunities and occasions for officials to respond more directly and even positively to patterns of public preferences on foreign policy questions. As we go on to discuss that, bear in mind that responsiveness does not mean simply doing the bidding of external groups; that, in a practical sense, is precluded most of the time. It means, rather, addressing themselves to the general concerns as well as the specific preferences of interested and attentive publics, to understand better what those concerns and preferences are, what convergences are possible, and how they might be obtained and at what cost.

INCR... ̄ ... POLITICAL VALUE
OF OP...

The core of [the problem of improving] responsiveness lies in *enlarging the util*[ity of outside opinion] for foreign policy officials. More specifically [increasing the value of] outside opinion as a preferential inp[ut into the decision making] process means improving its compe[titive standing against the] ny other considerations of bureaucrat[ic, material and inter-party] al politics that go into the formulation [of foreign policy]. But if [we] wish to magnify its utility, to increase it[s value, we have to start] with a realistic understanding of its pres[ent status, its present] value. Why, in brief, is external opinion im[portant to foreign policy] officials at all? Why do they respond t[o it as much (and as] little) as they do, and in the ways — substantial[, instrumental] and manipulative — that they do?

The answ[er to this] question is surprisingly obvious, though it is not easy to f[ix] in a simple sentence. It lies in the ordinary procedures of bureaucratic life, in the peculiar mixture of politics and administration that defines the opportunities that are open to an official to get something accomplished. The impulses of electoral ambition do not apply here; but that does not mean that men are without ambition here.[53] On the contrary, the force that moves the typical official is a *personal* ambition to *do* something that seems important to him and to do it well. To repeat a point I made earlier in this book, the official is not a "mindless bureaucrat" but a knowledgeable person with some convictions about the value and appropriateness of particular courses of action.[54] To accomplish his purposes, to prevail in a setting in which other officials may have equally strong convictions of a different stripe, he needs that elusive, undefinable variable, "support." In practice, "support" means two different things. First, it means the explicit agreement of individuals and groups, inside and outside the government, who are regarded as knowledgeable and "important" on the question by the various contenders — "important" in the sense that their views are disproportionately persuasive. Anyone who has ever participated, however remotely, in a decision making process of a substantially consensual variety will recognize the special weight accorded to the positions of a few people, a personal power that is based on such things as substantive knowledge and past experience with respect to the issue, reputation for fairness and for sound judgment, expressive capacity, as well as formal institutional authority. When these people align themselves with a particular proposal, apparent majorities coalesce, decisions acquire legitimacy, and officials can proceed in the expectation that others will take subsequent actions necessary to carry them out. Second, support means the absence of explicit disagreement of other individuals and groups, inside and outside the government, who are also regarded as knowledgeable and important by the contenders. When those who might be expected, by virtue of their known interests and their past behavior, to take a position against a proposal *fail* to do so, their silence is taken for consent, or at least as a tacit statement that they will not obstruct the execution of the decision.[55] "Support," then, is a variable mixture of the active agreement and cooperation of some people and the passive acquiescence of others; and where the mix is very different from this, where apparent majorities do not coalesce, where officials have no confidence that decisions will be met by affirmative "follow-up" action, they talk of "lack of support."

There is, of course, a very large subjective component in this process, since votes are rarely taken. Hence my use of the phrase "apparent majorities." Officials are obliged to make the best guesses they can concerning the alignment of relevant "others" and the resulting legitimacy and viability of proposed courses of action. Some things, to be sure, can be undertaken at almost any level in the absence of great attention to or conviction about majorities; experience *is* a reasonably good guide with respect to those matters which are, by virtue of the lack of sustained interest anywhere else, effectively within the discretionary power of officials. And at the higher levels some things can be done without lining up support in advance, because the persuasiveness of the President or the Secretary of State can be mobilized, in the event of untoward difficulty, to help sustain the decision. But for nonroutine problems at almost all levels and especially at the working level, rather more of consequence hangs on the capacity of officials to make correct guesses about the "alignment of forces," to use the Soviet expression. Officials, as I noted earlier, are motivated by the desire to see something develop, to make it happen with an economy of effort, to appear knowledgeable and competent and effective and not stupid or foolish. To the extent that external opinions — widely defined

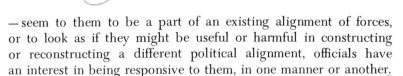

— seem to them to be a part of an existing alignment of forces, or to look as if they might be useful or harmful in constructing or reconstructing a different political alignment, officials have an interest in being responsive to them, in one manner or another.

How well do present practices in the assessment of opinion serve these purposes to which opinion is put? And what might be done differently to enlarge its usefulness to officials and thus their incentive to be responsive? To take the evaluative question first: on the face of it, one is tempted to say that officials are reasonably satisfied with what they "know" about outside opinion, and they make little effort to improve on that knowledge. Scattered, almost accidental, exposures to such opinion, and intuitions about its larger structure and significance, give them more information than they can in fact use, granted the primacy of other considerations in the formulation of foreign policy decisions. But to say that is simply to restate the problem, and in the process to suggest a quite different answer: external opinion has such a subordinate place in decision making, and needs for it are so easily and impressionistically met, precisely *because* so much of it is so useless so much of the time — because it is not readily convertible into political currency, because it has no major "clout," because it makes, or seems to make, little difference in any political alignment. At the risk of overstating the matter by treating opinion collectively, it does not address itself very precisely to the problems that are up for decision, it does not speak out knowledgeably and persuasively at points in time when matters are still fluid, and it brings to bear few sanctions or penalties of a political, bureaucratic or personal kind when it is ignored. Small wonder, then, that officials can comfortably disband their efforts to find out what people may be thinking, rely on their casual contacts and their intuitions and on convenient surrogates in the press and in the Congress, and be manipulative and instrumental in their approach to particular groups and to the public in general.

Is there any way to modify this situation? What might be done differently? There is quite clearly little point in urging officials to mend their ways, to pay more attention to external opinion. That merely encourages a patronizing attitude on their part and prompts them to construct more elaborate ways to try to shape that opinion into supportive postures — varieties of responsiveness that are sufficiently well developed as things are now. And there is little point in devising more elaborate mechanisms, in or out of government, for uncovering more and more information about the state of public opinion of the kind that is currently available; that merely makes the pile of useless information even higher. What we are looking for, rather, are ways to increase the political weight of those elements in public opinion that have some potentiality of participating in a policy (as distinct from simply a public) debate. This means, above all else, encouraging a deeper commitment to such participation on the part of those foreign policy "attentives" who have or who can acquire political resources — knowledge and information, experience and sound judgment, leadership, access to the media of mass communication, access to legislative power. In terms of the kinds of public sources I referred to earlier in this book, this means most particularly "notables," academic and other subject-matter specialists, either singly as individuals or in formal or informal advisory groups, and even interest groups, including those collectively referred to as the "peace movement." [56] It means a more assiduous cultivation of foreign policy problems, at an early stage in their development, by the media of communication, so that these participants would have better information resources at earlier phases in the policy making process. It means a more active exercise by members of Congress of their constitutional powers and political interests in foreign affairs — also at the formative stages of foreign policy. This is especially important because the Congress starts off with more than ordinary capabilities as a form of public opinion. It means, further, that some thought be given to the problem of how to improve the focus or the clarity of external opinions of a more general kind, so that their political relevance is better understood by foreign policy officials. One way that this might be accomplished, for example, would be through survey research teams whose mission would be to explore the cognitive and affective dimensions of opinion on diverse policy alternatives, rather than merely the distribution of opinion on the officially favored policy or some variants of it. The so-called "Stanford Poll" which performed this function with respect to Vietnam War alternatives in the spring of 1966 is a good example of the possibilities here, though they need not be limited to national samples.[57] A Congress that is concerned about the responsiveness of the Executive branch to public preferences in the foreign policy field may well reconsider its opposition to the use of public funds for opinion polling of this kind, under conditions of direction or control that keep it independent of Executive branch interests and perspectives.[58]

No foreign policy establishment, of course, could possibly incorporate all such public views, once these have been clarified and communicated more effectively.[59] But neither can it possibly incorporate all the views on any subject that are expressed *within* the establishment. To give something to everybody is, in the end, to give them nothing. What matters, rather, is that a wide range of relevant views and preferences both inside and outside the government get a reliable chance to be heard and to be seriously assessed before important commitments are made. This is what we mean by responsiveness — not simply that one's views get accepted in the final choices. One can devise mechanical ways to ensure a *chance* for private citizens as well as for government officials to be heard on issues of foreign policy; but if those views are to be seriously assessed, they must have substance and weight — they must be intellectually and practically persuasive in order to be politically meaningful, even if not, in the end, acceptable. It is in the cultivation of such skills and resources on the part of people outside of government that we might hope to find a key to greater responsiveness within it, on the part of foreign policy officials.

ACCOMMODATION OF MAJOR CHANGES IN OPINION

Perhaps the best way of summarizing and concluding this study of public opinion and foreign policy is to deal with the paradox that a policy making system which has mastered all the modes of resistance to outside opinion nevertheless seems, from a long-run perspective, to accommodate to it. The troublesome question, which has bedevilled an accurate assessment of the role of public opinion in foreign policy making, may be put as follows: given all the psychological and institutional mechanisms for cushioning, deflecting, and absorbing external opinion so that its day-to-day impact on foreign policy is minimal, and given the apparent immunity of the foreign policy establishment to electoral accountability, how can we account for occasional but important shifts in the ethos or ideology of foreign policy that seem to follow upon comparable shifts within the larger population? How, in other words, can we reconcile the lack of governmental responsiveness in the short run with an apparent responsiveness in the long run? Dean Acheson tells us he was once enjoined by an old lady to "remember that the future comes one day at a time." [60] But when it brings with it the daily compulsion to turn aside the uninformed or the critical or the ill-fitting views of "outsiders," how or when are the periodic shifts in direction managed?

Living in the midst of what appears to be a major shift in our basic approach to foreign policy makes us acutely sensitive to this problem, from a civic as well as a scholarly point of view. Yet it is uncommonly difficult to generalize about such circumstances: for one thing, historical experiences are comparatively few. In an earlier study that has recently been reexamined for its predictive insight, Frank L. Klingberg delineated only eight such shifts in the American approach to foreign policy since 1776.[61] And for another thing, relevant modern experiences are even fewer; the last such shift was the transition from isolationism to internationalism in the lengthening shadows of World War II, a passage that was abruptly eased by the attack on Pearl Harbor. For those who are uncomfortable with the notion of an automatic periodicity in these shifts, it is worth looking at what seems to be their underlying mechanism.

Changes in basic approach to foreign policy, in the priority to be given to the investment — in a broad sense — in foreign policy, are the responses of political elites to fundamental political phenomena which transcend the initiatives of public groups dealing with current issues or current problems, yet which grow out of a very large order of them. These changes emerge, at the highest levels, from a growing concern of leaders over their capacity to govern, to maintain reasonable control over events — either those abroad, which are perceived increasingly to threaten important values at home, or those at home, which are a consequence of growing political division involving events abroad. They emerge as leaders act, willingly (as in 1941) or reluctantly (as in 1968), on their felt needs to establish a new domestic political consensus that permits them to govern in the light of new problems, to take actions and make commitments in the normal expectation that these will be accepted as legitimate by politically attentive persons. These concerns, these felt needs, are a response not to raw opinion organized only by the artifice of polls but to opinion as mobilized by institutions with substantial political resources — by political parties, for example, or mass organizations like the Committee to Defend America by Aiding the Allies or the Vietnam Mobilization Committee. They are a response not to the substance of individual acts of public participation but rather to the temper of very large and persistent aggregations of them.

Officials have no way of accommodating private initiatives that differ sharply from established foreign policy — no way, that is, except by adopting a sharply different foreign policy. Such a radical development is incomprehensible when there is (apparently) solid support for established foreign policy, when customary actions and commitments are generally regarded as legitimate by the customary sources of external opinion. But such a radical development eventually becomes reasonable if the alternative is a more pervasive political disaster — if the pursuit of customary acts and commitments evokes overt hostility and explicit denials or withdrawals of support from the customary sources of external opinion. In our recent history, when political demonstrations attracted only a small subculture of the population which was not part of the customary sources, they were dismissed. Public information efforts having failed to avert them, what else could one do about them but ignore them? But when the customary sources left the old coalition and joined the opposition, as in March 1968, or when there were "straights," so to speak, in the streets, as in May 1970, the problem of legitimacy became acute, and the governors were impelled to find a new leadership, or a new policy basis, to reestablish it. In the preceding generation, when the supporters of an active internationalist foreign policy were only a small subculture of the population, they were all but ignored by President Roosevelt. What else could he do about them — or with them, depending on how one interprets Roosevelt's own preferences? But when the customary sources of external opinion began to leave the old isolationist coalition in 1940–1941, and to join the new interventionist one, the President was increasingly able to take new actions and make new commitments abroad in the expectation that they would be accepted as legitimate by politically attentive persons.

But a new legitimacy, a new approach to foreign policy, does not represent a new order of politics. Rather, and more simply, it is a matter of changing from one "conventional wisdom," which has effectively determined which external opinions were worth listening to and cultivating for their support and which ones were dismissable, to a new "conventional wisdom," which is comparably responsive to different viewpoints. Once the new wisdom is indeed conventional, opinions that support *it* are cultivated, and the modes of resistance to contrary opinions, so familiar in these pages, will be mastered once again.[62] In time, normal levels of unresponsiveness create new sources of opposition predisposed to a new order of priorities; and when a foreign policy problem develops for which the new conventional wisdom proves increasingly inappropriate or ineffective, the cycle of change and the reestablishment of legitimacy will reappear once again.

But are we condemned to repeat this cycle every generation or so, as if it had never happened to us before? Perhaps if we understand what it is that is happening, we can learn how to mitigate the dangers inherent in it. If the "normal levels of unresponsiveness" can be reduced, or replaced by higher levels of responsiveness, perhaps we can hope to moderate the transitions from old conventional wisdoms to new ones. With better vision and better sensitivity concerning what may lie around the bends in the road, perhaps we can learn how to negotiate the turns before disaster looms, without subjecting democratic institutions to strains and traumas beyond their capacity to absorb.

NOTES

1. E.g., V. O. Key, Jr., *Public Opinion and American Democracy*, New York: Knopf, 1961, p. 423.

2. Sheldon Appleton, *United States Foreign Policy*, Boston: Little, Brown & Co., 1968, p. 302.

3. See James N. Rosenau, "Foreign Policy as an Issue-Area," in James N. Rosenau, ed., *Domestic Sources of Foreign Policy*, New York: Free Press, 1967, pp. 11–50.

4. E.g., Robert A. Dahl: "Elected leaders keep the real or imagined preferences of constituents constantly in mind in deciding what policies

to adopt or reject." *Who Governs?* New Haven: Yale University Press, 1961, p. 164.

5. See the testimony of Richard E. Neustadt, dated March 25, 1963, in United States Senate, Subcommittee on National Security Staffing and Operations, Committee on Government Operations, *Administration of National Security*, Washington, D.C.: United States Government Printing Office, 1965, pp. 74–103.

6. See United States Senate, Subcommittee on National Security and International Operations, Committee on Government Operations, *The National Security Council: New Role and Structure, February 7, 1969*, Washington, D.C.: United States Government Printing Office, 1969.

7. Kenneth Prewitt, "Political Ambition, Volunteerism, and Electoral Accountability," *American Political Science Review*, Vol. 64, No. 1, March 1970, p. 10.

8. Warren E. Miller and Donald E. Stokes, "Constituency Influence in Congress," *American Political Science Review*, Vol. 57, No. 1, March 1963.

9. E.g., Angus Campbell, Philip E. Converse, Warren E. Miller, and Donald E. Stokes, *The American Voter*, New York: John Wiley, 1960; Kenneth Waltz, *Foreign Policy and Democratic Politics*, Boston: Little, Brown & Co., 1967; and Richard A. Brody, Benjamin I. Page, Sidney Verba, and Jerome Laulicht, "Vietnam, the Urban Crisis, and the 1968 Presidential Elections: A Preliminary Analysis," paper prepared for delivery at the annual meeting of the American Sociological Association, September 1969. In a subsequent paper, Benjamin I. Page and Richard A. Brody conclude that the infrequency of foreign policy issue-voting in Presidential elections has its roots in the failure of the electoral system itself to offer sharply differentiated choices to the electorate. See their "Policy Voting and the Electoral Process: The Vietnam War Issue," paper prepared for delivery at the annual meeting of the American Political Science Association, September 7–11, 1971.

10. Milton J. Rosenberg, "Images in Relation to the Policy Process: American Public Opinion on Cold-War Issues," in Herbert C. Kelman, ed., *International Behavior*, New York: Holt, Rinehart & Winston, 1965, p. 284.

11. See his *Bureaucracy, Politics, and Public Policy*, Boston: Little, Brown & Co., 1969, p. 3.

12. Kenneth Prewitt, "Political Representation and Political Accountability," paper prepared for delivery on the occasion of the 50th anniversary of the Department of Political Science, Stanford University, April 17–18, 1970. See also Hanna Pitkin, *The Concept of Representation*, Berkeley: University of California Press, 1967, pp. 57–58, for an incisive restatement of the accountability view.

13. See Glenn Paige, *The Korean Decision: June 24–30, 1950*, New York: Free Press, 1968, p. 141.

14. Cf. Joseph M. Jones's complaint from an earlier period: "To a degree far greater than is healthy each subordinate officer in the State De-

partment operates and makes recommendations on the basis of a personal estimate of what Congress or the American people will accept, and usually there are enough low estimates along the line to keep policy and action flying low, if not grounded." *The Fifteen Weeks*, New York: Viking, 1955, p. 149.

15. William O. Chittick, *The State Department, Press, and Pressure Groups*, New York: Wiley-Interscience, 1970, p. 237, citing Dean Rusk, "A Fresh Look at the Formulation of Foreign Policy," *Department of State Bulletin*, Vol. 44, No. 1134, March 20, 1961, p. 398.

16. *Department of State Newsletter*, No. 105, January 1970, pp. 2–5, 28–31.

17. *Department of State Newsletter*, No. 106, February 1970, p. 6.

18. Department of State Publication 8551, Washington, D.C.: United States Government Printing Office, 1970.

19. *Ibid.*, pp. 377–402.

20. *Ibid.*, p. 377.

21. *Ibid.*, p. 398.

22. *Ibid.*, pp. 397–402.

23. *Ibid.*, p. 391.

24. See also the remarks of Theodore L. Eliot, Special Assistant to the Secretary of State, Executive Secretary to the Department, and the new President of the American Foreign Service Association, at an Association luncheon on January 29, 1970, as reported in *Department of State Newsletter*, No. 106, February 1970, p. 26.

25. Tom Wicker, "In the Nation: Loud, Clear and Often," *The New York Times*, November 4, 1969. See also Townsend Hoopes, *The Limits of Intervention*, New York: McKay, 1969, esp. pp. 218–219; George E. Reedy, *The Twilight of the Presidency*, New York: World Publishing Co., 1970.

26. See Adam Yarmolinsky's remarks in Richard Pfeffer, ed., *No More Vietnams?* New York: Harper & Row, 1968, pp. 104–105.

27. Charles Frankel, *High on Foggy Bottom*, New York: Harper & Row, 1969, p. 84.

28. Walter Lippmann's is the classic contemporary expression of this argument: *Essays in the Public Philosophy*, Boston: Atlantic–Little, Brown, 1955. For more recent statements, see Waltz, *Foreign Policy and Democratic Politics*, esp. p. 279; and Doris A. Graber, *Public Opinion, the President, and Foreign Policy*, New York: Holt, Rinehart & Winston, 1968, esp. pp. 299–300.

29. Graber, *Public Opinion, the President, and Foreign Policy*, p. 300.

30. John Franklin Campbell had a different metaphor: *The Foreign Affairs Fudge Factory*, New York: Basic Books, 1971.

31. For such evidence, see Angus Campbell *et al.*, *The American Voter*.

32. E.g., Andrew Berding, *Foreign Affairs and You!* Garden City: Doubleday, 1962, p. 169; H. Schuyler Foster, "American Public Opinion

and U.S. Foreign Policy," *Department of State Bulletin*, November 30, 1959, p. 801; American Institute of Public Opinion, release dated October 24, 1965, reviewing thirty years of Gallup polling.

33. See Milton J. Rosenberg, Sidney Verba, and Philip E. Converse, *Vietnam and the Silent Majority: The Dove's Guide*, New York: Harper & Row, 1970, esp. Chap. 2; and Sidney Verba and Richard Brody, "Participation, Policy Preferences, and the War in Vietnam," *Public Opinion Quarterly*, Vol. 34, No. 3, Fall 1970, pp. 325–332.

34. See Key, *Public Opinion and American Democracy*, pp. 16–17.

35. Paul F. Lazarsfeld and Elihu Katz, *Personal Influence: The Part Played by People in the Flow of Mass Communications*, Glencoe: Free Press, 1955. See also Elihu Katz, "The Two-Step Flow of Communication: An Up-to-Date Report on an Hypothesis," *Public Opinion Quarterly*, Vol. 21, Spring 1957.

36. James N. Rosenau, *Public Opinion and Foreign Policy*, New York: Random House, 1961, pp. 7–8.

37. See Hoopes, *The Limits of Intervention*, p. 218.

38. E.g., H. Schuyler Foster, then Director of the Division of Public Studies: "Congress has acted favorably on various important international questions which have been little understood by the general public. . . . On all of these questions the positive approval of a majority of the general public was lacking. But support was forthcoming from the press and from national organizations." "American Public Opinion and U.S. Foreign Policy," p. 801. Townsend Hoopes even suggests that "the first real evidence of a consequential shift in public sentiment on the war" came not from anyone who claimed to represent "public sentiment" but from an unexpected *lack* of criticism from the right when several Congressmen moved against the war. *The Limits of Intervention*, p. 98.

39. E.g., Max Frankel, "Alternative in Vietnam: Democrats in Exile, Led by Kennedy, Step Up Calls for a Change in Policy," *The New York Times*, April 25, 1966.

40. See Morton Halperin's comment from the field of military policy: "Perhaps most important, the Gaither [Committee] episode demonstrated the inability of any group, either in opposition to the President or comprised mainly of private citizens (or, as in this case, both) to influence military strategy." *Contemporary Military Strategy*, Boston: Little, Brown & Co., 1967, p. 51.

41. See Chittick, *State Department, Press, and Pressure Groups*, p. 168. This dependency on external initiative marks the Department's approach to its press relations also; see Bernard C. Cohen, *The Press and Foreign Policy*, Princeton: Princeton University Press, 1963, p. 267.

42. See also Andrew M. Scott's discussion of the insulation of the Department of State, in "Environmental Change and Organizational Adaptation: the Problem of the State Department," *International Studies Quarterly*, Vol. 14, No. 1, March 1970, esp. p. 90.

43. See Carl J. Friedrich, *Man and His Government*, New York: McGraw-Hill, 1963, esp. pp. 199–215.

44. See Key, *Public Opinion and American Democracy*, p. 17; Milton J. Rosenberg, "Images in Relation to the Policy Process," p. 285; and Rosenberg, Verba, and Converse, *Vietnam and the Silent Majority*, p. 9.

✓ 45. Paige, *The Korean Decision*, p. 305.

46. Selig Adler, *The Isolationist Impulse: Its Twentieth-Century Reaction*, London and New York: Abelard-Schuman, 1957, p. 164.

47. Graber, *Public Opinion, the President, and Foreign Policy*, p. 363. Graber goes on to say that this is "the greatest public opinion influence on governmental decision-making."

48. E.g., Bernard C. Cohen, *The Political Process and Foreign Policy: The Making of the Japanese Peace Settlement*, Princeton: Princeton University Press, 1957, p. 29.

49. E.g., Raymond A. Dawson, *The Decision to Aid Russia, 1941*, Chapel Hill: University of North Carolina Press, 1959, *passim*.

50. Kenneth Prewitt has pointed out the paradox in theories which claim both that officials share the norms and policies of the larger society and that officials play a significant part in helping to establish those norms. See his "Political Representation and Political Accountability."

51. For a critique of "anticipated reaction" as an explanation of Presidential control in foreign policy, see Aaron Wildavsky, "The Two Presidencies," in Aaron Wildavsky, ed., *The Presidency*, Boston: Little, Brown & Co., 1969.

52. See Charles Frankel's perceptive account of his experiences as Assistant Secretary of State for Educational and Cultural Affairs, *High on Foggy Bottom*.

53. See Joseph Schlesinger, *Ambition and Politics*, Chicago: Rand McNally, 1966. For a different view of the role of ambition, see Kenneth Prewitt, "Political Ambition, Volunteerism, and Electoral Accountability," pp. 5–17.

54. Roger Hilsman's *To Move a Nation*, Garden City: Doubleday, 1967, speaks eloquently to this point.

55. See Hoopes, *The Limits of Intervention*, p. 98.

56. This position is not unlike that reached by Gabriel A. Almond nearly twenty-five years ago, in *The American People and Foreign Policy*, 1st ed., New York: Harcourt, Brace, 1950. It may seem retrogressive in a period when pluralism and "the power elite" are under serious attack. It is worth pointing out, however, that any regime, and especially a revolutionary one, would face comparable problems in the location of authority and responsibility for foreign policy making and that, *if* it were also to be held to some standard of continuing responsiveness to external opinion, the structural problem would persist even though its ideological content and the direction of policy had changed.

57. For a fuller analysis of the Stanford data following the initial release, see Sidney Verba *et al.*, "Public Opinion and the War in Vietnam," *American Political Science Review*, Vol. 61, No. 2, June 1967, pp. 317–333. For an analysis of press reactions to the Stanford Poll, see Nelson W. Polsby, "Political Science and the Press: Notes on Coverage of a

Public Opinion Survey on the Vietnam War," *The Western Political Quarterly*, Vol. 22, No. 1, March 1969, pp. 47–60.

58. See the recommendation of the National Policy Panel of the United Nations Association of the United States of America for "a federally-financed, but independently operated polling operation." *Beyond Vietnam: Public Opinion and Foreign Policy*, New York: UNA-USA, February 1970, p. 8.

59. See Frederick B. Hoyt's discussion of the contradictory demands made on the State Department by American groups in China in the period between the two World Wars, and of the Department's inability to meet them all: "Americans in China and the Formation of American Policy, 1925–1937," unpubl. Ph.D. dissertation, Department of History, University of Wisconsin—Madison, 1971.

60. Dean Acheson, "The President and the Secretary of State," in Don K. Price, ed., *The Secretary of State*, An American Assembly book, Englewood Cliffs, N. J.: Prentice-Hall, 1960, p. 36.

61. Frank L. Klingberg, "The Historical Alternation of Moods in American Foreign Policy," *World Politics*, Vol. 4, No. 2, January 1952, pp. 239–273. Samuel P. Huntington has recently reappraised Klingberg's forecast of a cycle of "introversion" beginning in the late 1960's, in Pfeffer, ed., *No More Vietnams?* pp. 39–41.

62. See J. David Singer, "Popular Diplomacy and Policy Effectiveness: A Note on the Mechanisms and Consequences (Comment on Birn)," *Comparative Studies in Society and History*, Vol. 12, No. 3, July 1970, pp. 320–325.

Index

Acheson, Secretary of State Dean, 35, 36, 38, 40, 72, 74, 84, 85, 127, 129, 155, 163, 169, 182, 183, 198, 206, 213

Adler, Selig, 35, 37, 76, 162, 164, 198, 212

advisory groups, 83, 204; composition of, 93; establishment of, by State Department, 95; as source of opinion, 92–95; use of, by State Department, 94–95

African Institute, 92

Agency for International Development, 33, 50

Alger, Chadwick F., 128

Almond, Gabriel A., 30, 34, 37, 73, 74, 126, 212

Alsop, Joseph, 61

American Institute of Public Opinion, 211

anticipated reaction, 151–152; as responsiveness to public opinion, 197–199

anti-proliferation treaty, 147

Appleton, Sheldon, 74, 164, 184, 208

audiences, as source of opinion, 80

Bailey, Thomas A., 37, 129

Ball, George, 127

Baltimore Sun, 107

Bauer, Raymond A., 36, 41, 76, 129, 161, 163, 164

Benson, Lee, 2, 8, 9, 34, 37

Berding, Andrew, 51, 55, 57, 73, 74, 128, 169, 182, 183, 210

Birn, Donald S., 37

Bonilla, Frank, 129

Borg, Dorothy, 71, 77, 163, 164

Bradley, General Omar, 127

briefings: as public relations device, 120; as source of opinion, 120–122

Brody, Richard A., 34, 209, 211

Browder, Robert P., 10, 13, 15, 36, 37, 38, 70, 76, 162, 164, 180, 183

Brown, Trevor R., 130

Bruck, H. W., 36

Brzezinski, Zbigniew, 151, 163

Bundy, McGeorge, 87, 127

Bureau of Public Affairs, 33, 44–50, 118, 159; decline of opinion-analysis role of, 44–46, 48–49; Division of News, 45 (*see also* Office of Press Relations); Division of Public Opinion Studies, 45, 47; Division of Public Services, 45, 47; Public Correspondence Branch, 117–118; public relations role of, 44–45, 63, 170

215